Preface

This book was initiated by a team of lecturers who have been teaching comparative and international education for postgraduate students at the University of South Africa and other prominent South African universities for the past ten years. It follows in the wake of the successful publication, *Critical issues for modern education*, which formed the basis for BEd courses in comparative and international education during the 1990s.

In the light of rapid developments in education and the challenges facing educators in the new millennium, *Contemporary education: Global issues and trends* aims at providing a fresh selection and discussion of key issues and trends of the contemporary scene in matters of educational policy and practice. Each chapter traces how these issues are being tackled in different contexts worldwide. The content of each chapter provides an overview of an educational issue rather than an in-depth analysis. In this way it is hoped that readers will be compelled to explore a topic further in greater detail or to expand their research in the direction of the education system of a particular country. Thus chapters do not attempt to provide the final word on educational issues nor all available information on a particular aspect. Rather a chapter is intended to act as a springboard for further research which could branch out in several related directions. Depth and a specific focus can be augmented by more extensive reading in the field. The themes which have been chosen for discussion in this book are by no means exhaustive but comprise a selection of topics identified collaboratively by lecturers and shaped by the interest and needs expressed by students who have already successfully completed courses in comparative and international education at South African universities.

Although reference is made throughout to recent developments in South Africa, the chapters are not written to provide an exclusively South African perspective. While South African education is certainly in the midst of a critical phase in the most momentous restructuring in its history, the authors maintain that it is important for educators at all levels to recognise the relevance and importance of maintaining a broader perspective on educational issues. International enquiry concerning issues and trends has become an integral part of policy studies in education, and intellectual exchange among policy makers has long provided a template for large-scale innovations. However, as a new millennium approaches, the degree and the tempo with which individual countries have turned their attention to what their neighbours are doing has increased dramatically, thus making cross national enquiry even more crucial. The issues presented and discussed in this book will thus be of interest not only to students of comparative education but also to policy makers, practitioners and academics. It is hoped that *Contemporary education: Global issues and trends* will contribute to an informed basis for decision-making in the educational sphere in the light of global developments.

Eleanor Lemmer

1999

Critical reviewers

Prof Philip Higgs, University of South Africa   (Chapter 1)

Mr Peter Southey, independant consultant (Chapter 2)

Dr Roger Deacon, University of Natal (Chapter 3)

Prof Ntombizolile Vakalisa, University of South Africa (Chapters 4 and 9)

Prof Ken Harley, University of Natal (Chapter 5)

Prof Tom Bisschoff, Rand Afrikaans University (Chapter 6)

Ms Leone van der Merwe, Pro Arte Alphen Park Academy (Chapter 7)

Prof Andrew van Zyl, University of South Africa (Chapter 8)

Dr Eulalie van Heerden, University of South Africa (Chapter 10)

Table of contents

CHAPTER 1

VALUES AND IDEOLOGIES

 Dr Petro van Niekerk
University of South Africa

Table of contents

1.1 Introduction

This chapter aims to deal with the role of values and ideologies in education and society. The main argument is to emphasise how important it is to consider the influence of underlying values and ideologies on the ongoing discourses in society and to be able to detect specifically what the effects of such underpinnings may be on educational dispensations within a broader societal context. Although reference will be made to other countries, the focus will be on South Africa. In order to reach these aims, values are briefly discussed in the context of the classroom situation with reference to South African education. Thereafter, ideologies will be explored in a conceptual sense. Finally, South African ideologies and their impact on education during times of transformation will be examined in order to understand the complexities of the current educational dynamic.

1.2 The role of values in formal education

Very often, abstractions such as definitions do not necessarily make a concept adequately clear. Therefore it is preferable to start with concrete examples of values and to give definitions later. Examples of values are legion: honesty, professional conduct, frugality, self-discipline, respect for human beings and nature, tolerance for different viewpoints, punctuality and so on are all examples of values which underpin people's behaviour. Pilch and Malina (1993:xviii) distinguish between core values and peripheral values. Core values are values expressed in all human interactions, although value preferences may differ from culture to culture. They illustrate this by pointing out that modern-day American society regards 'efficiency' as a core value, while more traditional societies as well as those in the ancient world would regard 'honour' and 'shame' as core values. Peripheral values are specific to certain conditions and interactions.

How then can values be defined? The word 'value' describes some general quality and direction of life that human beings are expected to embody in their behaviour. A value is a general, normative orientation of action in a social system. It is an emotionally anchored commitment to pursue and support certain directions of types of actions (Pilch & Malina 1993:xiii).

In addition to ways of behaving, humans' evaluation of behaviour towards certain objects also reveals values. This is called symbolising, that is, the way in which humans ascribe value to value objects. These value objects can be called symbols. What is important here is to realise that human beings neither relate to each other and their value objects, nor do they realise their values in a vacuum. They are always integrated in various structures or social institutions which help to give direction to certain social actions. For example, kinship or extended family life as is the custom in traditional, non-Western societies is a social institution that serves as a means of bringing new human beings into existence and then nurturing them for a lifetime (Botha 1997:165). In stark contrast are the ideals of the Western world, where family life is exemplified by a close-knit nuclear family with a father, a caring mother, two children (ideally a boy and a girl), and a dog – a family unit that is in a cordial but independent relationship with its extended family.

1.2.1 The purpose of education

The focus shifts to the impact of values, value systems and ideologies on formal education. If value systems which influence formal education can be identified and analysed, they will enable us to gain a better understanding of what is taking place in schools. This understanding can help to motivate teachers, community leaders, parents and learners to become positively involved in the transformation of the education system.

Firstly, it is necessary to think about the main purpose of a system of formal education in order to detect a dominant value system. If we reflect on schooling worldwide, it is astonishing that schools are so similar while the cultural contexts of societies in which they occur are so different. Various communities worldwide have a differing school ethos with regard to matters such as discipline, social class, codes of behaviour and those camouflaged by various forms of rhetoric. However, the universal basic aim of the school in general remains the preparation of children for their economic future, taking cognisance of a variety of aspects involved in such a future. The predicament of schools lies in the fact that they cannot accurately anticipate the future for which they have to prepare the learners. This is where it becomes relevant for educationists to reflect on perennial, core values essential for humanity and its survival on the globe which will remain the same, although circumstances may change (Badenhorst 1993:399). This poses an obvious question: why or how did the school attain its present character?

According to Hunter (1994:xvii), the contemporary school originates from two sources, namely Christian pastoral guidance (schools developed from Sunday schools in Britain) and monotorial schools (in Germany) where the state controlled teaching methods and content. This was during the time of the Enlightenment which saw, among other things, the growth of scientific enquiry and the rise of the European middle class. The industrial revolution was an outcome of the scientific developments of the Enlightenment and the Reformation which made it important to read the Bible. In general, the education movement emphasised the optimal realisation of the potential of the individual, prosperity of the state and a material view of the world (Badenhorst 1998:56-58).

Later, formal education became the tool whereby states trained workers to maintain and develop a common culture and to give citizens a shared national identity. It was believed that the best way of forging a nation was to supply mass education.

According to Eisner (1994:13) schools in the US had to provide a workforce that will make the country a competitive force and this means students need to be taught how to think. In the past, jobs made simple demands on workers. Schools needed to train learners to endure boredom as that was what they would experience in the workplace. Today new cognitive demands are being made in the workplace. In this regard, the business community in America is taking the lead in defining the educational agenda for American learners. Eisner (1994:14) goes on to say that the aims of schools in the USA and the content implied by these aims are rooted in the marketplace because the national identity is so closely linked to economic successes. Badenhorst (1993:403) agrees with this statement by stating that '[b]oth capitalists and non-capitalists regard the school as an important instrument in maintaining and expanding the economy'.

1.2.2 Conflicting value systems: implications for formal education

This section explores a range of conflicting value systems which complicates the task of formal education in general and South African education in particular.

Official and non-official values

In any community, two sets of values are usually apparent, namely *what ought to be* (the norm) and *what is* (facts of real life) (Van Dyk in Badenhorst 1993). The normative represents the official values, often included in school policy documents, and the values deducted from real-life observations represent the non-official values.

A South African example can be found in the claims made by conservative Afrikaner leaders who strongly emphasise the Christian values of their group as their official values. However, Joubert (1992:257-260) points out that if these values are examined closely, they are linked to ethnicity and individual privilege based on capitalism. He questions whether these values are not removed from biblical, Christian values which have more to do with love, communality and sharing. The case of Christian National Education (CNE) illustrates this point. The CNE Act promulgated all white schools in 1967. In practice schools had to be opened in the mornings by scripture reading and prayer and Biblical Studies was offered as a non-examining subject. The official values stated in the policy documents of the Education Department were stated as Christian, yet distinctly different from those of black or Indian schools, in order to justify separate systems to fit the apartheid ideology.

Another more recent example from a democratic South Africa can be cited. Many political organisations include the word 'democratic' in their names and slogans to denote an official value system. Yet, the real-life values of such organisations sometimes contradict the values of democracy by adopting the politics of coercion. Students therefore need to become critically aware of underlying value systems and the split between the official and non-official set of values in order to bring about change.

Conflicting value systems of adults and children

Conflicting values of parents and children are nothing new to South Africa. Ever since cultures have entered stages of transition, children have questioned their parents' values (Badenhorst 1993:407). The central role which education has played in the liberation struggle considerably complicated this particular situation in terms of education. Christie (1992:257-260) mentions the difficult shadows/side-effects of the struggle: youth militancy, the politics of immediatism (people want immediate effects) as well as the breakdown of a learning culture.

The parents of these politicised youths, who were obviously also against apartheid, at the same time objected to their children abandoning their education altogether because they feared that they would not be adequately prepared for future employment. The youths, on the other hand, embraced a largely Marxist-orientated ideology and wanted to transform society to conform to a socialist model before embarking on a radically different kind of education.

Another side-effect of this period, characterised by the breakdown of the culture of learning, is the fact that a variety of problematic assumptions about what education entails existed among many communities in South Africa, such as the notion of 'education as a commodity'. A commodity implies something which you can buy or be given. Heese (in Heese & Badenhorst 1992:3-4) maintains that this notion has led students to believe that education is something others can give to you or withhold from you. Students and teachers have consequently come to see themselves as passive receivers or disadvantaged non-receivers – a situation which can only be rectified by others, *inter alia* the government. In contrast to such a viewpoint, educationists worldwide commonly accept that active involvement in and personal responsibility for one's own learning are prerequisites for a successful education.

Different backgrounds and different value preferences

Differences in background and experiences include the different socio-economic and historical-political backgrounds of people depending on whether they come from sprawling urban black townships, rural villages or white privileged neighbourhoods in rural or urban areas. Claims have been made that background and exposure to different lifestyles have led to more differences in value systems and attitudes than our ethnic roots. For example, black people

5

living in villages exhibit more commonality in terms of values than ethnic groups like Xhosas or Zulus who live in crowded urban settlements.

Regarding these different experiences and how they have impacted on education, it is important to remember that black, urban, poverty-stricken townships were beset by police activity and violence during the apartheid years. This would inevitably have affected the psyche of school-going children in this context in a different manner from that of white children living in privileged, peaceful circumstances who were pursuing their schooling careers. Many white people were blissfully unaware of how widespread the struggle was and how it affected the lives of the majority of the South African people, especially before 1976 when TV was introduced in South Africa. In a democratic South Africa, where the school-going population is no longer homogeneous, the impact of these different experiences and acquired value systems and attitudes cannot be ignored by teachers, parents, youths and community leaders.

Conflicting ethnic and perceived ethnic values

In South Africa 'ethnicity' has become a derogatory term since it became stereotyped during the apartheid years. Diversity along ethnic lines was over-emphasised to the detriment of a common South African identity. Although ethnic clashes take place in many parts of the world, intra-ethnic struggles, like the faction fighting in KwaZulu-Natal, are often overlooked. The question that arises in this context is whether such clashes exist as the result of different values or as a result of an ideology where values are abused as a facade to disguise the struggle for power. Although the existence of ethnicity cannot be denied, the relevant question remains: what is its influence on education? How is it possible for people from different ethnic groups to live in harmony and at least work together for a common purpose without denying differences in values, customs and so on?

Other thorny issues are those of stereotyping and prejudice which are sometimes mistaken for ethnicity. In these cases, reference is made to perceived ethnicity. To illustrate: because some rural black South Africans have not been acculturated in terms of Western culture, others tend to stereotype all black people as non-Western. Alternatively, because many black people living in South Africa and in Africa are poor, it is assumed that all blacks are poor and all whites are rich. In a similar way, not all Afrikaners can be described as racists simply because the apartheid government, whose policies were inherently racist, comprised mainly Afrikaners. Beck and Linscott (1991:123-124) argue that different value preferences rather than race distinguish groups or individuals from each other.

Traditional and contemporary value systems

Traditional or conventional values are usually held by conservative people who are not comfortable with rapid social changes and usually want to maintain the status quo at all costs. Such persons often have rigid attitudes as a result of their isolation. Isolation often causes a stagnation of value systems and an alienation of surrounding dynamics due to the lack of exposure to the Other. Stagnation of values often leads to a mindset where stereotyping and prejudice is rife and, as a result, people in these circumstances tend to resist change (Thomas & Postlethwaite 1983:14). More open-mindedness is sometimes found in less remote and urban areas where people are more exposed to other views.

During the history of apartheid in South Africa, isolation on an international level as well as on an intra-national level prevailed. Intra-national isolation has also created alienation and suspicion among ethnic groups. It is clear that people who have been isolated and have not had the opportunity to share their views with others tend to think along traditional lines and are not flexible enough to change. It is thus advantageous for human beings to live in a situation of cultural diversity to counteract prejudice and stereotyping. Exposure to the Other and the different often serves as a balancing factor. In the words of Murray Gell-Mann (in Waldrop 1992:351-352) 'cultural diversity will be just as important in a sustainable world as genetic diversity is in biology. We need cross-cultural ferment'.

Modern and post-modern value systems

If one accepts that we are moving towards a more post-modern world where grand schemes are no longer considered to be as important as local, smaller and creative inputs (Rosenau 1992), then it stands to reason that the school needs to pay attention to these trends. For example, Toffler (1990) describes some of the main characteristics of a new economic dispensation worldwide, *inter alia* the availability and power of information. Creativity and entrepreneurship will become of vital importance. In order to survive the new era, people need to function successfully within an economy in which identifying and filling niches are more important than mass production according to the 'modern' way (Badenhorst 1993:411-413). (The concepts of modernity and post-modernity are examined in greater detail in subsequent chapters.)

Because of the diverse nature of South African society – both in terms of modern and post-modern needs – schools could vary on a continuum of old-fashioned schools functioning according to modern ideals to those designed according to post-modern ideals.

The advantage of post-modernism is that a plurality and multiplicity (multi = many) of models is accepted as legitimate and preferred to monolithic (mono = one) models of development, which facilitates tolerance towards plurality and fairness to everyone. Nyberg (1990:595) describes plurality in the American context as:

our blessing and our curse at the same time, for it means that we will have to live with conflict; we have no hope at all that everyone will agree on anything really important. ... on the other hand, we have the opportunity of using that conflict as a focus for open public educational debate and for protecting ourselves against the deplorably oppressive alternative of political, cultural, or religious orthodoxy.

According to this viewpoint, there is no such thing as purity of cultural values – only mixtures or hybrids of cultures. African traditional values and Western values can co-exist without being regarded as contradictory. Like many countries in the world, South Africa is part of a unique mosaic of relationships. Although the world is becoming increasingly complex it is, at the same time, becoming more interesting and challenging to cope with. Post-modernity requires a different conceptualisation of things in which linear causality must be relinquished in favour of non-linearity and a multiplicity of models and contexts.

The modernisation theory of development may have its merits in a developing world, but it also has its limitations. This particular theory proclaims a series of direct causal links including the following:

- *between education and the state of the economy*. If the education system is effective, the economy will grow.
- *between modernisation and Westernisation*. To be modernised necessarily implies that people need to discard their own traditions and acquire modern Western values.

Countries with relatively strong economies can easily upgrade their education systems (for example Germany, Japan and Australia). The opposite is not true. Education systems run by the state are expensive endeavours and there are no guarantees that they will instantly upgrade the economy. The case of Japan also serves as an example which raises questions about modernisation theory since the Japanese did not abandon their traditional beliefs and modernise according to Western beliefs, but still developed into a successful economic giant in the world.

1.2.3 The teacher and the application of values

According to Nyberg (1990:295) educators are important transmitters of values: neither teachers nor parents can avoid teaching values through their own words and actions. Thus what lives in the hearts of teachers and parents will colour their teaching or behaviour even if they remain silent about certain matters. Moreover, even young children observe and internalise adults' tacit values. In the present era, the educational task of the teacher comprises *inter alia* the reflection on which values should be inculcated in their students' lives.

Whatever policies may be intended by educational planners, it is ultimately what takes place in the classroom that matters in terms of the realisation of certain values. Since modern education strongly endorses middle-class Western values, children from such backgrounds have been found to have an obvious advantage over those from more traditional homes. As schools in South Africa become increasingly diverse, teachers will have to reflect on the implications of this diversity of values and their impact on teaching and learning (Badenhorst 1993:404).

The question remains: how can the teacher inculcate common, agreed-upon values that will help to bring about a positive learning environment? Perhaps teachers should become facilitators of value articulation in the classroom. Brooks and Kahn (1992:27) discuss various strategies for teachers to inculcate values in the classroom. They suggest that teachers should concentrate on positive aspects of values and attitudes in contrast to what happens in the 'normal' classroom where teachers pay considerable attention to learners who do things incorrectly. For example, learners could be encouraged to look for courageous behaviour which would then be praised and emphasised. Davies (1991:16-17) describes a case of a teacher who is punctual, well-prepared and succeeds in involving the learners actively in classwork. The so-called hidden curriculum sent to the learners is that this subject is worth studying. In contrast, where the teacher is ill-prepared the learners will have little enthusiasm for that subject which will result in minimal learning having occurred in that classroom. Davies (1991:16-17) states that teachers shape pupils' attitudes and values:

> if our professional conduct does not underscore the written content of the curriculum, then we have no alternative other than to admit that even the most relevant curriculum can become totally irrelevant if the teachers concerned are not themselves dedicated and competent professionals.

1.3 Theoretical aspects surrounding ideologies

The focus of the chapter now shifts to the concept of ideology because of its profound influence on society and education. It should be realised that new belief systems and ideologies will inevitably come into existence as human life deals with values and ideologies. Ideologies are always underpinned by values.

1.3.1 Definition and key concepts

Ideologies are systematised value systems which compel groups of people to act. In order to develop a comprehensive understanding of how the concept of ideology evolved, the following summary might be helpful:

- Ideologies accompany humankind's increased efforts to rationally explain political and social phenomena.
- Ideologies are the result of efforts to make political accommodations created by the industrial revolution.

- Ideology is a term originally used in an objective way to explain the origin of ideas. Later, however, ideologies came to be understood as subjective political rationalisations.

- Today ideologies are understood to be political statements that call on the masses to act in some way in order to improve political life.

Ashley (1989:2) defines an ideology as a set of beliefs and values which coheres in a systematic way, held by a group of people for whom it explains the nature of the reality they experience and which has the power to commit them to action: 'People act because they believe' (Ashley 1989:2).

Degenaar (1978:8) offers yet another version of the term. He proposes that ideology is:

- a system of ideas and values with priority usually given to one value which is used for the evaluation of theories and actions

- an action-related system of ideas intended to change or defend an existing political and social order

- a system of ideas which takes on a totalitarian structure linked with a corresponding state of mind

- a system of ideas in its social context, taking into account the possibility of concealing the political, economic and social interests of the group holding those views.

A system of formal education is a powerful tool for political leadership to shape a nation and thus is profoundly affected by ideological considerations with regard to its nature and purpose. Educational ideologies can thus be described as systems of beliefs and values about the purpose of education held by particular groups of educators and which result in educational action.

1.3.2 The role of attitudes and religion in supporting ideologies

A critical consciousness of the way in which particular ideologies intersect and support each other in maintaining forms of domination is vital. Often the interests of a specific group are presented as if they were representative of the entire nation. In this case ideology will operate by ignoring other groups' needs or withholding information which could be detrimental to the position of the dominant group. In other words, in this sense the ideologies will act only in their own interest, sometimes without even being aware of other people's interests (Mouton 1990:34).

Attitudes

From a psychological vantage point, Jordaan (1990:15-16) offers an interesting explanation as to why some ideologies tend to become more dogmatic and rigid than others. In his view people as participants in life hold either an attitude of openness or of closure. In the case of the former, a realisation of the tentative nature of life and the plurality of truth will prevail together with an open-ended and extending worldview. In the case of the latter, a more and more prescriptive and inflexible attitude towards life will eventually lead to 'frozen' perceptions of reality. Because of feelings of fear and uncertainty, such personalities tend to categorise people and events into inflexible dichotomies. The typical *us* against *them* situation develops because of an inability to understand or endure ambivalence and complexity.

Typical coping mechanisms in this regard would be to oversimplify matters and cling to old stereotypes as well as the reification of power especially in the militant sense of the word. Van Niekerk (1990:1) holds the view that a certain type of personality finds comfort in doing so because oversimplified formulae help to push the fear of the unknown future aside by taking on a brave facade and relying on rhetoric.

Religion

Proceeding to reflect on the influence of religion on the support and intersection among certain ideologies, the following overlapping characteristics which establish significant links between ideology and religion should be considered. Both religion and ideology:

- are matters of belief which should lead to action
- often consist of systematised and prescriptive rules
- claim a future-orientated vision
- deal with power.

Religion deals with power. Part of the attraction to faith is the power which a church or other religious institution can offer its members. All of these could easily be abused by power-hungry people:

> Religion could indeed help people to become independent, but they could likewise become bound by the church, by norms which are not above-board, by a social commitment which is aimed at one-sided interests and a suffocating morality (Du Toit 1991:9; translation – author).

Religion can also offer a powerful means to legitimise an ideology because it imbues a system with 'holiness' which cannot be challenged. In extreme cases, when a threat to social identity is perceived, the value system which underpins an ideology becomes fixated and a fanatic consciousness, which is fundamentally violent, starts to develop (Pillay 1991:7). The cause becomes a moral one and the territorial opponent becomes immoral. Thus a situation where *us* as directly opposed to *them* develops. A naïve form of religion could be abused by power-seekers in such a way that a specific group's interests could be legitimised and left unchallenged in order to maintain domination. This suggests how it is possible for ideologies to intersect and support one another, especially when they are justified by a 'holy' cause.

1.3.3 Ideologies and ideological fixations/dogmatisms and educational change

In practice, a group of people may find certain aspects in their belief systems on which they can commonly agree. Depending on how threatened they feel in terms of survival as a social group, they will construct an ideology to make sense of their existence as a defined collection of people. To make sense of life within a specific environment and time-frame in history is quite normal for a group and that would be called their 'ideological framework' or 'frame of reference'.

Sometimes ideologies arise when a group of people looks for a national identity – especially in cases where the group has had past experience of being treated unfairly and not recognised as a people, as has often happened in world history. Experiences of colonialism and imperialism have had a similar effect on national identity. When such a group of people feels threatened by others, it will go a step further and construct a clear-cut 'blueprint' ideology which it justifies in the name of religion, folklore and myths from the past often related to Utopian visions and ideals.

When such a people finds itself in a pluralistic environment, a struggle for land and government is usually initiated. Theodorson (in Botha 1989:21) says that ideology in a pluralistic society is usually linked to the value system of the dominant culture in order to legitimise the control which is enforced on the lives of the subordinate groups.

Ashley (1989:3) argues that although ideologies developed over time and therefore have an historical dimension, they often resist the challenge of changing circumstances and display a consistency of character. In such cases the underlying value system becomes rigid, static and dogmatic. The ideological framework consequently becomes impervious to revision and criticism, and at that stage the ideology fossilises into an ideological fixation or dogmatism which defies the dynamics of change.

In this context Van Niekerk (1990:2) suggests that people can be blinded by elevated or sublime ideals to such an extent that they lose their sensitivity to ordinary people and everyday life around them. Impaired vision is the inevitable result of fixing one's gaze on Utopia (Segal 1992:15). These groupings are almost irrational in their striving to achieve unrealistic ideals which usually boil down to the capture of supreme power.

To summarise: there are usually certain predominant factors involved when an ideological framework becomes an ideological dogmatism or fixation, that is, when abuse of power gradually takes place. In these cases:

- The former oppressed sometimes become the oppressors.
- Such a group of people demonstrates an inability to keep up with the changing times and surrounding realities.

- Utopian visions and mythical concepts tend to blind people so that they no longer recognise their irrational expectations in terms of the context in which they are functioning, resulting in the loss of ability to judge rationally and willingness to compromise.

In a more general sense, one could refer to various examples of acceptable ideological notions which could, with a different emphasis given by a power-abusive leader, become an ideological fixation/dogmatism. Such dogmatisms have inherent power to manipulate ordinary (uncritical) people. These are usually expressed as oversimplified slogans (formulae) and overoptimistic promises which make people believe in a better future which can only be achieved when followers adhere to such a system of thought and are slavishly obedient towards the visions of these systems. More concrete examples of economic ideologies are capitalism and socialism, both of which could become dogmatisms when power is seized to enforce them dogmatically and in a decontextualised way on a populace. In such cases, certain values within the system of thought are often elevated to absolutes, thus becoming impervious to criticism and oblivious to dynamic changes in their surrounding circumstances. Ideological dogmatism in this instance can then be enforced as a 'dogmatic blueprint' by a tyrannical, totalitarian state as was the case with applied Marxism in the former USSR and Eastern Germany. On the other hand, an example of resisting power abuse was when Roosevelt, president of the US, introduced the New Deal in 1930, whereby enough socialism was induced in America's economy to modify capitalism in such a way that it became a more humane system (Baradat 1995).

1.4 Common international fixated ideologies

In the following sections the ideologies of nationalism and racism which became fixations will be examined.

1.4.1 Nationalism

Nationalism is the theory of the nation-state and as such had an enormous influence on the modern world. In fact it is among the oldest and most fatal or virulent of all ideologies and affected most of the other important ideologies such as racism and fascism (Baradat 1995:42). 'Nation' is a sociological term related to nationality which refers to a group of people who have a sense of union with each other based on language, religion, customs and so on. One's nationality is often expressed in terms of ethnic background rather than citizenship. Loyal American citizens could easily formulate their nationality as 'Spanish' or 'Dutch'.

'State', however, is a political term that includes people, territory, government and sovereignty. Nationalism calls on people to identify with the interests of their national group and to support the creation of a state. Nationalism has become popular since the French Revolution. Leftists have supported it as a vehicle to promote the well-being of citizens, whereas rightists use it to encourage unity and stability. The end of the Cold War has seen many of the people who were formerly controlled by the USSR assert their right to national self-determination. Western European countries and North America, on the other hand, have taken steps towards international unions, and for some time the Muslim world has toyed with the idea of a huge reactionary Pan-Islamic state (Baradat 1995:42).

Some arguments maintain that a nation need not be organised into any particular state, but evolves solely because its people identify with one another on the grounds of residing in the same country. The US, for example, has a population of enormous racial and ethnic diversity. Though American English is a common language which everybody can use, many other valuable things tie them together as humorously stated by Baradat (1995:43-45): hot dogs, apple pie, baseball and Chevrolet. This could be called a moderate patriotism – love for the familiar and a feeling of commitment to a common location.

According to Degenaar (1978:30), patriotism should not be equated with nationalism. Nationalism is itself an ambivalent concept. If one focuses more on the values and less on the ideology, certain values can be linked to historical phenomena.

Nationalism is valuable insofar as it:

- locates the highest political authority in the people
- inspires people to liberate themselves from internal or external domination to a more equal distribution of power as well as the fruits of economic growth
- helps individuals to define themselves and creates a feeling of security and belonging
- has a formal juridical function in laying down legal relationships between individuals and the state
- functions symbolically and cultivates a healthy patriotism towards the country which provides space for one's birth and spiritual growth.

In stark contrast to this moderate view, the theory of nationalism has an inherent potential for destruction. In the name of nationalism, millions of people's lives have been sacrificed, and the property, resources and infrastructure of countries demolished. Nationalism in itself is an abstraction. The ideological components in nationalism, which people tend to ardently believe and act upon, are its world-view or vision of a better life. Nationalism is usually exclusivist and asks for unity with the national group with an extraordinary degree of loyalty. It asserts the right of a nation of people to be served by a state that complements their interests. It maintains that national interests should take supremacy over individual interests and the interests of other national groups. The emotional attachment to nationalism is so strong because it gives the individual an identity which extends itself into something greater than the self. Thus nationalism also has transcendental qualities, evoking a sense of purpose for its followers (Harber 1998:52-53).

How is one to distinguish between a 'healthy' nationalism and a dogmatic nationalism? According to Degenaar (1978:30-31), there are certain mythical justifications for nationalisms. He mentions three – theologism, romanticism and racism:

- Theologism is related to the myth that God has created certain chosen people who believe they have a superior mission (cf the ideology of CNE).
- Romanticism assumes the existence of a national spirit or *volksgeist* which is the inexhaustible source of the individual's life and outside of which man loses his moral value.
- Racism assumes a mystical bond with the 'blood and land' as the basis of nationality.

Viewed critically, these mystical justifications have no real validity.

Another concept used in the ideology of nationalism is the concept of identity. There are two ways in which this concept can be viewed: mystically or more rationally without denying emotions. The mystical way would be to claim that a nation has a spirit or a soul and that the individual born into this nation is identical with that spirit which is usually endowed with superior virtues. Such a view is not open to a rational approach and potentially has very dangerous implications.

If I say that I identify with my sports team or my school or my university, this statement can be rationally unpacked. In speaking in a rational manner about a national or other identity, it loses its assumed fixed, metaphysical nature with which members of that team or nation need to identify themselves. It furthermore does not assume that the nature of human beings is fixed. Human beings are seen to be capable of identifying themselves in a variety of ways with a variety of aspects, of which a nation is but one example. Open identification with other values and other groups simultaneously becomes possible. This is when pluralism comes into play. A plurality of identifications becomes an option and this demonstrates why the identification with the nation-state need not be the only and highest act of identifying oneself. Degenaar (1978:6) proposes that pluralism should become a priority over nationalism as a frame of reference for politics and that an open society is more conducive to the cultivation of democratic values than a closed one.

1.4.2 Racism and fascism

Race is a biological concept, and although one speaks of the human race as distinct from the animal kingdom, the human species is further divided into different races on the basis of specific biological characteristics. The most common are: the Caucasian, Negroid and Mongolian groups, also called the white, black and yellow races. As a socio-psychological term race relates to group consciousness, manifesting characteristics such as social distance, racial discrimination and racial prejudice. Closely related to this is the attitude of racism which can be defined as the view that one racial group is by nature hereditarily inferior and another racial group hereditarily superior. If nationalism is linked to racism, one can talk of racialistic nationalism (Degenaar 1978:51).

When race is used as the dominant feature to explain all aspects of society, as was the case in Nazi Germany, one can talk of the ideology of racism. Basically it boils down to a theory of ethnocentrism, where all other peoples (races) of the world are regarded as inferior and impure. The national socialist ideology of Hitler is an example which explains how the combination of racism, German mythology which legitimised the superiority of the German *volk* (based on a long tradition) and irrationality were used to unite people in the common goal of purging the world of all its evils.

1.5 Ideologies in the context of third-world countries

Because of their past experiences of exploitation by colonial masters, one of the most striking political realities among third-world countries is their enthusiasm for nationalism. It is especially important because they have often suffered a severe identity crisis. The tragic economic realities of many developing countries do not make ruling, for often inexperienced leadership, very easy. The overabundance of people is paired with a scarcity of resources required by modern life. Most newly emerging states are plagued by a high illiteracy rate, cultural traditions and attitudes that hinder modernisation, few skilled people, a lack of an experienced civil service, little modern technology and scarce domestic capital. The demands of the 'have-nots' who are able to observe other societies' wealth through the media create great tension in world politics. The inevitable failure of leaders to meet their citizens' unrealistic expectations and ambitions usually results in either a rapid succession of unstable governments or in military dictatorship.

Although many factors, such as national traditions and cultural habits are important, the most fundamental source of problems plaguing democratic states is economics. As Baradat (1995:271) puts it, 'perhaps more than any other political system, democracy depends for success on wealth'.

Democracy, with its need for tolerance and its requirement for public consensus, often does not fare well during periods of severe economic hardship. For example, if a country lacks a basic infrastructure to allow people to contest issues, or people are so poverty-stricken that they do not see how debates can change their lives and do not have the capacity to participate (e.g. high levels of political illiteracy) in shaping their own destinies, democracy cannot survive.

The term 'guided democracy' is often applied to the centralised systems that tend to develop among third-world states. This centralisation of power happens for the following reasons:

- The communal spirit of tribalism encourages a collective rather than a competitive approach.

- The politically active people in a developing country are often united in a single movement organised to liberate society from colonial control. After independence such a liberation movement usually benefits from politically aware popular leadership and tends to dominate the political system in the form of a centralised system.

- Third-world leaders have to face serious political and economic conditions together with urgent demands for material progress resulting in a Catch 22 situation. If the government fails to overcome the problems quickly, the impatient masses become negative and violent. The ruling party has to decide between two evils: either run the risk of being overtaken by a coup or stay in power, but deal sternly with dissidents and thereby stifle political activity. This kind of authoritarian government is still seen by the people as being 'democratic' because the concept of the basic equality of the citizens has great political resonance. Coming from the same origins and social group as the people, the rulers suggest that they are united by common interests and goals constituting the 'common good'. They continually remind the people that they are united in their experiences of the previous exploitation of the colonial masters (Baradat 1995:273-274). Thus people value the idea of being 'one', or equal, to such an extent that they equate that idea with democracy (participative government). Individuals identify so strongly with the state that they believe that to be as it should be.

We should ask ourselves whether South Africans would find it comfortable to fit into this picture of democracy, whether the concept of 'guided democracy' will eventually be applicable or whether we will adopt another, unique version of democracy altogether.

1.6 South African ideologies and their impact on education

In times of transition, levels of uncertainty are high and stability is a sought-after condition. What is important in this context is to guard against the captivating force of ideological fixations by people in positions of power. Moreover, in any educational situation one is dealing with the emotional, cognitive and psychological dimensions of children's and young adults' learning. During transitional times, such as is the case in South Africa, it is especially important that the different 'masks' of ideological frameworks within educational discourse (debates, curricula, policies) should be closely examined, recognised and demystified to determine their role in the process of educational change.

1.6.1 Ideological roots in the pre-democratic era

The history of ethnically-based education systems in South Africa has resulted in inequalities, backlogs and imbalances regarding both human and financial resources. The present government is endeavouring to address these with its recent policies (The South African Schools Act, the National Education Act, The South African Qualifications Authority Act and the Curriculum 2005). However, the aftermath of the struggle for liberation has left us with an over-politicised educational discourse. The culture of teaching and learning in schools has not yet adequately been re-established and nor has the ethical fabric of a disrupted society been healed.

In light of this, 'nationalisms' within prevalent ideologies in South Africa are discussed. Examples are Afrikaner nationalism and African nationalism. Afrikaner nationalism has demonstrated a fixed, closed and mystical understanding of national identity at the cost of others sharing the same country. According to Walshe (1987) the history of African nationalism demonstrates a far more open-ended approach, although a clear analysis of concepts such as non-racialism, rainbow nation, and *simunye* should be made since these appear to be based upon Utopian ideals. Scholars should become aware of the constant need for a clear analysis of the underpinning value system of a political ideology.

As far as educational ideologies are concerned, educationists from a variety of disciplines should participate in transformation processes of policy formulation debates on national curricula. Attitudes within different viewpoints may range through conservative, moderate and radical (Christie 1992:18-25) or conservative, moderate, radical and reactionary (Baradat 1995:22-27).

Ashley (1989) conducted research on three mainstream educational ideologies which were influential during the pre-democratic era. The following are the main ideas as far as educational goals are concerned:

- Christian National Education was embodied within the white education system and enforced in all former white schools, especially in Afrikaner schools. The official value system was that schools should have a broad Christian and national (meaning Afrikaner nationalist) character. The non-official value system was that of inculcating ethnocentrism and attitudes of both superiority and obedience (or not questioning) towards the state. The aim was obvious – namely to legitimise an own separate education system and maintain white supremacy and privileged social and economic positions.

- Liberalism was mainly concerned with the realisation of the potential of the individual with regard to his obligations to society. The freedom of expression of the individual as well as the development of a critical rationality are regarded as the main value preferences of liberals. These values were mainly inculcated in upper-class English-speaking schools and private schools. Western countries, especially the Anglo-Saxon worlds of the United Kingdom, Australia and the US, cherish liberal values and, apart from English-speaking communities, many black people who took part in the broad democratic movement in South Africa went abroad into exile and were exposed to liberal views expressed there.

- Liberation socialism encapsulates all the viewpoints of the liberation struggle, including those of English liberals, the Black Consciousness Movement (with Steve Biko as the main leader), Cosatu and other trade unions, as well as moderate, idealistic African nationalists who envisioned a democratic, non-racial, non-sexist society. The People's Education Movement emanated from this quarter and embodied the following educational ideals:

  O to prepare people for participation in a non-racial, democratic system

  O to eliminate capitalist norms of competition, individualism and stunted intellectual development

  O to encourage collective input and active participation by involving the community in decisions on the content and quality of education

  O to stimulate critical thinking and bridge the gap between theory and practical life, making education relevant to democratic struggles (Ashley 1989).

1.6.2 Mainstream ideology prevalent in new curriculum policies

It is necessary to investigate the underpinning value system of recent educational policy documents. A number of academics have analysed outcomes-based education within the National Qualifications Framework. Constructive criticisms emerging from these studies have stimulated a debate on the envisaged directions of the South African education system.

Parker and Harley (1998:11-12) argue that the importation of OBE policies and the NQF have not recognised the true nature of the relationship between school and society in South Africa, especially with respect to aspects such as teachers' personal and professional identities. They suggest that staff and students might experience a loss of structure, boundaries and continuity in a way that will make the implementation of Curriculum 2005 extremely problematic. The imported model has emerged in very different societies with a highly advanced division of labour and strong, stable economies. The assumed conditions for the successful implementation of OBE are aspects like well-resourced schools, supportive parents, and efficient and co-operative management. The obvious danger is that those schools most affected by apartheid may well be further disadvantaged by the new approach because the assumed pre-conditions to implement OBE successfully do not exist. Christie (1997:64) agrees on this point, when she remarks that 'there is always a danger that changed curriculum formulations will do little more than introduce new enclosing orthodoxies which continue to privilege the social groups with cultural capital'.

Much will depend on the teachers. To implement OBE within the NQF, teachers will need to shift their own identities – their understanding of who they are and how they relate to others. This requires a high degree of interpersonal skills, self-reflection and adaptation. In-service training needs to be carefully implemented because it needs to look at the level of consciousness and identities of the teachers. In-service training programmes will have to pay urgent attention to this facet before they can tackle curriculum issues as such.

Skinner (1998) has examined the epistemological underpinnings of OBE (assumptions about the kind of knowledge which is valued). She maintains that although the official values show some resemblance to the principles of People's Education (influenced by the Freirean ideal), namely critical thinking and problem-solving skills related to the world of work and so on, the non-official values are about capitalism and the value which knowledge, skills and competencies can contribute to the marketplace. A reason for adopting this particular model of education was the predominant role which the trade unions played when important curricular and policy choices had to be made.

Skinner's findings reveal that the overriding perception of knowledge which is favoured the most in the new envisaged curriculum documents on OBE is no different than before, namely that of positivism and the teaching methods of neo-behaviourism. In stark contrast to this kind of epistemology, Freirean 'critical pedagogy' provided an awareness of issues of power which is potentially a transformative epistemology. It provided a sense of empowerment to individuals formerly excluded from society and of transcending society's assumptions. For this reason Skinner (1998:4) subsequently urges teachers and educational planners to regard educational theories with respectful but skeptical consideration, that is, to analyse the underpinning value system which are often not explicit (the non-official value system). Teachers should not hesitate to question the assumptions of policies. They should also be encouraged to interpret policy directions in a creative way by utilising directives only as a broad framework and not as a blueprint which has to be rigidly obeyed. For example, South African teachers should not only focus on competencies, but also on values and attitudes to build the moral fibre of the society.

1.7 Conclusion

Transformation of education in South Africa implies a radical break with the past and a reconstruction of the system of education within its wider social context, partly because of its loss of legitimacy among the majority of its users. Inbar (1993:166-183) maintains that transformation operates on at least three levels, namely symbols, frames of reference and ultimately behaviour. Lagerwij (1993:26-29) pleads for education as transformation on a different level, meaning that both society and the persons involved (learners, educators, parents) should not be left untouched by educational efforts, but ultimately undergo radical change or personal growth. On a philosophical level, transformation can also be seen as an ongoing worldwide process of evolution, which is essentially a differentiating process, against the backdrop of a continuously changing landscape (Waldrop 1992). Educational change can thus only be properly understood within a broader social context. More importantly, the role of attitudes, value systems and ideologies in identity formation should not be overlooked. A paradox may unexpectedly emerge.

According to Degenaar (1978), the general direction of the democratic transformation of South Africa should be towards cultivating a democratic culture rather than nation building in order to avoid the malaise suffered by some third-world countries. He cautions against a dogmatic understanding of identity formation which leads to an oversimplified and monolithic interpretation of nationalism based on mythical justifications. Instead, he advocates that values of fairness, equality, participating in communities' upliftment and acting out civil responsibility be inculcated.

The development of a democratic culture depends on values and behaviours that are supportive of the practice of democracy in several group settings of civil society. The underlying values should be based on tolerance of diversity, fairness, justice for all, peace, and mutual respect between individuals and groups based on equal social, political and human rights. In a democracy there should be an emphasis on reason, evidence, a critical open-mindedness, fairness, co-operation, negotiation, compromise and accommodation. Such values and attitudes are acquired rather than inherited through social interaction and learning. Education – formal and informal – can play a role in developing these values. For example, schools have been successful in promoting or combating racism, and racism is a prime example of the negation of such democratic values as fairness, equality, tolerance and mutual respect (Harber 1998:2-3).

Comparative educationists more often study collective education in a global context. This enables them to use insights gained from this 'bird's-eye view' in their own educational situation. Noah (1984:154) contends that 'Comparative Education can help us understand better our past, locate ourselves more exactly in the present, and discern a little more clearly what our education future may be'.

Recent trends in comparative education indicate that educational issues should become the focus of educational studies (Thomas 1990:294). International comparisons are done with the specific purpose of looking at similarities and differences in educational aims and policies to learn lessons which could be useful for countries' own systems. Although direct 'transplants' and borrowing from one system to another are not being advocated, valuable insights can be gained from others' experiences. Jallade (1989:103) formulates this succinctly:

> This is perhaps the real value of comparative studies: revealing the existence of alternatives when a real national debate has become bogged down and at the same time suggesting some general principles – carefully expressed, naturally – which could be applied to specific national circumstances.

In other words when an education system experiences a problematic phase such as transition, the importance of asking the correct questions is far more crucial than finding instant solutions. Only by asking questions can alternatives and creative solutions arise. Moreover, De Clercq (1997:165) warns against the mechanical transplantation of other countries' policies, saying that South African policy work will benefit significantly 'if it roots itself more firmly in local realities, dynamics and constraints on the ground and if it promotes a dialogue and debate among the social actors involved at all different levels of policy-making'.

Educational discourses should not be left entirely to politicians (Ginsburg et al. 1990:498). All role players within the educational arena should become participants in shaping the formal and informal educational scene. Educators who are particularly influential as community leaders should be able to recognise the importance of underlying value systems (both official and non-official), the role of power struggles and vested interests in debates. Educators should develop the capacity to detect these concealed factors as well as influence debates and directions of change processes in order to make a difference in their own communities.

References

Ashley, M (1989) *Ideologies in schooling in South Africa*. Rondebosch: South African Teachers Association.

Badenhorst, DC (1993) Exploring the role of values in formal education. In EI Dekker and EM Lemmer (eds) *Critical issues in modern education*. Durban: Butterworths.

Badenhorst, DC (1998) The socialising role of the school in society. Study guide for OSO431. Pretoria: Unisa.

Baradat, LP (1995) *Political ideologies: their origins and impact*. Fifth edition. New Jersey: Prentice Hall.

Beck, D and Linscott, G (1991) *The crucible: forging South Africa's future*. Denton: New Paradigm.

Botha, JE (1997) Biblical social values and African social values today. In CW du Toit (ed) *Images of Jesus: A compilation of papers at the twenty-first symposium of the Research Institute for Theology and Religion* held at the University of South Africa, 3-4 September 1997.

Botha, TR (1989) Multikulturaliteit en onderwys: ideologiese alter egos. *Aambeeld*, 17(2):1-25.

Brooks, BD and Kahn, ME (1992) Value-added education. *The American School Board Journal*, December 179(12):24-27.

Christie, P (1992) *The right to learn: the struggle for education in South Africa*. Pretoria: Sached Trust.

Christie, P (1997) Globalisation and the curriculum: proposals for the integration of education and training in comparative context. In P Kallaway, G Kruss, G Donn and A Fataar (eds) *Education after apartheid: South African education in transition*. Cape Town: UCT Press.

Davies, EH (1991) Curricular enterprise. Unpublished paper delivered at a seminar held by NAPTOSA and PRU, 26 September.

De Clercq, F (1997) Effective policies and the reform process: an evaluation of South Africa's new development and education macro policies. In P Kallaway, G Kruss, G Donn and A Fataar (eds) *Education after apartheid: South African education in transition*. Cape Town: UCT Press.

Degenaar, JJ (1978) *The roots of nationalism*. Cape Town: University of Stellenbosch.

Drucker, PF (1993) *Post-capitalist society*. New York: Harper.

Du Toit, CW (1991) *Kontoere van 'n teologie van mag*. Paper delivered at Faculty of Theology, Unisa.

Eisner, EW (1994) *Cognition and curriculum reconsidered*. Second edition. New York: Teachers' College, Columbia.

Ginsburg, MB; Cooper, S; Raghu, R and Zegarra, H (1990) Focus on educational reform: national and world-system explanations of educational reform. *Comparative Education Review*, November:474-499.

Harber, C (1998) *Racism in two countries: racism and civic education for democracy in Britain and South Africa*. Paper delivered at the WCCES conference held in Cape Town, July 1998.

Heese, C (1992) In C Heese and DC Badenhorst *South Africa: the education equation. Problems, perspectives and prospects.* Pretoria: JL van Schaik.

Hunter, I (1994) *Rethinking the school: subjectivity, bureaucracy, criticism.* New York: St Martin's Press.

Inbar, DE (1993) Educational planning: the transformation of symbols, frames of reference and behaviour. *Education Policy,* 7(2):166-183.

Jallade, JP (1989) Recent trends in educational education and training: an overview. *European Journal of Education,* 24(2):103-125.

Jordaan, W (1990) Die bevrore psige van regse radikaal. *Insig,* April:15-16.

Joubert, SJ (1992) Van werklikheid tot werklikheid: die interpretasie en interkulturele kommunikasie van Nuwe Testamentiese waardes. *Scriptura,* 41:55-56.

Lagerwij, N (1993) *De lange adem van onderwijs vernieuwing.* Vakgroep onderwijskunde. Universiteit Utrecht: Utrecht.

Mouton, J (1990) Wanneer is sosiaalwetenskaplike oortuigings ideologies? *Aambeeld,* 18(1):31-35.

Noah, H (1984) The use and abuse of comparative education. *Comparative Education Review,* 28(4):550-562.

Nyberg, D (1990) Teaching values in the school: the warrior and the lamp. *Teachers' College Record,* 91(4):595-612.

Parker, B and Harley, K (1998) *Curriculum and teacher development in an outcomes-based National Qualifications Framework: a study of South Africa in the 1990s.* Paper delivered at the Tenth World Conference of Comparative Education Societies (WCCES), Cape Town, 12-17 July.

Pilch, JJ and Malina, BJ (1993) *Biblical social values and their meaning: a handbook.* Peabody: Hendrickson.

Pillay, GJ (1991) Theology and the fanaticised consciousness. Inaugural lecture in the Department of Missiology, Unisa, 8 March.

Rosenau, PM (1992) *Postmodernism and the social sciences: insights, inroads and intrusions.* Princeton: Princeton University Press.

Segal, S (1992) *The logic of fear in Christian Nationalism.* Paper presented at the Kenton Conference held at Broederstroom, October.

Skinner, J (1998) *Critical outcomes – political paradoxes.* Paper presented at the Tenth World Congress of Comparative Education Societies (WCCES), Cape Town, 12-17 July.

Thomas, M (ed) (1990) *International comparative education: practices, issues, prospects.* Oxford and California, US: Pergamon Press.

Thomas, RM and Postlethwaite, TN (eds) (1983) *Schooling in East Asia: forces of change.* Oxford: Pergamon Press.

Toffler, A (1990) *Powershift: knowledge, wealth and violence at the edge of the 21st century.* New York: Bantam Books.

Touwen, A (1996) *Gender and development in Zambia.* D.Ed. thesis. Rijks University, Groningen.

Van Niekerk, A (1990) Die invloed van ideologieë op die alledaagse lewe. *Roeping en Riglyne,* 38(1):1-3.

Van Niekerk, MP (1993) Ideology and educational change in Spain and South Africa. In EI Dekker and EM Lemmer (eds) *Critical issues in modern education.* Durban: Butterworths.

Waldrop, MM (1992) *Complexity: the emerging science at the edge of order and chaos.* London: Penguin.

CHAPTER 2

THE STATE, GLOBALISATION AND EDUCATION

Prof Chris Claassen
University of South Africa

Table of contents

2.1 Introduction

The state plays an important role in the life of an individual. You are a citizen of a state and your nationality is often your primary identification. For example, if a foreigner asks you who you are, you are likely to answer, 'I am a Kenyan' or 'I am a German', whatever the case may be.

Traditionally, the state has been instrumental in the provision of education. In every single state of the world there is a national education system which is administered and funded by the state. To be sure, some national education systems are not monolithic, in that they have subsystems (such as the French, German and Italian subsystems in Switzerland) or are decentralised systems (such as the 50 state or provincial subsystems in the US).

This traditional role of the state is being challenged by the rise of so-called globalisation or internationalisation. In its most extreme form, globalisation theory predicts the following:

- National economies and states will fade into oblivion.
- The world will become borderless and national cultures will become hybrids of each other.
- National education systems, key institutional supports of the state, will lose their function to transmit national cultures and to reproduce national labour power and thus become obsolete.

In this chapter we will examine this prediction by questioning the effect of globalisation on the role of the state as a provider of mass education. A good starting point is to examine the historical development of states and education systems.

2.2 Historical overview

Since the dawn of history there have been civilisations, empires, dynasties, countries, city-states and other political entities. Similarly, education has been practised in a rudimentary form ever since humankind climbed from savagery to some form of accumulated culture. Wilds and Lottich (1970:3) believe that 'education occurred long before anyone thought about it; people thought about education long before anyone wrote about it'.

However, it is only from the 1600s that sovereign, territorially-bounded states were created out of the many often-disorganised political entities which existed until then. Thus, modern states have been created only during the past three centuries. New nations had to be forged out of these states. National symbols such as flags and anthems were adopted in order to unite the nation. The citizenry was conscripted and disciplined in the national defence force and nationalist wars were waged.

However, the best way of forging a nation was to supply mass education. For this purpose, national education systems were created. Thus, the creation of modern states simultaneously led to the introduction of national education systems. 'The history of national education is very much the history of the nation state in formation' (Green 1997:31).

Education became the tool which states used to train workers, to maintain and develop a common culture and to give citizens a shared national identity. In short, the overall aim of the national education system was, and still is to a large extent, *citizen formation*. Education is quite logically an excellent tool to achieve this benign form of national social engineering.

State involvement in education is attested to by the fact that in each country there is a minister of education who is the political head of the state education enterprise. The state is involved at all levels here, in both pedagogical matters (curriculum content, teacher training, national goals) and non-pedagogical matters (funding, support services, administration). There are extensive education bureaucracies (usually called departments of education) and a huge amount of public funds is spent on education. In developing countries like South Africa, such expenditure readily amounts to more than 20% of the national budget, frequently becoming the largest single item of that budget.

This process of state and nation formation is continued to this day. Look at a map of the world drawn in 1950 – it is vastly different from that created at the end of the century. At its inception in 1947, the United Nations consisted of 67 member states. This number grew to 193 in 1998. The Soviet Union alone has broken up into more than 20 states in the last decade.

The proliferation of states has produced a concomitant increase in national education systems. Developing countries attach special significance to the role of the state in education. Green (1997:143) states that 'in the developing world there has been an even more explicit link between education and state formation, with education unequivocally linked with both citizen formation and national economic development'. A sizable proportion of public funds is directed to education. Those states that cut down on public spending on education are regarded as pariahs.

In conclusion, there is not a single state which reneges on its responsibility to provide education, although the level of state involvement varies from country to country. However, recent global developments are impacting on the traditional connection between the state and education.

2.3 The decline of the state

There are signs that the significance of the state is declining:

> At the beginning of the twentieth century we saw the development of the nation-state as the natural focal point for government and the control of

peoples ... indeed many would argue that the twentieth century has been 'the age of the nation-state'. Now, as we come to the end of the twentieth century and approach the twenty-first century, the concept of the nation-state is coming under threat from a variety of sources. These changes have major implications for the provision of public education systems, since these have hitherto developed with one major purpose which is to develop a sense of national identity and mass allegiance to the concept of the state. (Watson 1994:1)

The reasons for this decline are interconnected and represent different sides of the coin called globalisation. Other facets which erode the traditional notion of the state include:

- localisation
- technology
- the changing workplace
- post-modernism.

Globalisation and its related influences are first discussed, followed by a critical analysis of the implications for education.

2.3.1 Globalisation

Reich (1992:112) supplies the following example of globalisation at work: 'A sports car is financed in Japan, designed in Italy, and assembled in America, Mexico and France'.

Companies become transnational in this *economic* globalisation process. They owe allegiance to no particular state and their employees belong to different states. In this process, the economies of states have become interlinked and interdependent (Pretorius 1996:141). A country's success depends on how many of the nation's citizens can sell high-value skills and insights in the world market. The countries that fail to compete fall behind and become economically marginalised (Maraj 1996:9). Quite logically, the importance of the state dwindles in such an environment, creating a so-called post-national world. Supranational forces ('larger-than-national forces') exceed national ones.

Thus, globalisation theory has its origins in the New Right view of *laissez faire* free-market capitalism. Fukuyama's controversial 'end of history' thesis holds that all successful countries will ultimately adhere to free-market capitalism (Fukuyama 1992). All societies will become similar, there will be no more wars and a globalised one-world system will be in place, thus leading to the end of history as the record of competing nations.

Although globalisation is a process which has its origins in economics, it has spread to influence spheres such as culture and education. For example, a global popular teenage culture has developed. A teenager in Bombay can look similar to one in Soweto. They may wear the same clothes, eat hamburgers from the same international hamburger franchises, listen to Michael Jackson's music and can share many similar attitudes and views on life.

Cultural globalisation becomes a process of hybridisation which gives rise to a global *mélange*, for example Moroccan girls practising Thai boxing in Amsterdam. The process is actually one of so-called glocalisation, in which the global and the local interpenetrate. But while it seems that a global culture is developing, this is only superficially so.

Our civilisation has essentially globalised only the surface of our lives. Our inner self continues to have a life of its own. Because of this, individual cultures, increasingly lumped together by contemporary civilisation, are realising with new urgency their own inner autonomy and their differences with others (Havel 1994).

The ultimate claim of globalisation is the demise of the nation-state. This claim is debatable. It is evident that there is a global market in goods, capital and communications. However, this does not necessarily mean the end of the state. For one, the nation-state has always co-existed with international markets. While the role of the state may be changing, globalisation does not necessarily reduce the importance of its functions, such as the provision of mass education (Green 1997:165). Furthermore, the number of new states would not indicate the demise of the state. More than 100 nation-states have been established in the last 40 years, the very era in which globalisation has taken effect. Paradoxically, more nation-states are being formed, even as their internal influence wanes (Naisbitt 1994:66).

2.3.2 Localisation

An interesting and seemingly contradictory development is taking place simultaneously with globalisation, namely localisation. Even as people are losing their national attachments and becoming more internationalised, they are also becoming more attached to their primary cultural group. This group may be ethnic, religious or linguistic, or a combination of these. Naisbitt (1994) uses the term *global paradox* to describe this seemingly contradictory development. There are many examples of cultural and ethnic resurgence across the globe, such as the break-up of the former Soviet Union into more than 20 autonomous countries, and the special rights accorded to the French in Quebec, Canada, and to the Native Americans in the US.

Both globalisation and localisation erode the all-pervasive hold of the nation-state on the citizenry. The reason for localisation is perhaps that the global environment is simply too impersonal for individuals to relate to, and that they long for something more tangible with which to identify, a group in which they feel secure. The nation-state falls between two chairs as it were, being 'too big for the small problems and too small for the big problems' (Degenaar 1995:9).

Thus, localism brings subnational forces ('smaller-than-national forces') to the fore, while globalisation underscores supranational forces.

2.3.3 Technology

Information technology (IT) such as the computer, the Internet and e-mail, fast transport and global television channels such as CNN are examples of modern technology. Without technology the process of globalisation would have been impossible. Technology creates a so-called *information revolution*, so that knowledge production rather than the production of material things is becoming the major economic activity.

The widespread use of technology undermines the traditional role of the state. On the one hand, people across the globe are brought into close contact with one another by technology. In this global village the influence of the state wanes:

> States once relied on their ability to shape what citizens thought and believed, by control over the information received. Today many states have lost that control. Information enters their countries freely. (McGinn 1997:548)

On the other hand, people are exposed to enough information to decide for themselves where they want to live and work. Job skills are becoming portable – one can easily take one's skills across international borders, which are becoming penetrable. As job opportunities become internationalised so people are growing less attached to their countries of birth. The global village has become too small and too familiar for people to give their loyalty blindly to the piece of soil where they happen to be born. In a sense, people are becoming global citizens rather than national citizens.

In other words, there is a shift of power away from the state, which used to control the lives of people. Because people can obtain knowledge and skills from various sources, and because they can easily move around, they take control of their own lives. Toffler (1990) coined the term *powershift* to denote this trend. Totalitarian states do not tolerate this powershift, fearing that the citizenry will become too empowered.

Technological progress is closely intertwined with globalisation, being both a cause and an effect of globalisation. On the one hand, technology brought the world in close contact. On the other hand, growing globalisation demands even more advanced technology to support it.

2.3.4 The changing workplace

We are entering the fourth stage in the economic development of humankind. Initially, people were nomadic *hunter-gatherers*, constantly on the move in search of food and shelter. Gradually, agriculture was introduced, and people practised a subsistence economy: your work was to produce your own food and to barter for other products. Most people were involved in farming. In Western countries, about 50% of the population was involved in agriculture in the *agrarian, pre-industrial age*, while this number shrank to 3% in 1980. The *industrial age*, which started in the nineteenth century (the 1800s), brought about a powerful change. People moved from the farms to cities where they offered their labour in factories and industries which manufactured products. After World War II, 50% of all jobs in Western countries were in the manufacturing sector (Maraj 1996:5).

Currently another massive shift is taking place in the workplace. We are moving into the *post-industrial* or *post-Fordist era*. The Fordist era derives its name from the typical production line of the Ford car factory, which has become a metaphor for the conveyor belt factory jobs of the industrial era.

The difference between the Fordist and the post-Fordist work environments can be summarised as follows:

Fordist	Post-Fordist
isolated work	team work
fixed markets	flexible, competitive markets
mass products	niche products
fragmentation of work	multi-skilling
formality	informality
following orders	negotiation

As a result of post-Fordism, people are moving from the manufacturing sector into the service and information sector. Examples of service and information jobs are those of waiter, travel agent, banker and computer programmer. Instead of making tangible things like cars, more people are now delivering intangible services. Improved mechanisation and technology have lessened the need for physical toil. Simultaneously, technology has created the need and the means for more services.

Technological progress has brought about changes in workforce patterns (Titmus 1989:393). Since the first half of the twentieth century the working week has been shortened and the age of the work force has been increasing. Furthermore, new technology makes some jobs obsolete while creating other ones. While being trained for a single career or trade in the past, it is estimated that many workers will in future have to change jobs as many as four times during their working lives (Dekker 1993:298).

In section 2.4.2 below the educational implications of the changing workplace will be discussed.

2.3.5 Post-modernism

Post-modernism is the overall philosophical framework within which the above trends take place. It reacts against modernism (cf Van Niekerk 1996), which had its beginnings in Europe during the Renaissance some 500 years ago. This was a period of classical scholarship, scientific and geographical study characterised by a sense of individual human potential. 'Knowledge increased humanity's confidence that it was the Lord of the Universe, and improvements in conditions of life were possible through the application of intelligence' state McGinn and Cummings (1997:18). Rationality and objectivity became central tenets of Western thinking.

Scientific discoveries and inventions have improved the quality of our lives immensely. The modern nation-state, the national education system and the modern school are products of modernism (Badenhorst & Claassen 1995:66; McGinn & Cummings 1997:33). Rust (1991:619) argues that the national education system has been designed to fit modernist purposes, stating that 'Schools served as universalizing institutions, promoting unifying ideals and fostering notions of nationalism and civic pride'.

However, modernism has also brought about catastrophic developments (Bosch 1991:350). The global environmental crisis is attributed to modernism. Because modernism stresses expansion and growth, natural resources have been recklessly depleted in an effort to achieve this. Humanity itself has developed in an unbalanced way. Although modernism has improved the quality of some people's lives, it has occurred at the expense of that of others. Furthermore, an over-optimistic belief in the power of science to solve all problems has reduced people's sense of spirituality and awe. They mistakenly believe that humankind can ultimately control everything in nature. In the past few decades there has been a gradual shift away from the so-called grand narratives and strict dogma (a thing is either right or wrong) of modernism to a new value system which acknowledges paradoxicality, complexity and relative truths.

In post-modernism, everybody has an autonomous voice regardless of their position in the hierarchy of power. There are many discourses. This leads to cultural pluralism and fragmentation. The post-modern state is almost a contradiction in terms. The state can no longer be a unifying project as a single nationalism is unwarranted in a post-modern age (Hinkson 1991).

There is an interesting convergence between the views of the New Right and post-modernism. Both are sceptical of state education, albeit for different reasons. The New Right rejects the idea that a common, state-driven education system should be used for a progressive social end, such as increasing social equality. They criticise state education as an inefficient market monopoly, and would rather that market mechanisms dictate education policy, which would bring about greater diversity. Post-modernism, again, rejects state education for its imposition of a uniform culture on diverse populations.

2.4 Education and globalisation

In the previous section, globalisation and its corollaries – localisation, technology, the changing workplace and post-modernism – were discussed. These issues are now more directly related to education by raising the following questions:

- What are the general effects of globalisation on education?
- What are the educational implications of the changing workplace?
- How does globalisation influence the role of the state in providing education?

2.4.1 General effects of globalisation

At a first level, globalisation will make and, indeed, has already made changes to traditional patterns of education provision, for example:

- Rust and Kim (1997:565-572) cite numerous global education tendencies, at higher, secondary and primary levels. These include international oversight and standards councils, student exchanges, recognition of credits, internationalisation of qualifications, branch campuses in foreign countries, the dramatic growth of distance education, international research, school partnerships, multicultural curricula, language instruction, values training and universal standards for vocational training.

- The curriculum reflects the global context. The selection of knowledge for the curriculum is not confined to localised facts: 'Schooling will have increasingly less to offer in terms of preparing oneself for a role in the community, and will become more focused on preparing one for a prescribed life in the global economy' (Ilon 1997:620).

- An approach to education, called *global education*, has been devised for this purpose:

  Global education requires an understanding of the values and priorities of the many cultures of the world ... Global education leads to the implementation and application of the global perspective in striving for just and peaceful solutions to world problems. (Brown-Guillory & Guillory 1989:58)

- Mathematics, science and technology are strongly influenced by the global context. Many studies indicate that proficiency in these disciplines is a prerequisite for economic success. Ramirez (1997:57) believes that 'the expansion of math and science students in higher education should increase the technological quality of the labor force, and hence, generate greater economic growth'.

One response to this global demand is the National Education Goals project launched in the US in 1990. The following goals to be attained by 2000 were formulated:

- Learners in grades 4, 8 and 12 will be nationally assessed in English, mathematics, science, history and geography.
- American learners will be first in the world in science and mathematics.
- Every adult American will be literate and will have the knowledge and skills to compete in the global economy and to be responsible citizens.
- Multiculturalism, that is, knowledge and appreciation of cultural diversity, infuses the curriculum. Learners should understand and appreciate cultural differences, not only between other cultures within the country, but between cultures across the globe.
- Learners are introduced to technology through technology education and technology-aided education (e.g. teaching maths, science, geography and history with the aid of computers). An effective education system will constantly be in touch with the demands of the world of employment. In virtually all developing countries, technology, and especially the use of the computer, has become an integral part of daily teaching. For example, in the United Kingdom each learner, in addition to having access to the Internet at school, is supplied with a free personal e-mail address.
- Learning will be separated from its traditional institutional locations. In other words, physical schools will be replaced by virtual schools or cyber schools, because close proximity will not be required when information is delivered electronically.

Many of these predictions have partly been realised. Information technology does open up new possibilities for education (cf Kamil 1994). Learning is no longer constrained by the limitations of time and space. This has an interesting parallel with the invention of print by Gutenberg in the 1400s: 'Just as Gutenberg paved the way for the independent itinerant scholars of Renaissance Europe, so the global web can create a new generation of mental travellers, only this time they need not leave their terminals' (Green 1997:171).

However, it seems unlikely that education will be completely de-institutionalised. For example, at least at the compulsory levels (primary school and part of the secondary school), there will still be a classroom and a teacher. Socialising and tutoring will always require close proximity. At tertiary level, on the other hand, more separation not only is feasible but is already happening, as evidenced by the many traditional residential institutions which are offering distance education. Even at this level, however, fields of study like science, medicine and engineering require laboratories and other expensive resources which can only be cost-effective in a physical group context. At some point, a medical student has to cease computer simulations and operate on a real patient under physical supervision.

2.4.2 Educational implications of the changing workplace

The modern school arose out of a desire to link with a larger world and to access the opportunities it promised (Ilon 1997:619). However, globalisation has changed this larger world from the community or region to the world itself. It is obvious that not everyone can have a job directly or indirectly tied to a global economy. Ilon (1997:620) proposes that 'One's ability to access a job and that job's linkage to a global economy will be the primary determinant of one's demand for education'.

Labour will continue to be stratified (divided into classes and categories of different status and income) as it has always been. However, in a global context the room for stratification will be much larger. For example, at the one end of the spectrum a person from a remote area or an undeveloped country will have access to even more limited job opportunities than in the last three decades. At the other end, a person in a developed country with access to information technology will have a wide array of attractive, well-paying job opportunities.

Ilon (1997:620) identifies five basic categories in a global job stratification. Each of these categories demands a different level and type of education:

- *World-class jobs*. These jobs are often called *symbolic analysts*. This recent concept, which has been popularised by Reich (1992), involves problem-solving, problem-identifying and strategic-brokering activities. It involves sophisticated analyses, most often in the service sector. Symbolic analysts identify, broker and solve problems by manipulating symbols. They simplify reality into abstract images that can be rearranged and experimented with, and eventually transformed back into reality. These workers trade in symbols – data, words, and oral and visual representations (Reich 1992:178). Typical jobs are research scientists, design engineers, information technology workers, civil engineers, biotechnologists, public relations workers, marketing strategists, journalists, musicians, television producers, bankers, lawyers and real estate developers. These workers will demand a world-class education for their children.

- *Internationally linked jobs*. Located primarily in one area, these jobs are closely linked to a global economy, such as banking executives and travel industry specialists. Although they may not be able to pay for world-class schooling, they demand the best of local schooling, which is often private education.

- *Local support jobs*. These jobs support the local economy. Examples are service shops and manufacturers of locally used products. They are not directly linked to the global economy and exist largely for local demand. These workers will use such resources as are available to make sure that their children have the best education possible.

- *Community-supported jobs*. These jobs are defined by community needs. Examples are farm workers and butchers. These workers generally attend only public schools.

- *Non-participatory jobs*. People in these jobs live on the fringes of a formal economy and only occasionally participate in work and schooling.

It is clear that retraining will be needed for workers in labour-declining industries. It can be assumed that those modes of education which emphasise retraining such as continuing education, adult education and lifelong learning will become more significant in future.

Reich (1992:229) lists several skills which world-class jobs in particular will require:

- *Abstraction*. The real world contains a vast jumble of noises, shapes, colours, smells and textures which are actually meaningless until the human mind imposes some order on them. Education should develop the capacity for abstraction, the very skill needed by symbolic analysts. The learner should be skilled in wielding equations, formulae, analogies, models and metaphors to create possibilities for reinterpreting and rearranging the data to create new solutions.

- *System thinking*. This carries abstraction a step further. Traditional teaching is often aimed at reductionism – seeing things apart, almost as a series of snapshots, and as belonging to disciplines. System thinking requires learners to see relationships among phenomena. For example, instead of teaching learners how to travel from one place to another by following a prescribed route, learners should rather familiarise themselves with the entire terrain so that they can find shortcuts to wherever they want to go. They should generate their own problems and solutions, as it were.

- *Experimentation*. Traditional schooling often discourages experimentation, an urge which is innate in young children. Metaphorically speaking, learners should explore a city on their own, often getting lost, rather than following a guided tour.

- *Collaboration*. Symbolic analysts typically work in teams. Learning activities should be designed in such a way that learners collaborate, communicate and achieve consensus.

Many countries have reformed their education systems to meet these challenges (Pretorius 1996). Learners are made aware of the brave new world they will be facing in the workplace. New curricula stress creative thinking and problem-solving skills instead of mere rote learning to enable learners to adapt to the ever-changing demands of the workplace.

One such response is the introduction of a new outcomes-based curriculum in South Africa, the so-called Curriculum 2005. This aims at seven critical outcomes, including problem-solving skills, team work, communication by means of mathematics and language, and the application of science and technology. To a large degree, this curriculum is a response to the demands of globalisation.

Generally, curricula are becoming more vocationally orientated. However, this does not imply a narrow focus in which the learner is trained for a single job such as a car mechanic. Cars may become obsolete during the learner's working life! Instead of a narrow vocational education, career education may be a better option. Career education provides learners with broad, portable skills which they can carry over from one job to the next (Department of Education and Culture 1990:24). Although career education is not far removed from a traditional academic education, it is more in touch with the world of work.

Both education *demand* and education *supply* will be affected by the changing work environment. Economic circumstances of a country or a region will directly affect the impetus for education. The emphasis on education is quite different at the two ends of the spectrum, namely low-income, low-growth (LILG) countries at the one extreme and high income, high growth (HIHG) countries at the other. In LILG countries the social welfare aspect of education will be emphasised, while job preparation will be emphasised in HIHG countries.

In LILG countries, there is little need to train people for a growing labour market which barely exists. The jobs that do exist will require only minimum levels of education. On the other hand, in HIHG countries labour demand will often outpace labour supply, favouring intellectual/analytic skills over manual skills. Where job growth is highest, education focused on job training will be highest.

Sadly, the gap between HIHG countries and LILG may be widened by the demands of globalisation. Education inequality may actually increase, despite efforts to decrease it. The most desirable jobs – world class jobs and internationally linked jobs – will be catered for by the education systems of HIHG countries, while the education systems of LILG countries are highly unlikely to cater for non-existing jobs.

In addition, the imbalance between in-groups and out-groups within a country may also increase as a result of globalisation. The stratification of schools may increase, leading to wide divergence from national norms. Élite public and private schools may provide educational levels, content and quality above the average. On the other hand, neighbouring schools of poorer means may find the needs of their learners quite different.

Thus, globalisation may have the very real effect of the rich becoming richer, and having better education and, conversely, the poor becoming poorer, with inferior education (Reich 1992:208). Although it is not impossible to break this vicious cycle, it is decidedly more difficult to do so for newly emerging countries competing against established 'old' nations.

2.4.3 The role of the state in providing education

At the outset, it should be noted that there are divergent responses to this issue, all of which are supported by research and practical developments. In the discussion below both sides of the issue are given.

Kenway (1992) and Usher and Edwards (1994) are authors who predict the extremist effects of globalisation on the state. In a nutshell, these predictions are as follows:

- The demise of the state in providing mass education is imminent. The demands of the international economic market will carry more weight than the culturalist voice of the state.

- Schooling will be shifted away from central state control (McGinn & Cummings 1997:31). Control over major practices and policies will move to the school level and parents will play a larger role.

- The traditional statist goal of transmitting common cultures will become obsolete. The multitude of cultures and subcultures undermine the modernist goals of national education as a unifying project.

- Education can no longer control or be controlled: 'Education can no longer function as a means of reproducing society or as an instrument of large-scale social engineering' (Usher & Edwards 1994:211).

Again, many of these predictions are partly feasible. Policy borrowing between states will grow as the world becomes smaller. In fact, this has always been the case. For example, Cousin advised the French about Prussian (German) education policies in the 1700s, and Marc-Antoine Jullien, the father of Comparative Education, observed education systems across Europe in order to improve the education system of his home country, France. More recently, the past 20 years have been a period of huge international trading in educational ideas. For example, the newly introduced curriculum in South Africa which is premised on outcomes-based education has been influenced by experiences in Australia, Canada, New Zealand and the US. Similarly, Japan has internationalised its curriculum, increased educational exchanges, promoted foreign languages and supported education in developing countries.

This process of internationalisation has brought about a larger degree of similarity in the way in which states provide education. The phrase *educational isomorphism* ('sameness') is used to describe the global standardisation of education. Ramirez (1997:54) illustrates this standardisation in terms of compulsory schooling, the expansion of primary enrolments and primary school curricula. Inkeles and Sirowy (1993) have found international convergence in areas such as administration and finance. In Europe, mass post-compulsory and higher education has been developed in virtually all the European Union member states. In many Western countries a single ladder in compulsory education and a standardised, national curriculum are now followed in contrast to the widely divergent curricula of the past. At the same time, schools provide for a greater diversity of learners. For example, European post-compulsory schools are classified into three main fields, namely general and academic, broadly vocational or technical, and vocational.

McGinn (1997:548) contends that supranational organisations have a four-fold impact on education:

- Competition between the mass media (controlled by transnational corporations) and schools for the attention of youth. For example, it is the mass media, and no longer the school and education, which defines heroes.

- Transnational corporations define the need for human resources, making it increasingly difficult for national education systems to anticipate the kinds of graduates who will find employment.

- They undermine state control of public education. Most world bodies, such as Unesco and the World Bank, are avid supporters of decentralisation and privatisation.

- They are directly involved in national decisions about education. For example, when Mexico became a member of the North American Free Trade Agreement (NAFTA), its government had to give the 'productive sector' a direct role in planning education.

Despite these growing similarities, there are still many distinct national features in all education systems. These features cut across the entire education endeavour, such as knowledge traditions, curricula, types of schools and outcomes. For example, in countries with rationalist traditions, such as France, there are broad curricula up to a later stage, while countries with more humanist traditions, like England, introduce specialisation at an early stage. Post-compulsory education is work-based in some countries (for example, Germany and Austria), while it is school-based in other countries (for example, the US and France). It is unlikely that globalisation will ultimately cause all schools across the globe to have similar curricula and approaches.

It is apparent that anti-state forces such as decentralisation and privatisation are growing stronger. For example, many alternatives to traditional funding are sought such as more privatisation, education vouchers, performance-linked salaries and the closure of non-performing schools. However, even in this regard there is an interesting paradox (McGinn 1997:549). There are simultaneous processes of decentralisation and centralisation. For example, in the United Kingdom and other countries, local schools were given control of management, but at the same time national curricula were introduced. Thus, it seems that states assume a more differentiated role in providing education, delegating those functions in which they are ineffective while assuming more power in areas where they can and should exert an influence.

The final question remains: Will the role of the state decline to the extent that the national education system disappears and is replaced by some hybridised global education system? Current evidence points to the contrary. Even though there is greater international penetration of national education systems, and even though the demands of the international market have influenced education more directly, these systems are still firmly entrenched.

Green (1997:179) disagrees with McGinn (1997:550) on the influence of supranational organisations. Despite their undoubted influence, supranational bodies have only a limited say in the education affairs of member states (Green 1997:179). Not a single state has combined with a neighbouring state to form a joint education system. There are still as many education systems as there are nations:

> For all the postmodern protestations to the contrary, and despite the effects of globalizing trends, governments across the world still exercise considerable control over their national education systems and still seek to use them to achieve national goals. (Green 1997:181)

Even though the goal of citizen formation has been largely replaced by the goal of skills formation in developed countries, this has an interesting 'national' slant to it. Developed nations with high wages such as the US and EU member states cannot compete with low-wage nations such as Taiwan and Thailand in making products. Developed countries must rely on high value-added, knowledge-based products and especially services. This requires high levels of skill and flexibility among its humanpower. At the same time, it is difficult for these governments to manage their national economies through fiscal, monetary and trade regulations. They turn to skills formation in the education system which they can at least control. Paradoxically, skills formation is just another way of achieving national preservation and citizen formation.

Even the argument derived from post-modernism does not necessarily erode the role of the state. The notion of the national education system as a unifying project is untenable in a post-modern context, as a universal and unifying education are anathema to the plural discourses of post-modernism. However, this is a distorted view of post-modern society, which is both more diverse and more homogeneous than the traditional modern world. Globalisation provides ways for local cultures to express themselves. However, at the same time it makes them more visible to other cultures, which creates a common discourse. Sharp distinctions between groups based on ethnicity, class and language have decreased and led to greater social uniformity.

This argument is even more complex when the new identity of the *individual* is considered: the demise of group identities in one respect has led to greater individuation and greater diversity at the individual level. The state must provide an education which is commensurate with this diversity. Individuals must be allowed to be themselves, but they must also show awareness of a collective identity:

> For the individual it means constructing identities and negotiating loyalties within the complex constellation of collectivities defined by geography, ethnicity, age and nationality, as well as cultivating the skills which enable active participation in democratic society at community and national levels. (Green 1997:186)

State-promoted mass education will play a role in this: it provides opportunities for individual development and it promotes civic identity and competence; it promotes both citizen formation and skills formation.

2.5 Conclusion

In section 2.3.1 globalisation was criticised for being a purely economic, market-driven response to changes in the world. This criticism is substantiated by the effects on education listed above. Virtually all the changes in response to globalisation point to a utilitarian response to education. It would seem that the traditional goal of education, *citizen formation*, makes way for a new goal, namely *skills formation*. When citizen formation is the aim of education, the importance of the state is entrenched – education, state formation and nation building are complementary. When skills formation becomes the main focus of education, the role of the state declines. Although this is not necessarily a negative development, its proponents should at least be aware of its pitfalls.

The skills formation view of education, which is largely a result of globalisation, is part of the neoclassical paradigm in economics. According to this paradigm or 'thought framework', there is a positivist, linear link between education, societal change and development. By simply providing the right economy-driven curriculum, free marketeers assume that there will be development. This link is often not so clear-cut, as many other variables influence both education efficiency and development.

Furthermore, education becomes a mere handmaiden of the economy, vulnerable to the cult of efficiency – that is, the values of businessmen and scientific management – and school administration becomes far more concerned with hierarchy, control and efficiency than with issues of curriculum, pedagogy and educational values (Boyd 1992:509).

Wielemans (1992:8-9) questions the globalist view that the behaviour of people has to be interpreted only in terms of private benefit/profit/use/utility. For them the only type of human being seems to be 'homo economicus'. Development and well-being is seen as economic progress and welfare. Values are restricted to exchange values.

Thus, the globalisation of education has the real danger that the economic free enterprise metaphor is uncritically applied to education (Rust & Kim 1997:572). Ultimately, democracy loses its power. Education is no longer managed by governments (the voice of the people) but rather by efficiency and other economic motives.

Perhaps there is a middle road. On the one hand, teachers should be aware of the demands of globalisation and prepare their learners for the merciless competitiveness of the global marketplace. Learners should *know* and *do*. On the other hand, teachers should be aware of the deeper dimensions of being, of humankind's moral responsibilities, individually and collectively. Thus, they should teach their learners to live together harmoniously with others and *to be*, in other words, to know themselves and develop their talents (Maraj 1996:13).

References

Badenhorst, DC and Claassen, JC (1995) Reinventing education. Paper read at the International Conference on Education and Change, Unisa, Pretoria, 15-17 September.

Bosch, DJ (1991) *Transforming mission: paradigm shifts in theology of mission*. Maryknoll: Orbis Books.

Boyd, WL (1992) The power of paradigms: Reconceptualizing educational policy and management. *Education Administrative Quarterly*, 28(4):504-528.

Brown-Guillory, E and Guillory, LM (1989) Demistifying global education. *Momentum*, 20, February.

Degenaar, J (1995) Suid-Afrika kan nie nasie bou nie. *Insig*, 9 Mei.

Dekker, E (1993) The provision of adult education. In E Dekker and E Lemmer (eds) *Critical issues in modern education*. Durban: Butterworths.

Department of Education and Culture (1990) *The evaluation and promotion of career education* (The Walters Report). Pretoria: Government Printer.

Fukuyama, F (1992) *The end of history and the last man*. London: Hamilton.

Green, A (1997) *Education, globalisation and the nation state*. London: Macmillan.

Havel, V (1994) The new measure of man. *New York Times*, 8 July.

Hinkson, J (1991) *Postmodernity: state and education*. Geelong: Deakin University Press.

Ilon, L (1997) Educational repercussions of a global system of production. In

WK Cummings and NF McGinn (eds) *International handbook of education and development: preparing schools, students and nations for the twenty-first century*. Oxford: Pergamon Press.

Inkeles, A and Sirowy, L (1993) Convergent and divergent trends in national education systems. *Social Forces*, 62(2).

Kamil, BL (1994) *Delivering the future: cable and education partnerships for the information age*. Cable in the Classroom: Alexandria.

Kenway, J (1992) Market education in the post-modern age. Paper read at the AARE Conference, San Francisco.

Maraj, J (1996) Glimpses of tomorrow – the challenges for education. Annual Faculty Lecture, Unisa, 6 September.

McGinn, NF (1997) Supranational organizations and their impact on nation-states and the modern school. In WK Cummings and NF McGinn (eds) *International handbook of education and development: preparing schools, students and nations for the twenty-first century*. Oxford: Pergamon Press.

McGinn, NF and Cummings, WK (1997) Introduction. In WK Cummings and NF McGinn (eds) *International handbook of education and development: preparing schools, students and nations for the twenty-first century*. Oxford: Pergamon Press.

Naisbitt, J (1994) *Global paradox*. New York: Morrow.

Pretorius, SG (1996) Hervormingstendense in die onderwys: 'n internasionale ondersoek. *Suid-Afrikaanse Tydskrif vir Opvoedkunde*, 16(3):134-143.

Ramirez, FO (1997) The nation-state. Citizenship and educational change: institutionalization and globalization. In WK Cummings and NF McGinn (eds) *International handbook of education and development: preparing schools, students and nations for the twenty-first century*. Oxford: Pergamon Press.

Reich, RB (1992) *The work of nations*. New York: Vintage Books.

Rust, V (1991) Postmodernism and its implications for comparative education. *Comparative Education Review*, 35:610-625.

Rust, V and Kim, A (1997) Free trade and education. In WK Cummings and NF McGinn (eds) *International handbook of education and development: preparing schools, students and nations for the twenty-first century*. Oxford: Pergamon Press.

Titmus, CJ (ed) (1989) *Lifelong education for adults: an international handbook*. Oxford: Pergamon Press.

Toffler, A (1990) *Powershift: knowledge, wealth and violence at the edge of the 21st century*. New York: Bantam Books.

Usher, R and Edwards, R (1994) *Postmodernism and education: different voices, different worlds*. London: Routledge.

Van Niekerk, EJ (1996) Enkele aspekte van die postmodernistiese kritiek teen die modernisme en die relevansie daarvan vir die opvoedkunde. *Suid-Afrikaanse Tydskrif vir Opvoedkunde*, 16(4):210-215.

Watson, K (1994) *Educational provision for the 21st century: who or what is shaping the agenda and influencing developments?* Paper read at the SACHES Conference, Gaborone, 25-27 October.

Wielemans, W (1992) *The consequences of free-market principles for educational policy*. Paper read at the University of Pretoria, Pretoria.

Wilds, E and Lottich, K (1970) *The foundations of modern education*. New York: Holt, Rinehart and Winston.

CHAPTER 3

EDUCATION AND THEORIES OF DEVELOPMENT

Prof Clive Harber
University of Birmingham, UK

Table of contents

3.1 Introduction: the nature of 'development'

Despite frequent use of the terms 'developed' and 'developing' countries the nature of 'development' remains a controversial and much-debated issue. In general terms 'developed' has traditionally referred to the richer, primarily industrial countries of the northern hemisphere, while 'developing' has referred to the poorer, primarily agricultural countries of the southern hemisphere. In effect this meant that the category of 'developing' countries would include the whole of Africa, Latin America, the Caribbean and most of Asia excluding Australia, New Zealand and Japan, while 'developed' would include North America, Europe, the countries of the former Soviet Union and Japan, Australia and New Zealand.

However, this initial emphasis on wealth and production in conceptualising development has gradually given way to attempts to measure development based on more diverse criteria such as social indicators concerned with health, education, the environment and gender equity. It has also led to a less rigid bipolar classification of development and a much broader understanding in terms of a broad continuum of development. The annual United Nations Human Development Report, for example, ranks countries individually according to what they term the 'human development index', which is a composite measurement based on certain basic indicators – life expectancy, adult literacy, proportions of enrolment in the different levels of education and the gross domestic product (economic output). On these indicators, for example, Canada is rated top of the human development index and Sierra Leone bottom – South Africa is ninetieth out of 175 (see Table 3.1). They then analyse the same indicators in terms of gender equality to provide a gender-related development index which is given in Table 3.2 (UNDP 1997). More recently political indicators such as human rights and political choice have been included in considerations of development, though these are inevitably more difficult to measure and quantify than economic and social indicators.

HDI rank	Life expectancy at birth (years) 1994	Adult literacy rate (%) 1994	Combined first, second- and third-level gross enrolment ratio (%) 1994	Real GDP per capita (PPP$) 1994	Adjusted real GDP per capita (PPP$) 1994	Life expectancy index	Education index	GDP index	Human development index (HDI) value 1994	Real GDP per capita (PPP$) rank minus HDI rank
High human development	74.6	97.0	80	17,052	6,040	0.83	0.91	0.98	0.907	-
1 Canada	79.0	99.0	100[b]	21,459	6,073	0.90	0.99	0.99	0.960	7
2 France	78.7	99.0	89	20,510	6,071	0.89	0.96	0.99	0.946	13
3 Norway	77.5	99.0	92	21,346	6,073	0.88	0.97	0.99	0.943	6
4 USA	76.2	99.0	96	26,397	6,101	0.85	0.98	0.99	0.942	-1
5 Iceland	79.1	99.0	83	20,566	6,071	0.90	0.94	0.99	0.942	9
6 Netherlands	77.3	99.0	91	19,238	6,067	0.87	0.96	0.99	0.940	13
7 Japan	79.8	99.0	78	21,581	6,074	0.91	0.92	0.99	0.940	0
8 Finland	76.3	99.0	97	17,417	6,041	0.85	0.98	0.98	0.940	15
9 New Zealand	76.4	99.0	94	16,851	6,039	0.86	0.97	0.98	0.937	s15
10 Sweden	78.3	99.0	82	18,540	6,064	0.89	0.93	0.99	0.936	11
11 Spain	77.6	97.1[c]	90	14,324	6,029	0.88	0.95	0.98	0.934	19
12 Austria	76.6	99.0	87	20,667	6,072	0.86	0.95	0.99	0.932	1
13 Belgium	76.8	99.0	86	20,985	6,072	0.86	0.95	0.99	0.932	-1
14 Australia	78.1	99.0	79	19,285	6,068	0.89	0.92	0.99	0.931	4
15 United Kingdom	76.7	99.0	86	18,620	6,065	0.86	0.95	0.99	0.931	5

HDI rank	Life expectancy at birth (years) 1994	Adult literacy rate (%) 1994	Combined first, second- and third-level gross enrolment ratio (%) 1994	Real GDP per capita (PPP$) 1994	Adjusted real GDP per capita (PPP$) 1994	Life expectancy index	Education index	GDP index	Human development index (HDI) value 1994	Real GDP per capita (PPP$) rank minus HDI rank [a]
High human development	74.6	97.0	80	17,052	6,040	0.83	0.91	0.98	0.907	-
16 Switzerland	78.1	99.0	76	24,967	6,098	0.88	0.91	0.99	0.930	-12
17 Ireland	76.3	99.0	88	16,061	6,037	0.85	0.95	0.98	0.929	8
18 Denmark	75.2	99.0	89	21,341	6,073	0.84	0.96	0.99	0.927	-8
19 Germany	76.3	99.0	81	19,675[d]	6,069	0.86	0.93	0.99	0.924	-3
20 Greece	77.8	96.7[c]	82	11,265	5,982	0.88	0.92	0.97	0.923	15
21 Italy	77.8	98.1[c]	73	19,363	6,068	0.88	0.90	0.99	0.921	-4
22 Hong Kong	79.0	92.3	72	22,310	6,075	0.90	0.86	0.99	0.914	-17
23 Israel	77.5	95.0	75	16,023	6,037	0.87	0.88	0.98	0.913	3
24 Cyprus	77.1	94.0	75	13,071[e,f]	6,021	0.87	0.88	0.98	0.907	8
25 Barbados	75.9	97.3	76	11,051	5,979	0.85	0.90	0.97	0.907	11
26 Singapore	77.1	91.0	72	20,987	6,072	0.87	0.85	0.99	0.900	-15
27 Luxembourg	75.9	99.0	58	34,155	6,130	0.85	0.85	1.00	0.899	-26
28 Bahamas	72.9	98.1	75	15,875	6,036	0.80	0.90	0.98	0.894	0
29 Antigua and Barbuda	74.0	96.0	76	8,977[e]	5,947	0.82	0.89	0.97	0.892	16
30 Chile	75.1	95.0	72	9,129	5,950	0.83	0.87	0.97	0.891	13
31 Portugal	74.6	89.6[c]	81	12,326	6,014	0.83	0.87	0.98	0.890	3
32 Korea, Rep. of	71.5	97.9	82	10,656	5,974	0.77	0.93	0.97	0.890	5
33 Costa Rica	76.6	94.7	68	5,919	5,853	0.86	0.86	0.95	0.889	27
34 Malta	76.4	86.0[g]	76	13,009[e,f]	6,021	0.86	0.83	0.98	0.887	-1
35 Slovenia	73.1	96.0	74	10,404[e]	5,970	0.80	0.89	0.97	0.886	3
36 Argentina	72.4	96.0	77	8,937	5,946	0.79	0.90	0.97	0.884	10
37 Uruguay	72.6	97.1	75	6,752	5,895	0.79	0.90	0.96	0.883	15
38 Brunei Darussalam	74.9	87.9	70	30,447[e,f]	6,125	0.83	0.82	1.00	0.882	-36
39 Czech Rep.	72.2	99.0	70	9,201	5,951	0.79	0.89	0.97	0.882	3
40 Trinidad and Tobago	72.9	97.9	67	9,124	5,949	0.80	0.88	0.97	0.880	4
41 Dominica	72.0	94.0	77	6,118[e]	5,868	0.78	0.88	0.95	0.87	16
42 Slovakia	70.8	99.0	72	6,389	5,882	0.76	0.90	0.96	0.873	12
43 Bahrain	72.0	84.4	85	15,321	6,034	0.78	0.85	0.98	0.870	-14
44 United Arab Emirates	74.2	78.6	82	16,000[h]	6,036	0.82	0.80	0.98	0.866	-17
45 Panama	73.2	90.5	70	6,104	5,868	0.80	0.84	0.95	0.864	14
46 Fiji	71.8	91.3	79	5,763	5,763	0.78	0.87	0.94	0.863	16
47 Venezuela	72.1	91.0	68	8,120	5,930	0.79	0.83	0.96	0.861	1
48 Hungary	68.8	99.0	67	6,437	5,884	0.73	0.88	0.96	0.857	5
49 Saint Kitts and Nevis	69.0[g]	90.0[g]	78	9,436	5,955	0.73	0.86	0.97	0.853	-9
50 Mexico	72.0	89.2	66	7,384	5,913	0.78	0.81	0.96	0.853	0
51 Colombia	70.1	91.1	70	6,107	5,868	0.75	0.84	0.95	0.848	7
52 Seychelles	72.0[g]	88.0[g]	61	7,891[e]	5,925	0.78	0.79	0.96	0.845	-3
53 Kuwait	75.2	77.8	57	21,875	6,074	0.84	0.71	0.99	0.844	-47
54 Grenada	72.0[g]	98.0[g]	78	5,137[e]	5,137	0.78	0.91	0.83	0.843	17
55 Qatar	70.9	78.9	73	18,403	6,063	0.76	0.77	0.99	0.840	-33
56 Saint Lucia	71.0[g]	82.0[g]	74	6,182[e]	5,872	0.77	0.79	0.95	0.838	-1
57 Saint Vincent	72.0[g]	82.0[g]	78	5,650[e]	5,650	0.78	0.81	0.92	0.836	6
58 Poland	71.2	99.0	79	5,002	5,002	0.77	0.92	0.81	0.834	14
59 Thailand	69.5	93.5	53	7,104	5,906	0.74	0.80	0.96	0.833	-8
60 Malaysia	71.2	83.0	62	8,865	5,945	0.77	0.76	0.97	0.832	-13
61 Mauritius	70.7	82.4	61	13,172	6,022	0.76	0.75	0.98	0.831	-30
62 Belarus	69.2	97.9	80	4,713	4,713	0.74	0.92	0.76	0.806	13
63 Belize	74.0	70.0[g]	68	5,590	5,590	0.82	0.69	0.91	0.806	1
64 Libyan Arab Jamahiriya	63.8	75.0	91	6,125[e]	5,869	0.65	80	0.95	0.801	-8
Medium human development	67.1	82.6	64	3,352	3,352	0.70	0.76	0.54	0.667	-
65 Lebanon	69.0	92.0	75	4,863[e,f]	4,863	0.73	0.86	0.79	0.794	8
66 Suriname	70.7	92.7	71	4,711	4,711	0.76	0.85	0.76	0.792	10
67 Russian Federation	65.7	98.7	78	4,828	4,828	0.68	0.92	0.78	0.792	7
68 Brazil	66.4	82.7	72	5,362	5,362	0.69	0.79	0.87	0.783	0
69 Bulgaria	71.1	93.0	66	4,533	4,533	0.77	0.84	0.73	0.780	9
70 Iran, Islamic Rep. of	68.2	68.6[c]	68	5,766	5,766	0.72	0.68	0.94	0.780	-9
71 Estonia	69.2	99.0	72	4,294	4,294	0.74	0.90	0.69	0.776	8
72 Ecuador	69.3	89.6	72	4,626	4,626	0.74	0.84	0.75	0.775	5
73 Saudi Arabia	70.3	61.8	56	9,338	5,953	0.76	0.60	0.97	0.774	-32
74 Turkey	68.2	81.6	63	5,193	5,193	0.72	0.75	0.84	0.772	-4
75 Korea, Dem. People's Rep. of	71.4	95.0	75	3,965[e,f]	3,965	0.77	0.88	0.64	0.765	10
76 Lithuania	70.1	98.4[g]	70	4,011	4,011	0.75	0.89	0.65	0.762	8
77 Croatia	71.3	97.0	67	3,960[d]	3,960	0.77	0.87	0.64	0.760	10
78 Syrian Arab Rep.	67.8	69.8	64	5,397	5,397	0.71	0.68	0.87	0.755	-12
79 Romania	69.5	96.9[g]	62	4,037	4,037	0.74	0.85	0.65	0.748	3
80 Macedonia, FYR	71.7	94.0	60	3,965[f]	3,965	0.78	0.83	0.64	0.748	5
81 Tunisia	68.4	65.2	67	5,319	5,319	0.72	0.66	0.86	0.748	-12
82 Algeria	67.8	59.4	66	5,442	5,442	0.71	0.62	0.88	0.737	-17
83 Jamaica	73.9	84.4	65	3,816	3,816	0.82	0.78	0.61	0.736	7
84 Jordan	68.5	85.5	66	4,187	4,187	0.73	0.79	0.68	0.730	-3
85 Turkmenistan	64.7	97.7[g]	90	3,469[g]	3,469	0.66	0.95	0.56	0.723	12
86 Cuba	75.6	95.4	63	3,000[e]	3,000	0.84	0.85	0.48	0.723	17
87 Dominican Rep.	70.0	81.5	68	3,933	3,933	0.75	0.77	0.63	0.718	1
88 Oman	70.0	35.0	60	10,07[g]	5,965	0.75	0.43	0.97	0.718	-49
89 Peru	67.4	88.3	81	3,645	3,645	0.71	0.86	0.59	0.717	5
90 South Africa	63.7	81.4	81	4,291	4,291	0.64	0.81	0.69	0.716	-10

Table 3.1 Human development index

HDI rank	Gender-related development index (GDI) rank	Life expectancy at birth (years) 1994		Adult literacy rate (%) 1994		Combined primary, secondary and tertiary gross enrolment ratio (%) 1994		Earned income share (%) 1994[a]		GDI value 1994	HDI rank minus GDI rank[b]
		Female	Male	Female	Male	Female	Male	Female	Male		
High human development	-	77.7	71.4	96.6	97.4	80.0	78.9	34.7	65.4	0.874	-
1 Canada	1	81.7	76.3	99.0	99.0	100.0[c]	100.0[c]	37.8[d]	62.2[d]	0.939	0
2 France	6	83.0	74.3	99.0	99.0	91.0	87.0	39.0	61.0	0.926	-4
3 Norway	2	80.4	74.6	99.0	99.0	93.0	92.0	42.1	57.9	0.934	1
4 USA	5	79.5	72.8	99.0	99.0	98.0	93.0	40.7	59.3	0.928	-1
5 Iceland	4	80.8	77.4	99.0	99.0	81.0	82.0	42.0	58.0	0.932	1
6 Netherlands	11	80.2	74.3	99.0	99.0	88.0	93.0	33.5	66.5	0.901	-5
7 Japan	12	82.8	76.6	99.0	99.0	77.0	79.0	33.9[d]	66.1[d]	0.901	-5
8 Finland	7	79.9	72.4	99.0	99.0	100.0[c]	92.0	41.5	58.5	0.925	1
9 New Zealand	8	79.2	73.6	99.0	99.0	96.0	91.0	38.8	61.2	0.918	1
10 Sweden	3	80.9	75.8	99.0	99.0	84.0	81.0	45.1	54.9	0.932	7
11 Spain	19	81.3	73.9	97.1	97.1	94.0	87.0	29.4[d]	70.6[d]	0.874	-8
12 Austria	15	79.6	73.2	99.0	99.0	85.0	88.0	33.7[d]	66.3[d]	0.890	-3
13 Belgium	14	80.2	73.3	99.0	99.0	86.0	86.0	33.4	66.6	0.891	-1
14 Australia	9	81.0	75.2	99.0	99.0	80.0	77.0	39.8	60.2	0.917	5
15 United Kingdom	13	79.3	74.1	99.0	99.0	86.0	85.0	35.0	65.0	0.896	2
16 Switzerland	20	81.5	74.6	99.0	99.0	73.0	78.0	30.2	69.8	0.874	-4
17 Ireland	29	79.0	73.6	99.0	99.0	89.0	87.0	25.8	74.2	0.851	-12
18 Denmark	10	77.8	72.6	99.0	99.0	90.0	87.0	41.7	58.3	0.916	8
19 Germany	16	79.3	72.8	99.0	99.0	78.0	83.0	34.8	65.2	0.886	3
20 Greece	21	80.4	75.2	96.7	96.7	80.0	83.0	31.2	68.8	0.873	-1
21 Italy	23	80.9	74.6	98.1	98.1	74.0	72.0	31.0[d]	69.0[d]	0.86	-2
22 Hong Kong	28	81.8	76.0	89.1	96.0	73.0	72.0	27.1	72.9	0.852	-6
23 Israel	22	79.1	75.7	95.0	95.0	74.0	74.0	92.9[d]	67.1[d]	0.872	1
24 Cyprus	33	79.2	74.9	94.0	94.0	75.0	75.0	27.1	72.9	0.837	-9
25 Barbados	17	78.2	73.2	96.6	97.9	76.0	74.0	39.5[d]	60.5[d]	0.885	8
26 Singapore	27	79.3	74.9	87.2	95.6	71.0	73.0	30.7	69.3	0.853	-1
27 Luxembourg	38	79.1	72.5	99.0	99.0	59.0	57.0	25.3	74.7	0.813	-11
28 Bahamas	187	6.5	70.1	97.7	98.4	77.0	73.0	39.5[d]	60.5[d]	0.880	10
29 Antigua and Barbuda	-	-	-	-	-	-	-	-	-	-	-
30 Chile	44	77.9	72.1	95.0	95.4	71.0	72.0	21.9[e]	78.1[e]	0.785	-15
31 Portugal	30	78.3	71.0	89.6	89.6	84.0	77.0	34.1	65.9	0.850	0
32 Korea, Rep. of	35	75.2	67.7	96.8	99.0	78.0	86.0	27.7	72.3	0.826	-4
33 Costa Rica	36	78.9	74.3	95.0	94.6	67.0	69.0	27.2	72.8	0.825	-4
34 Malta	48	78.6	74.1	86.0	86.0	75.0	79.0	20.9[d]	79.0[d]	0.773	-15
35 Slovenia	24	77.5	68.4	96.0	96.0	76.0	72.0	39.3[d]	60.7[d]	0.866	10
36 Argentina	47	76.0	68.9	96.0	96.0	79.0	76.0	22.0[e]	78.0[e]	0.777	-12
37 Uruguay	31	75.9	69.4	97.3	96.7	80.0	70.0	33.4[e]	66.6[e]	0.84	25
38 Brunei Darussalam	-	-	-	-	-	-	-	-	-	-	-
39 Czech Rep.	25	75.2	69.2	99.0	99.0	70.0	69.0	38.1	61.9	0.859	12
40 Trinidad and Tobago	32	75.4	70.8	97.2	98.6	67.0	67.0	29.7[d]	70.3[d]	0.84	16
41 Dominica	-	-	-	-	-	-	-	-	-	-	-
42 Slovakia	26	75.5	66.3	99.0	99.0	73.0	71.0	40.7[d]	59.3[d]	0.859	13
43 Bahrain	56	74.5	70.1	77.6	87.7	87.0	83.0	14.7[d]	85.3[d]	0.742	-16
44 United Arab Emirates	61	75.7	73.3	77.9	78.0	85.0	80.0	10.0[d]	90.0[d]	0.727	-20
45 Panama	41	75.3	71.3	89.7	91.2	71.0	69.0	27.5[d]	72.5[d]	0.80	21
46 Fiji	53	74.1	69.9	89.2	93.7	78.0	80.0	21.4[d]	78.6[d]	0.763	-10
47 Venezuela	43	75.1	69.3	90.3	91.6	69.0	66.0	26.8[d]	73.2[d]	0.79	21
48 Hungary	34	73.8	64.2	99.0	99.0	68.0	66.0	39.5	60.5	0.837	11
49 Saint Kitts and Nevis	-	-	-	-	-	-	-	-	-	-	-
50 Mexico	50	75.0	69.1	86.7	91.5	65.0	67.0	25.1[d]	74.9[d]	0.770	-4
51 Colombia	40	72.8	67.4	91.3	91.1	72.0	67.0	33.3[e]	66.7[e]	0.81	17
52 Seychelles	-	-	-	-	-	-	-	-	-	-	-
53 Kuwait	51	77.5	73.5	72.6	80.4	57.0	56.0	24.5[d]	75.5[d]	0.769	-3
54 Grenada	-	-	-	-	-	-	-	-	-	-	-
55 Qatar	64	74.6	69.1	78.3	78.2	74.0	71.0	9.7[d]	90.3[d]	0.713	-15
56 Saint Lucia	-	-	-	-	-	-	-	-	-	-	-
57 Saint Vincent	-	-	-	-	-	-	-	-	-	-	-
58 Poland	37	75.8	66.6	99.0	99.0	80.0	79.0	38.9[d]	61.1[d]	0.818	13
59 Thailand	39	72.2	66.8	90.7	95.6	53.0	53.0	37.2	62.8	0.812	12
60 Malaysia	45	73.5	69.0	77.5	88.2	63.0	61.0	30.2[d]	69.8[d]	0.78	27
61 Mauritius	54	74.2	67.4	78.4	86.8	62.0	61.0	25.4[d]	74.6[d]	0.752	-1
62 Belarus	42	74.6	63.8	97.9	97.9	81.0	79.0	41.6[d]	58.4[d]	0.792	12
63 Belize	-	-	-	-	-	-	-	-	-	-	-
64 Libyan Arab Jamahiriya	77	65.8	62.3	57.2	88.9	90.0	91.0	16.0[d]	84.0[d]	0.655	-22
Medium human development	-	69.5	64.7	76.1	88.9	60.8	65.2	35.7	64.4	0.643	-
65 Lebanon	66	70.9	67.1	89.5	94.3	76.0	74.0	22.5[d]	77.5[d]	0.708	-10
66 Suriname	-	-	-	-	-	-	-	-	-	-	-
67 Russian Federation	46	72.2	59.2	98.7	98.7	82.0	75.0	41.3[d]	58.7[d]	0.778	11
68 Brazil	60	70.5	62.5	82.5	82.8	72.0	72.0	28.7[e]	71.3[e]	0.728	-2
69 Bulgaria	49	74.9	67.7	93.0	93.0	69.0	64.0	41.0[d]	59.0[d]	0.772	10

HDI rank	Gender-related development index (GDI) rank	Life expectancy at birth (years) 1994		Adult literacy rate (%) 1994		Combined primary, secondary and tertiary gross enrolment ratio (%) 1994		Earned income share (%) 1994[a]		GDI value 1994	HDI rank minus GDI rank[b]
		Female	Male	Female	Male	Female	Male	Female	Male		
70 Iran, Islamic Rep. of	-	-	-	-	-	-	-	-	-	-	-
71 Estonia	52	75.0	63.3	99.0	99.0	74.0	69.0	42.0[d]	58.0[d]	0.764	8
72 Ecuador	73	72.0	66.8	87.8	91.8	71.0	73.0	18.4[e]	81.6[e]	0.675	12
73 Saudi Arabia	95	72.1	69.0	47.6	70.6	53.0	59.0	9.7[d]	90.3[d]	0.581	-33
74 Turkey	58	70.6	68.9	71.1	91.7	55.0	70.0	33.2	66.8	0.737	5
75 Korea, Dem. People's Rep. of	-	-	-	-	-	-	-	-	-	-	-
76 Lithuania	55	75.9	64.2	98.4	98.4	72.0	68.0	40.8[d]	59.2[d]	0.750	9
77 Croatia	57	75.8	67.1	97.0	97.0	68.0	67.0	36.5[d]	63.5[d]	0.741	8
78 Syrian Arab Rep.	84	69.9	65.8	53.0	84.8	59.0	68.0	20.6[d]	79.4[d]	0.646	-18
79 Romania	59	73.3	65.9	96.9	96.9	62.0	62.0	37.5[d]	62.5[d]	0.733	8
80 Macedonia, FYR	62	73.9	69.4	94.0	94.0	61.0	60.0	33.9[d]	66.1[d]	0.726	6
81 Tunisia	74	69.4	67.4	50.4	77.9	64.0	71.02	4.5[d]	75.5[d]	0.668	-5
82 Algeria	92	69.0	66.6	43.5	71.8	61.0	70.0	19.1[d]	80.9[d]	0.614-	22
83 Jamaica	63	76.1	71.7	88.4	79.6	67.0	64.0	39.2[d]	60.8[d]	0.726	8
84 Jordan	-	-	-	-	-	-	-	-	-	-	-
85 Turkmenistan	65	68.1	61.3	97.7	97.7	90.0	90.0	38.2d	61.8[d]	0.712	7
86 Cuba	68	77.5	73.7	94.8	95.9	65.0	61.0	31.1d	68.9[d]	0.699	5
87 Dominican Rep.	75	72.1	68.0	81.2	81.2	69.0	67.0	23.1d	76.9[d]	0.658	-1
88 Oman	-	-	-	-	-	-	-	-	-	-	-
89 Peru	76	69.9	65.1	82.2	94.5	77.0	84.0	22.9d	77.1[d]	0.656	-1
90 South Africa	71	66.8	60.8	81.2	81.4	82.0	80.0	30.8d	69.2[d]	0.68	15

Table 3.2 Gender-related development index

The measured level of development of a country therefore depends on the indicator or indicators used to define and measure development. The use of a different indicator can change one country's ranking in relation to another. For example, a country may be relatively wealthy and so rank high on this index but the wealth may be very unequally divided between extremes of rich and poor so the same country would rank much lower in terms of equality. This shows that describing and analysing levels of development using indicators is not a neutral or technical exercise but instead involves value judgements and political choices about the essential ingredients of development and contending priorities for development. Moreover, certain agencies and organisations, such as the United Nations, are in a more powerful position to define what counts as an indicator of development than others. An emphasis on economic growth and wealth production as development, for example, would lead to the use of very different indicators in ranking countries than those used when the emphasis is on ecological sustainability and protecting the natural environment.

Debates about the nature of development are therefore intimately connected with different sets of ideas or theories about how development takes place or, perhaps more accurately, how it ought to take place. Although such theories purport to 'explain' how development takes place they do so primarily either from a particular emphasis or priority (e.g. economic development rather than social or political development) or from a preferred ideological model such as capitalism or socialism. It is often difficult to separate 'is' and 'ought' questions in discussions of development, since how it actually takes place cannot easily be separated from an understanding of its ultimate goal – the nature of a 'developed' society – and this is a matter of opinion, preference, judgement and power rather than fact.

One key social institution believed to make a significant difference in the way societies operate and individuals behave is education. Formal education has been linked to different theories of development because schools help to create the citizens and workforce of the future and therefore to define the direction of development. The remainder of this chapter examines the role of education in the context of a number of key theories of development – human capital theory, modernisation theory, dependency theory, correspondence theory, liberation theory, capitalism, socialism, green development, democratisation and post-modernism. For purposes of clarity of analysis the different theories are dealt with under separate sub-headings but it must be borne in mind that there are overlaps and links between the theories. While the formulation of general theories of development (and education and development) goes back to ancient times (Fagerlind & Saha 1989), this chapter is primarily concerned with post-1945 debates. The end of the Second World War was a catalyst for anti-colonial movements leading eventually to independence in a wide range of formerly colonial countries, particularly in Asia, Africa and the Middle East, and thereby creating a focus on the difference between the newly independent, 'developing' states and the 'developed' states of Europe and North America.

3.2 Human capital theory

One major and enduring emphasis within development theory has been the concern with economic development and in particular economic growth. Even within the broader understanding of development now espoused, for example, by the United Nations, economic growth continues to be given conceptual importance as one of four essential processes or components of development. (Equity, sustainability and democratic participation, the other three, are all further discussed below.) The United Nations Development Programme (1995:12) argues that 'people must be enabled to increase their productivity and to participate fully in the process of income generation and remunerative employment. Economic growth is, therefore, a subset of human development models'.

Human capital theory was initially perhaps most cogently expressed by the American economist Theodore Schultz (1961). It is based on the idea that the key to economic development is to see the increased education of the human workforce as a capital investment. Education is not only a good investment for individuals (in terms of future returns in the form of higher income) but an educated population is necessary for industrial development and economic growth because such a population is more productive. The skills and motivation for productive behaviour are therefore imparted through formal education. Increased educational expenditure and increased participation rates in education would therefore improve economic productivity and set the economy on a path of growth. One important implication of this is that both the causes of, and the cure for, lack of economic development lie within countries themselves.

However, even if it is accepted that there is a relationship between levels of education and productivity and economic growth, the theory is questionable on several points. One problem is the assumption that the higher earnings of more educated people are a consequence of their greater productivity. This assumes a perfect fit between education and the labour market in that the better-educated get the better jobs and higher salaries. Yet certain occupations may have higher incomes simply for historical reasons, perhaps maintained by restricting the amount of new entrants, or more educated people may come from more well-off families which have better contacts in the world of employment.

Income differentials are also affected by social structures – in many societies racial and gender discrimination affects both employment and promotion prospects. 'Screening theory' on the other hand goes further and argues that, while it is true that more educated people earn more, this is not because education makes people more productive, but because people differ in their innate productive potential. Education does not add to the market value of its products but simply provides a screening or filtering mechanism to identify and select those with this natural potential and ability for future employers (Oxenham 1984:31-33).

Perhaps the biggest problem with human capital theory, however, is one of cause and effect. Simply because high levels of education have been associated with economic growth and employment in certain countries does not mean that education causes economic growth – indeed, it may just as well be that economic growth allows a country to afford education. Many developing countries, including South Africa, spend a high proportion of their national budgets on education yet the result is simply more people who are both educated and unemployed. 'Africa already spends a higher percentage of the government budget and gross national product on education than any other continent' (Fay Chung, United Nations Children's Fund, quoted in *The Mercury* 27/5/98).

Yet many countries in Africa are afflicted by relatively poor economic performance and high levels of unemployment. Increased expenditure on education in itself is not therefore a guarantee of economic growth. It is the economy which must generate economic growth with education perhaps best being seen as either hampering or facilitating this growth through the quantity, nature and quality of provision.

3.3 Modernisation theory

Modernisation theory takes a more sociological approach to the notion of economic growth as the basis of development. Here the main contention is that economic prosperity comes with modernisation and that this will only occur when the majority of the population holds 'modern' values. An example of this would be the 'achievement motive' (McLelland 1961) where the values of hard work, punctuality, competition and capability of divorcing work from family ties would lead to economic and technological development. This was further developed by Inkeles and Smith (1974) who developed what they termed a 'modernity scale' differentiating a 'modern' person from a 'traditional' one. Examples of the characteristics of a modern person would be their universalism (the belief that social rules should apply equally to everyone regardless of gender, age or family background); openness to new experience and social change; an acceptance of diversity of opinion; a readiness to base and justify opinions on empirical information; an orientation towards the present and future rather than the past; a readiness to plan ahead and a belief in individual efficacy or influence over one's situation and a rejection of fatalism.

In their empirical research Inkeles and Smith (1974) found education to have the strongest correlation with individual modernity of all socialisation agencies. Their explanation for this relates to the nature of school organisation and the way young people are socialised through the school into modern bureaucratic norms and behaviours:

> School stops and starts at fixed times each day. Within the school day there generally is a regular sequence for ordering activities: singing, reading, writing, drawing, all have their scheduled and usually invariant times. Teachers generally work according to this plan, a pattern they are rather rigorously taught at normal school. The pupils may have no direct knowledge of the plan, but its influence palpably pervades the course of their work through school day and school year. Thus, principles directly embedded in the daily routine of the school teach the value of planning ahead and the importance of maintaining a regular schedule. (Inkeles & Smith 1974:141)

While there are general criticisms of modernisation theory – for example, that it is simply based on a model of existing Western, capitalist and industrialised society and assumes that this model of development is suitable for all societies – the present focus is on the role of education. In regard to education, a major problem with modernisation theory is the reality of school organisation in developing countries. In practice, social organisations tend to reflect the actual values and behaviours of their surrounding society so it would be surprising if schools in developing countries were to act autonomously as modernising change agents independently of their society, i.e. if the society is marked by non-modern strictures and behaviours then why should schools be any different?

Riggs (1964) described developing countries as having 'prismatic societies'. By this he meant that the societies of most developing countries, and the organisations that exist within them, are a synthesis – though not always a harmonious one – of traditional, long-lasting indigenous values and practices and relatively new ones imported during and after colonialism. They are neither fully modern nor fully traditional. As a result, within the form or facade of modern, bureaucratic organisation much that happens in schools will reflect older priorities and needs emanating from family and village as well as newer ones emanating from the Ministry of Education. For example, a basic tenet of modernity is regular attendance at a place of work and punctuality. However, staff and student absenteeism and lack of punctuality are marked problems in schools in developing countries where harvests, markets and family responsibilities can take priority over schooling. Evidence from a range of developing countries suggests that schools primarily reproduce the values and behaviours of the existing 'prismatic' society rather than acting as independent agents of modernisation (Harber & Davies 1997).

One important response to the emphasis on economic growth and wealth creation manifested in human capital and modernisation theories was a need to recognise the importance of social justice. The criticism is that a country as a whole may develop economically but contains large sections of the population who remain poor and underprivileged. The poor, it is argued, should be given access to and have the opportunity to both engage in and benefit from production processes. Rather than simply hoping that the benefits of a wealthy minority will trickle down to the poor, there should be public investment, including education, in disadvantaged groups in order to provide greater equality of opportunity. Equity has also become, therefore, a key component of human development. Conceptually, the United Nations includes equity as one of its four essential components of human development: 'People must have access to equal opportunities. All barriers to economic and political opportunities must be eliminated so the people can participate in, and benefit from, these opportunities' (UNDP 1995:12).

3.4 Dependency and correspondence theories

Dependency theory (Baran 1957; Frank 1967) rejects the basic tenets of modernisation theory. Based on Marxist ideas of the exploitation of the poor by the rich (further discussed below), dependency theory does not see all poorer countries as 'developing' towards some future developed goal. It argues that they are underdeveloped because other, industrial countries are developed. It posits that the relationship between the 'metropole' or rich and powerful northern countries and the 'periphery' of poorer, southern countries is based on exploitation and domination. Rather than poor countries being poor because they are not 'modern', they remain poor because the more powerful capitalist countries of the metropole (Western Europe and North America) can use their financial, organisational and technological supremacy to control the terms of trade. This means that they can buy primary goods (agricultural and mining products) at low prices and sell manufactured goods at prices favourable to themselves. Within the underdeveloped societies, ruling élites are not so much post-independence as neo-colonial in that they retain attitudes, interests and allegiances consistent with the countries of the metropole. As a result imported consumer goods are favoured over locally produced ones, and the interests of multi-national corporations are favoured over small local producers and employers. Therefore both poorer countries and rich élites within the countries become dependent on the more powerful countries.

In educational terms:

> ... because of the power of world languages such as English, developed country publishers are able to sell textbooks and educational resources at competitive rates, undermining the establishment of indigenous publishing firms. The textbooks and northern examining boards drive the curriculum and local assessment, and schools become more locked in a cycle of neo-colonial education which may not fit the culture of their people. (Harber & Davies 1997:86)

There is a number of criticisms of dependency theory, the most important of which are its deterministic and static nature and its resultant failure to provide a coherent strategy for change:

> Perhaps the most serious difficulty with dependency theory has been its failure to provide a viable strategy for development ... the important question is what kind of dependency and what kind of development should be pursued in any given context. The dependency theorists have given very few guidelines in this regard. (Fagerlind & Saha 1989:25)

It also notably fails to explain the economic growth and development of the 'peripheral' capitalist countries of South East Asia like Singapore, Hong Kong, Taiwan and South Korea.

While dependency theory has implications for education, 'correspondence theory' focuses entirely on education in attempting to explain how economic and political élites within countries maintain and reproduce their position. While this theory was originally based on an analysis of America (Bowles & Gintis 1976), it can be applied to developing countries as well. It is called correspondence theory because, it is argued, the social relations of school mirror, or correspond to, the social relations of production in the workplace. Pupils from different social backgrounds are provided with different education to fit the future role they will play in the workforce. The children of élite groups go to élite schools whose buildings and resources are superior and whose hidden curriculum emphasises leadership, superiority, separateness, independent thought, confidence and the giving of orders. The children of the working class, on the other hand, go to schools which teach routine, subservience and the taking of orders, summed up in the phrase 'Learning to Labour' (Willis 1977).

The imposition of Western forms of schooling during colonialism and their perseverance in the post- or neo-colonial period has meant that similar patterns of social relations are found in schools in developing countries. In Africa, for example, the children of political élites have tended to go to certain schools modelled on the British public (independent) schools or the French *lycées*. One example would be Kamuzu Academy in Malawi founded by the then President of Malawi, Dr Hastings Kamuzu Banda. This school, which was highly selective, was closely based on a British public school. Classics (the study of the ancient Greek and Latin languages) was compulsory and all instruction was in English; pupils heard speaking Chichewa were liable to be punished. The school was deliberately and explicitly created for the minority that Banda hoped would go on to become the leaders of Malawi (Harber 1989:6-9; 1997a:9).

Conversely, schooling for the mass of children from ordinary backgrounds in developing countries has been organised bureaucratically to teach the impersonal, contractual values and relationships that typify the transition from agricultural to industrial society. The values and behaviours reinforced by the school were those needed for the maintenance of social order – obedience, abiding by the rules, loyalty, respect for authority, punctuality, regular attendance at place of work, quietness, orderly work in large groups, response to orders, bells and timetables and tolerance of monotony (Shipman 1971). Evidence from a wide range of African and other developing countries strongly suggests that as a result the educational experience for most young people outside of an élite school is authoritarian, designed for those who take orders and follow rather than give orders and lead (Harber 1997a; Harber & Davies 1997).

As with dependency theory, it is possible to argue that correspondence theory again concerns explanation of how education contributes to élite-mass relationships, but does not provide a theory of how education can contribute to development away from such relationships. This issue has been confronted at length in liberation theory and in particular in the writings of Paulo Freire.

3.5 Liberation theory

Liberation theory is about taking sides with the oppressed in developing countries against the oppressors and working with the former to overcome the latter in order to remove all forms of oppression and exploitation:

The theory entails certain solutions: the transformation of the balance of power in the poor countries as well as on the international scene. This will only come about if the oppressed succeed in smashing the power of their enemies, starting in their own countries. (Kruijer 1987:5)

The oppressors are identified as either the colonial power or the rich neo-colonial power-holders who succeed them, both of whom share the values of the former colonists and need to perpetuate inequality, injustice and authoritarianism in order to serve their own interests and protect their privileges. The oppressed, on the other hand, are the poor, often illiterate peasants and workers. The emphasis therefore is on the need for radical change and the need to sever all external and internal ties with international capitalism and develop a form of socialist society based on equality.

There is a number of major problems with liberation theory including, in the writing of Kruijer at least, an uncritical admiration for state socialist societies, such as Cuba, China and North Korea, as viable alternatives to capitalism despite serious concerns about their records on freedom and human rights. (Capitalist and socialist models of development will be further discussed below.) For present purposes, however, the main concern is with education as a means of liberation in developing countries and in this respect the most influential writer was the Brazilian, Paulo Freire (1972; 1985).

For Freire the essence of education about society is that social reality is made by people and can be changed by people. It is important that learners see that social and political reality is not fixed, immutable and inevitable but that it can be changed and transformed. This is because the social and political reality facing most young people in developing countries is often one of inequality, exploitation and oppression. All too often schools are part of what Freire refers to as a 'culture of silence' where young people are taught to accept what is handed down to them by the ruling élite. Their education aims to socialise them so that they carry out orders from above in an unquestioning and unthinking manner. Their understanding of social and political reality is limited to what they are told to accept and believe – the myths that keep them silent and in ignorance. Freire argues that, instead of this, education should be a process of 'conscientisation', an attempt to raise critical consciousness so that learners both understand their social reality and act upon it.

Education can never be neutral – people are educated either for domestication in an oppressive culture of silence or for liberation through conscientisation. Education for liberation is not compatible with traditional, didactic forms of teaching where the teacher formally transmits information from the front of the classroom or lecture hall and where the learners passively receive it, memorise it and repeat it in examinations. This is referred to by Freire as 'banking education' whereby knowledge (as defined by the teacher) is 'deposited in' the student and on which he or she is later expected to 'capitalise'. It implies a view of knowledge as static, as made and finished, and of learners as empty and lacking consciousness. Critical education, on the other hand, means involving students in their own learning and interpretation of the world through dialogue, questioning, participation and discussion.

However, a major problem in Freire's writing concerns the issue of educational outcomes. It often appears from his writing that there are clear-cut, 'correct' answers to the questions of whether or not there are oppressors, who the oppressors are, and what the way forward should be. Once these answers have been established the oppressed masses must be 'educated' to see them. The answers to these questions may be more straightforward in a colonial situation, or even a military or one-party regime, but in a post-colonial situation, especially where citizens have the vote, they are a question of value rather than fact. If there is a predetermined 'answer' to education for critical consciousness, i.e. the correctness of the post-colonial party of liberation and its version of socialism, then much of what Freire has to say about doubt, uncertainty, investigation and dialogue is rendered meaningless. Paulo Freire's writings on education retain important insights into the political nature of education and the need for critical educational method, but the question of outcomes needs to be reconsidered in the light of debates surrounding democratic political development which are discussed below.

3.6 Goals of development

3.6.1 Capitalism and socialism

Theories of economic growth, and in particular modernisation theory, were strongly influenced by the historical development of Western, industrialised and capitalist countries from the seventeenth and eighteenth centuries onwards. As a result they implicitly tended to assume that the goal of development and the means of achieving it within developing countries would be based on similar experience. Dependency, correspondence and liberation theories, on the other hand, stress capitalism as the cause of underdevelopment and therefore have leaned towards alternative, socialist models of development as a preferable way of combining economic growth with greater justice and equity. In this section these two models of development are examined in relation to their implications for education. First, however, it is necessary to examine what these two terms mean.

Capitalism is based on the idea that each person is the best judge of his or her own interests and that the free pursuit of economic self-interest will result in higher productivity and in greater benefits all round. Thus the free market should be allowed to decide the level of supply and demand in an economy with profits going to the most efficient and productive entrepreneurs. Profit maximisation is assumed to be the most important motivating force in economic life. Entrepreneurs should be free to accumulate profit in the free market and this will provide the capital to finance further economic enterprises aimed at making profit. Social and economic inequality is important because there must be greater rewards for those who merit it by working harder and being more productive, enterprising and efficient.

The mid-nineteenth century writer Karl Marx, however, saw the inequality associated with capitalism as a form of oppression of one social class – the proletariat or working class – by another, the bourgeoisie or middle class. The bourgeoisie owned the means of production (the factories, land, companies and mines) and the proletariat sold their labour to the bourgeoisie for wages. Marx (1967) predicted the overthrow of capitalism and its replacement with a socialist society. The resulting one-party socialist state model is based on a belief that the maximisation of production and the rational distribution of resources requires a central production plan determined by the government. This is possible because ownership of the means of production and distribution of goods is in the hands of the state.

There is a belief in the importance of the collectivity over the individual and hence industrial and agricultural production is removed from private ownership. The state extracts the profits from state-owned enterprises for reinvestment in the economy. There is an emphasis on social equity over economic growth but in practice some inequality is tolerated, though usually less than in a capitalist state. A first step for a developing country is detachment from dependency on the world capitalist system. This means expropriation of foreign-owned holdings and control over consumption which prevents capital outflow from the economy as a result of the importation of foreign goods. Additional economic independence is maintained by restrictions on the flow of capital, whether in the form of purchases of goods or travel to, and investment in, other countries.

Fagerlind and Saha (1989:238) have described some of the educational differences typically found under capitalist and socialist systems in developing countries. Under capitalist systems, for example, there is an emphasis on individual achievement, an orientation towards employment in the public service sector and a hidden ideology supportive of capitalism is learned through the 'hidden curriculum' of competition within and between schools. In socialist education there is more emphasis on collective achievement, on a vocational curriculum (especially agriculture) and on an overt political ideology of education (the new socialist citizen).

Kenya and Tanzania provide examples of two neighbouring countries based on different systems which are reflected in some ways in their education systems (Harber 1989). In capitalist Kenya, for example, education plays a role in legitimating inequality through the promotion of a strong meritocratic belief in equality of opportunity:

> People can accept ultimate inequalities of wealth if they believe that they have a chance to enter the school system, will be judged by objective criteria within it and will have an equal chance to enter employment outside it. To the extent that the ethos of equal opportunity and social mobility can be shown to coincide with reality, tensions arising from inequalities of wealth and status are correspondingly fewer. (Court 1984:284)

Those who fail to find employment after school see themselves as unlucky or personally at fault in a basically just system even though the vacancies for paid employment in the modern sector can absorb but a fraction of school leavers each year. Conversely, from 1967 Tanzania followed a path of African Socialism supported by a policy of 'Education for Self-Reliance' (Nyerere 1967). In contrast to Kenya this policy rejected education based on competition and individualism and the phenomenon whereby educated Africans became estranged from the problems of their society by their wish to obtain the comforts and privileges of salaried employment. Instead, each school would possess a farm or other productive enterprise so that pupils did not become divorced from the agricultural production of the surrounding society and retained a respect for manual labour. In order to help achieve the change in attitudes required, political education in the values of African socialism became compulsory throughout education.

For most of the post-1945 period capitalism and socialism provided the main models of development. However, poor economic performance and a rejection of the autocratic one-party, communist state led to the political and economic collapse of the Soviet Union and its satellite state socialist countries in Eastern Europe in the late 1980s. As a result of this collapse, the range of countries following a path of socialist development has declined over the last decade. In Africa, for example, Ethiopia, Mozambique and Benin have rejected this model of development. Indeed, economic problems in developing countries, particularly in Latin America and Africa, have led to the widespread adoption of capitalist economic reforms. In order to secure a loan from world financial institutions such as the World Bank or the International Monetary Fund such countries are usually obliged to adopt a 'structural adjustment plan' based on the principles of capitalist economics – a decreased role for the state, greater emphasis on private enterprise and free markets (including privatisation of state industries) and cuts in both taxation and public expenditure by the government on such items as social welfare and education. Reference to 'globalisation' or a world economic order often means the current dominance of capitalist economics, though developing countries with structural adjustment programmes have varied in the extent to which they have had to adopt World Bank priorities and policies (Samoff 1994).

Educationally, however, what is more interesting than any differences between the nature and processes of schooling under capitalism and socialism is the similarities between the two in practice. Ironically, public schools in both capitalist and socialist countries have operated as authoritarian bureaucracies – schools in capitalist Nigeria, South Korea and Brazil operate in the same routine orientated, teacher-centred and non-participatory manner as schools in socialist Cuba, Tanzania or China (Harber & Davies 1997:48 52; 89-91; 159-60). The implications of this for democratisation will be further discussed below.

3.6.2 Green development

Both capitalist and socialist models of development are concerned with economic growth, though as we saw above, capitalism has become the dominant world economic model. However, not everybody thinks this is desirable. There are those who argue that unchecked capitalist development would be disastrous for the planet. 'Green' or 'ecological' writers fear that the self-interest, greed and ever-expanding consumption at the heart of capitalist markets will eventually destroy the planet by over-exploiting resources such as water, soil and minerals and by polluting the environment. What good, it is argued for example, is the freedom to buy a car if the city is choked with traffic and nobody can move or breathe? Yet unregulated, free-market policies have led to this situation in a number of cities, for example Bangkok in Thailand. And what happens when the oil runs out? These debates have led to an increasing emphasis on sustainability in debates on development. Conceptually the United Nations, for example, includes sustainability as one of its four essential components of development: 'Access to opportunities must be ensured not only for the present generations but also for future generations as well. All forms of capital – physical, human, environmental – should be replenished' (UNDP 1995:12).

Moreover, green indicators are increasingly being used to monitor damage to the world's resources. The World Wide Fund for Nature, for example, has produced the first Living Planet Index which contains data from over 150 countries and which measures declines in such resources as the world's natural forests and fish populations (*The Mercury* 1/10/98).

Hart (1997:6) draws on the work of Korten (1990) to compare the growth-centred vision of development with a green or 'people-centred' vision. The former assumes that the earth's physical resources are, for all practical purposes, inexhaustible or, if not, that science will provide a substitute. Growth theories also assume that the environment has an infinite ability to absorb waste. On the other hand, people-centred development assumes that the earth's physical resources are finite and that there is a limit to the productive and recycling capacity of ecological systems. There is a preference for national investment in small, locally-based and ecologically sustainable forms of production over mass production for export. So for green educationalists, education for development would place a strong curriculum priority on environmental education, would prefer small, 'human scale' local schools over large, impersonal ones and schools would practise what they preach in terms of environmentally auditing school policies (such as a recycling programme for paper, cans and bottles or purchasing environmentally friendly products only).

Green educators have also argued for a more 'holistic' approach to education and a move away from 'fragmentationalist' thinking. Greig, Pike and Selby (1989:45), for example, define a fragmentationalist world-view as one where humanity is seen as separate and divorced from nature and can therefore exploit the environment. Nature is seen as being made up of a series of isolated building blocks. Individuals are encouraged to compete in the marketplace as free agents. Associated with this is a 'transmission' model of curriculum and instruction where education is a one-way, top-down movement of knowledge skills and values. Its focus is on the traditional school subjects taught in the traditional way. The student is seen as a passive recipient of conveniently packaged and programmed blocks of teaching labelled 'maths', 'science' or 'history'.

A 'holistic' world-view, on the other hand, sees all life on the planet as interconnected and interdependent. Meaning is derived from understanding relationships. Individuals cannot act in isolation as the actions of any one impact on the system. Associated with this world-view is a 'transformational' model of curriculum and assessment where education is a process of personal and social development which focuses on the aesthetic, moral, physical, emotional and spiritual development of a student as well as on cognitive attainment – the student is seen as a whole person and an integral part of the natural environment.

Particular stress is also laid on the need to move away from hierarchical and authoritarian forms of educational organisation to ones that stress participation and education for democracy. Hart (1997), for example, argues for education to involve young people in environmental action projects in their local communities:

> ... children now need to be investigating their own communities in ways that will heighten their awareness of the need for a people-centred approach to development. At the same time, through their community research and action, children will develop a sense of shared responsibility and skills that will enable them to continue to participate as adults and to recognise the importance of their participation in local, national and even global environmental decisions. This fundamental democratisation of children is the most important aspect of their

participation in the environment of their communities, more than the particular impact of any of their projects. (Hart 1997:8)

However, while green education stresses the importance of education in democratic political skills, these are primarily for a particular purpose – environmental protection. Like capitalism and socialism there is a broadly defined outcome or predetermined answer for education – the green citizen and the green society. An education for democracy, on the other hand, does not have a predetermined outcome but encourages debate and a choice between alternatives or combinations of alternatives.

3.6.3 Education, democratisation and political development

One significant theme running through development theory is the contrast between democratic and authoritarian forms of development, and this theme has important implications for education. The formal structures of democracy include mechanisms of representative and accountable government which protect human rights and the rule of law. They include, for example, a choice of political parties, the freedom to organise into pressure groups and a free and diverse mass media. However, there are also important procedural values underlying democracy both at the level of macro-formal structures and at the level of everyday institutional, group and individual interaction. These include, for example, tolerance of diversity and mutual respect between individuals and groups, a respect for evidence in forming opinions, a willingness to be open to the possibility of changing one's mind in the light of such evidence, the possession of a critical stance towards political information and the regard of all people as having equal social and political rights as human beings.

In other words in a democracy there should be an emphasis on reason, open-mindedness and fairness. This is why there are nevertheless some limits to complete freedom of choice in a democracy: unlike rival economic or environmental policies, for example, racism, ethnic prejudice and sexism contradict the basic tenets of democratic procedural values of human equality and therefore should not be acceptable in a democracy or as an outcome of education for democracy.

In contrast to democracy, authoritarianism is a political system in which a government does not represent the people and in which there are no genuine elections, resulting in the final power to remove the government being taken out of the hands of the voters. There is no free political choice and the government is not accountable – it can do as it wishes and there are therefore no guaranteed human rights. Citizens have little say in how the country is run and rule is by edict and dictate. Military and one-party regimes fall into this category. The culture supportive of this is characterised by the availability of part (not all) information, and a lack of regular discussion and tolerance of a range of viewpoints. Diversity, critical thought and participation are suppressed. The leaders know they have the solutions to all problems and the role of the people is to obey their rules. Communication is top-down and hierarchical. The ideal citizen is submissive, behaves according to the wishes of the regime, respects authority and does not ask questions.

These broad models of a political system form either end of a continuum that has been a recurring theme in theoretical debates about political development. The most influential writing on political development theory emerged in America from the late 1950s to the early 1970s (Higgott 1983). While initially clear that the goal of political development was some form of representative democracy, the conspicuous fragility of post-colonial political institutions leading to a pattern of civil war, revolution and military *coups d'état* brought about an increasing emphasis on stability and order as more desirable than representation, accountability and human rights. Authoritarian regimes were considered acceptable, even preferable, as a means of providing the stability necessary for social and economic development (O'Brien 1972; Leys 1996:67).

American writers on political development were strongly influenced by general theories of modernisation and, in their concern for stability and order, defined political development and political modernisation primarily in terms of the bureaucratic efficiency of the state in delivering effective (stable) government. Participation, for example, was seen as important to the efficient working of any modern or developed state but was also seen in one key text on education and political development as '… affectively neutral, that is, not loaded in favour of either a democratic or non-democratic direction' (Coleman 1965:15).

For these writers a modern state is a participatory one – this can be participation either in the forced, centrally directed and monolithic fashion of an authoritarian state or by free and voluntary association in a democratic state. As a result, and in tune with modernisation theory, education is seen as contributing to a modern, participatory state essentially through the mass development of political skills: 'Formal education has a cardinal role to play in producing the bureaucratic, managerial, technical and professional cadres required for modernisation' (Coleman 1965:17).

Education for democracy was not necessarily a fundamental goal for political development. Since the late 1980s, however, some form of democracy has become increasingly acknowledged as *the* goal of political development. Publications of the United Nations are consistently clear on this, for example, and the fourth of the UN's four essential conceptual components of the human development paradigm is 'empowerment': 'Development must be by the people, not only for them. People must participate fully in the decisions and processes that shape their lives' (UNDP 1995:12).

This growing international consensus has been the result of the collapse of state socialism in Eastern Europe. Not only have the former countries of the

Warsaw Pact become democracies but the one-party socialist state model of the former Soviet bloc has become much less attractive to developing countries. Despite using a certain amount of Marxist rhetoric during the struggle for independence, for example, Eritrea, Namibia and South Africa have all adopted policies supporting multi-party democracies. Moreover, the West has been much less willing than they were during the period of the cold war to support authoritarian and dictatorial regimes in developing countries simply because they were anti-communist and pro-Western. Increasingly, aid and loans from Western development agencies have, in principle at least, been contingent on democratic political reform. Within developing countries themselves internal pressures for democratic change have come from trade unions, lawyers, intellectuals, students, religious groups and the media. Many countries in Asia, South and Central America, and Africa have, with varying degrees of success, begun a process of democratisation as a result of a combination of these factors.

As a consequence of democratic reform in developing countries there has been a renewed interest in the question of how to create a political culture that is composed of values and behaviours both supportive of democracy and able to help to sustain it in the long run. Such values and behaviours are learned, not genetically acquired, and cannot be taken for granted. There has therefore been a renewed international interest in education for democracy (Harber 1997b).

A democratic education has implications for both school management and the curriculum. In a democratic school students would be expected to be involved in some way in school management, usually through some form of elected school council with at least some responsibility in matters of significance to students and in which their views are represented along with those of parents and teachers. Legislation in South Africa, for example, has made such councils mandatory in all secondary schools. In terms of curriculum it means at least some choice for students of what they learn, though here there is a long continuum of possible levels of freedom of choice from complete freedom at the one end to subject options and courses in which students are allowed some self-direction through negotiated study and project work at the other. The democratic classroom indicates greater variety in teaching method with students being actively engaged in learning on a regular basis. Discussions, group work, projects, visits, simulations and independent study will all be used more frequently than in an authoritarian school. Also, a more diverse range of assessment techniques will be used in addition to examinations based on memorisation.

3.7 Post-modernism and contextuality

It might at first seem strange to end with a theoretical stance that rejects 'modernism' in a discussion of societies which are still in the process of becoming 'modern'. However, the purpose of this final, brief section is not to provide a full account of post-modern debates but to make a link in one particular way between some of the ideas of what has been termed post-modernism and education in developing countries.

Post-modernism is something of an umbrella term bringing together a collection of ideas from a variety of sources – interactionist sociology, qualitative research approaches in the social sciences, gender studies and the green movement (Siraj-Blatchford 1997). For present purposes its importance lies in its rejection of what have been termed 'meta narratives', i.e. grand, sweeping explanatory theories of historical development. Post-modernism received a boost from the fall of one-party state socialism in Eastern Europe and what was perceived as the demise of one of the great explanatory theories of social development – Marxism. At the same time, post-modernism would reject any single macro theory of development, including modernisation, dependency, capitalism, socialism and green development. Instead, post-modernism would argue that '... all knowledge claims are partial, local and specific rather than universal and ahistorical' (Usher & Edwards 1994:10). There is a rejection of unity and homogeneity and a celebration of plurality, difference and diversity in human experience.

Many would take issue with an extreme post-modernist 'anything goes' position which totally rejects any form of universalism. This is due to, for example, the need for universal principles such as human rights in order to guard against dictatorship and oppression. Indeed, it can equally well be argued that it is only within the universal principle of democracy that pluralism and diversity can flourish in the first place. Nevertheless, the post-modern negative reaction to over-certain, universal 'iron laws' of development or progress does help us to recognise that, although there may well be a need for universal broad principles in education, such as the need to educate for democracy, there is great danger in the assumption that, for example, a particular school management technique that works well in one context necessarily works well in another.

Educational issues, problems and resources can vary considerably from one context to another. The need to recognise a plurality of contexts is of particular importance in discussions of techniques of educational innovation in developing countries. This is because of the tendency for educational formulas or recipes for school effectiveness, educational management or curriculum development that originate in Europe or North America to be imported uncritically and unadapted into the very different educational contexts of developing countries. Often such packages do not address relevant questions, let alone provide suitable answers. Rather, contextual theory would stress above all the need first of all to understand the realities of the educational context and secondly the necessity for flexibility in finding relevant educational solutions to meet the plurality of national, local, institutional and individual needs in developing countries (Harber & Davies 1997).

3.8 Conclusion

This chapter has provided a broad overview of complex debates about national development and the role of education. At the beginning of the chapter it is stressed that these debates are as much about values and judgement as about 'facts'. For this writer, the key goal of development is democracy since, although still an ideology, the paradox of democracy is that it allows for plurality, debate, choice between alternatives and peaceful change. Thus states, and institutions and citizens within states, to an extent can choose between various capitalist, socialist and green alternatives or combinations of these and the balance can shift over time.

Few political and economic systems are uniform or homogeneous. Democracy has meant, for example, that there are significant differences between the levels of public expenditure and state intervention in the economy and society of welfarist capitalist countries such as Norway and Sweden on the one hand and more free-market, privatised economies such as Britain and America on the other. Moreover, legislation in all these countries has increasingly, though not exclusively, been influenced by green ideas and policies. Education therefore, in the eyes of this writer, must above all else be a preparation for life in a democracy though, in the democratic spirit, readers are, of course, free to differ.

References

Baran, P (1957) *The political economy of growth*. New York: Monthly Review Press.

Bowles, S and Gintis, H (1976) *Schooling in capitalist America*. New York: Basic Books.

Chung, F (1998) quoted in *The Mercury*, 27 May.

Coleman, J (1965) *Education and political development*. Berkeley: University of California Press.

Court, D (1984) The education system as a response to inequality. In J Barkan (ed) *Politics and public policy in Kenya and Tanzania*. New York: Praeger.

Fagerlind, I and Saha, L (1989) *Education and national development*. Oxford: Pergamon Press.

Frank, G (1967) *Capitalism and underdevelopment in Latin America*. New York: Monthly Review Press.

Freire, P (1972) *Pedagogy of the oppressed*. London: Sheed and Ward.

Freire, P (1985) *The politics of education*. London: Macmillan.

Greig, S; Pike, G and Selby, D (1989) *Earthrights*. London: Kogan Page.

Harber, C (1989) *Politics in African education*. London: Macmillan.

Harber, C (1997a) *Education, democracy and political development in Africa*. Brighton: Sussex Academic Press.

Harber, C (1997b) International developments and the rise of education for democracy. *Compare*, 27(2).

Harber, C and Davies, L (1997) *School management and effectiveness in developing countries*. London: Cassell.

Hart, R (1997) *Children's participation*. London: Earthscan.

Higgott, R (1983) *Political development theory*. London: Croom Helm.

Inkeles, A and Smith, D (1974) *Becoming modern*. London: Heinemann.

Korten, D (1990) *Getting to the 21st century*. West Hartford: Kumarian Press.

Kruijer, G (1987) *Development through liberation*. London: Macmillan.

Leys, C (1996) *The rise and fall of development theory*. London: James Currey.

Marx, K (1967) *The communist manifesto*. Harmondsworth: Penguin.

McLelland, D (1961) *The achieving society*. New York: The Free Press.

Nyerere, J (1967) *Education for self-reliance*. Dar Es Salaam: Government Printer.

O'Brien, D (1972) Modernisation, order and the erosion of a democratic ideal: American political science 1960-1970. *Journal of Development Studies*, 8.

Oxenham, J (1984) *Education versus qualifications?* London: George Allen and Unwin.

Riggs, F (1964) *Administration in developing countries: the theory of prismatic society*. Boston: Houghton Mifflin.

Samoff, J (1994) *Coping with crisis*. London: Cassell.

Schultz, T (1961) Investment in human capital. *American Economic Review*, 51.

Shipman, M (1971) *Education and modernisation*. London: Faber.

Siraj-Blatchford, I (1997) Postmodernism. In R Meighan and I Siraj-Blatchford (eds) *A sociology of educating*. London: Cassell.

UNDP (1995) and (1997) *Human development report*. Oxford: Oxford University Press.

Usher, R and Edwards, R (1994) *Postmodernism and education*. London: Routledge.

Willis, P (1977) *Learning to labour*. Farnborough: Saxon House.

Worldwide Fund for Nature (1998) Living Planet Index in *The Mercury*, 1 October.

CHAPTER 4

SCHOOLING

Dr Noleen van Wyk
University of South Africa

Table of contents

4.1 Introduction

The origins of formal education go back many centuries and in most settings derive from the initiatives of religious groups who established such institutions as the *madrasah*, the *terakoya*, the parish school, or the English 'public' school (Cummings 1997:63). However, while these schools were associated with religious groups, they tended to be supportive of the established authorities and many of their graduates took up positions in state bureaucracies, courts and armies.

Compulsory schooling began in the early 1700s in Europe, where one by one states defined a certain number of years of schooling as the responsibility of the state and as both the right and obligation of citizens (Williams 1997:120). As primary enrolment increased, secondary education began to expand to incorporate some of the graduates of primary schooling. All countries have followed at least the initial stages of this 'model', although it is not clear whether all countries will, or desire to, achieve truly universal schooling for their citizens in the near future.

4.2 School phases/structure of schooling

The schooling system of a country includes many different institutions for education and training which strive to meet the diverse needs of learners. In accordance with the learners' ages and developmental stages, there are pre-primary schools, primary or elementary schools, secondary schools and institutions for higher education such as universities and technikons. Furthermore, schools may specialise according to various fields of interest of the learners, such as general academic schools, agricultural schools and technical schools.

In addition to the above, the literature also differentiates between *basic education* and *further education*. In 1990 the *World Conference on Education for All* (Ahmed et al. 1991:23) defined basic education as:

> ... education intended to meet basic learning needs; it includes instruction at the first or foundation level, on which subsequent learning can be based; it encompasses early childhood and primary (or elementary) education for children, as well as education in literacy, general knowledge and life skills for youth and adults; it may extend into secondary education in some countries.

Where countries can afford to do so, basic education is compulsory. However, in many developing counties, this is not always possible.

There are many measures which may be used to determine whether the levels of schooling in a country are adequate. Benson (1994:1790) includes the following:

- The proportion of the relevant age group enrolled in primary education. In Ethiopia, for example, a figure of 36% was reported in 1985.

- The balance of gender, that is whether educational opportunities are provided for women. In Morocco, 98% of the age cohort of males were enrolled in primary school, but only 68% of females.

- The adult literacy rate. The industrial nations report no adult illiteracy to speak of, with the illiteracy rate typically at 99%; poorer nations generally have illiteracy rates of 50% or less.

In South Africa, the first democratically elected government of 1994 accepted in principle that basic education should be offered to all citizens. At this stage it is defined as including the reception year plus nine years of schooling. After completion the learner is to receive a *General Education Certificate*. This phase is equal to level one on the newly established National Qualifications Framework (NQF).

4.2.1 Pre-primary schools

Education at the pre-primary level has become a most important issue with changing family structures, single-parent families, varied forms of living arrangements, different cultural and social backgrounds, and diverse levels of parental involvement in children's upbringing and education (Lingens 1997-1998:3). Moreover, early child care and education are thought to be particularly significant in compensating children at least partially for the disadvantages of a poor home and family environment. Because of these and various other factors, the proportion of children enrolled in preschool education has been steadily increasing over the past decades.

No single definition of preschool education is universally acceptable, among other reasons because the starting age of primary schooling varies between five years old (e.g. the United Kingdom and Israel), and seven years old (e.g. Scandinavia). There is also considerable variation in the institutional arrangements of preschools and the extent of professionalisation of staff. Preschool education is most often considered an integral part of the education system (as in France and Belgium), but may also be community-based (as in the 'Head Start' programmes of the United States of America), or run by employers (as in the mobile crèches for construction workers in India), or managed by and for parents (as in the British playgroup movement) (Woodhead & Weikart 1988:49). However, most educationists agree that preschool programmes should be designed to increase children's intellectual, social and language competence and to provide them with skills in self-expression, thereby preparing children for elementary school as well as for participation in society at large. In many ways the preschool acts as a bridge between a child's family and the larger community.

Many preschool programmes use play as a learning medium, thereby assisting children to organise what they learn, to create conceptual schemes and to develop new modes of self-expression. However, as children grow older there is less emphasis on play in preschool and more on required activities. Some of these programmes are built upon specific developmental theories; others have a more elective base. There is no clear evidence that one programme approach is better than another. In addition, the different goals and values underlying alternative programmes make comparison difficult (Spodek 1988:105).

A major justification for preschool education has been its potential to modify school achievement and life prospects. This claim has been born out by most longitudinal studies on the effectiveness of preschools. It has been found that early childhood programmes play an indispensable role in introducing children, particularly those from poor or minority backgrounds, to school organisation, the official language of the school, the universe of print, and to future cognitive and expressive behaviour. In addition, the rate of dropout and repetition in primary school is significantly reduced. This has resulted in many governments throughout the world giving increased attention to the development of early childhood services.

Preschools in industrialised countries

In industrialised countries the benefits of preschool education have received attention for many years. In addition, many young women in industrialised nations continue their careers after childbirth and need to have satisfactory childcare and preschool facilities at their disposal (Bennet 1994:4671). The emphasis placed on this phase of education and the resources allocated to pre-primary education will, however, differ from one country to the next. For example, in the United States of America (US) a two-tier system of childcare is offered: a publicly funded system for poor minority children, and private childcare and educational arrangements funded by parents for the majority middle class. When children reach the age of five years kindergarten is provided free to all children in the US. In addition, a growing number of employers in the United States are beginning to provide childcare and education centres for the children of their employees (Bennet 1994:4674).

In Japan childcare and education is highly organised. Japan succeeds in enrolling almost 50% of its three-year-olds, 89,7% of four-year-olds, and 94,5% of five-year-olds in publicly funded day nurseries and kindergartens (Bennet 1994:4675). This tendency of providing preschool facilities is found to a varying extent in most developed countries.

Preschools in developing countries

Amongst developing countries, where in many cases universal basic education is still being established at the same time as the preschool sector is emerging, the priorities are somewhat different. The central issue is whether scarce resources should be diverted to early childhood education in the hope that it will improve primary education by preparing children for the demands of schooling, thereby reducing the wastage through dropout and grade repetition.

Conditions in developing counties also make the provision of early childhood care and education particularly important. These countries are often characterised by poverty, large rural communities and populations increasing faster than the national resource base can allow. In addition, family breakdown caused by wars, migratory movements, AIDS or social upheavals have become so common that tens of millions of children live without schooling or assistance of any kind. Because of these and other problems, a multi-dimensional approach to childcare and education has evolved in many developing countries. Through mobilising parents and volunteers, and with governmental and/or external support, communities are starting to initiate low-cost, community-based programmes in childcare and parental education (Bennet 1994:4673). Often women come together to organise social and educational services for their children, examine child-rearing practices, improve their own level of education, and institute educational follow-up for their children. This approach has the following advantages:

- Community-managed programmes tend to cater for a multiplicity of needs such as nutrition, basic health, hygiene, etc. Instead of preschool education operating in isolation, care and education are linked.

- The community approach is low-cost because of its voluntary nature. Likewise, community programmes generally start from the real needs of the local population, which are not always met by formal centralised systems.

- Because of the multi-ethnic nature of many countries, voluntary and community-based child care is culturally more appropriate.

- Though aimed essentially at young children, locally managed early child development programmes educate mothers and allow them to gain self-confidence.

This type of initiative is needed in South Africa, as the *South African Congress for Early Childhood Development* estimates that there are between 5,5 and 6 million children under the age of six years in South Africa, of which only about 560 000 are accommodated in child-care facilities (Shindler 1998:8). The remaining children are either left unattended or are being cared for by older siblings.

4.2.2 Elementary/Primary schools

The primary purpose of the elementary school is to provide an environment in which each learner can develop as an individual and as a functioning member of society. Because these pupils differ in their mode of learning, elementary school teachers must vary their teaching styles and their use of teaching materials and resources to suit the developmental needs of the learners. In order for the elementary school curriculum to serve learners appropriately, an effort is made to keep the student-teacher ratio low. However, the organisation and the age groups included in primary or elementary education differ between countries. In the US, for example, elementary schools encompass pre-kindergarten through grade 6, thus including learners between the ages of four and twelve. In Canada, elementary education is free and compulsory, while the starting age is six in four provinces and seven elsewhere (Wickremasinghe 1992:147). In Germany, compulsory school attendance begins when children reach the age of six (Führ 1997-1998:7).

Likewise, the approach to primary school education also differs. In the US, for example, the concept of individualised instruction has received expression in such experiments as open classrooms and programmes for the gifted and talented as well as for those with learning disabilities or cultural disadvantages (Cummings 1997:73). This has led to a preference in the US for small classes where teachers and students can experience intensive interaction. In contrast, in Japan, the education system is characterised by a uniform curriculum with virtually no electives until secondary tracking. In addition there is a national system for the production of textbooks which relies on professional educators and writers to develop the drafts, while bureaucratic committees make the final judgement on content (Cummings 1997:75).

Although there is a trend towards universal primary school enrolment in developing countries, this is not the case in some of the countries in sub-Saharan Africa, where the school enrolment rates started falling in the 1980s. This historical decline has been attributed to stagnant or declining economies, declining returns to education and the substantial withdrawal of government investment in education (Williams 1997:120). This tendency is not applicable to South Africa, where the introduction of free and compulsory education for six-year-olds in 1996 placed between 150 000 and 300 000 pupils in school (Bot 1996:5).

4.2.3 Secondary schools

A key policy issue which has formed the core of public discussion over secondary schooling is the debate around the purpose of secondary education. Major competing orientations have been that secondary schools should:
- prepare students for admission to higher education
- prepare students for the world of work
- seek to fuse academic studies with practical, work-orientated studies (Owens 1988:138).

In addition, secondary schools increasingly have been expected to expand their mission to implement other, broader social policies through educational offerings. These range from teaching sex education and the effects of alcohol and drugs to the nutritional benefits of a healthy diet.

Another issue concerning secondary education has been the question of whether there should be open and equal access to high/secondary schools. In developed countries the present trend is towards the belief that all youth, regardless of where they live, their social status, sex, ethnicity or religion, should have free access to secondary education (Owens 1988:138). Unfortunately, this is as yet impossible within developing countries. Thus the proportion of the age cohort enrolled in secondary school in the industrialised nations runs from 70 to 90% while in the poorer nations a figure of around 35% is typical (Benson 1994:1790).

The formal length of secondary education varies between three and nine years and usually concerns all or part of the ten- to 19-year-old cohort. For example, in the United Kingdom and Russia learners generally leave school at 17, whereas the age is 19 in Germany (Kallen 1997:3). In the United States, a three-year junior high school and a three-year senior high school is the norm. However, changing demographics have led many school districts to modify the 3:3 plan in favour of a 'middle school' plan which allows greater flexibility in shifting groups of students from overcrowded buildings to those which are under-utilised.

In the USA secondary education is also characterised by individualised programmes of instruction, made possible by the comprehensive high school and its generous offerings of electives. A typical high school will accommodate students interested in both academic and vocational studies, and within each of these tracks will provide numerous combinations of subjects and subject quality levels (Cummings 1997:72). Critics of this system argue that many students elect frivolous combinations, while the economic burden of providing such a diverse programme is often staggering.

In Canada secondary education has traditionally been academic in nature, although there is an increasing trend towards composite secondary schools offering academic, commercial and technical classes (Wickremasinghe 1992:147). Because free, compulsory schooling exists in Canada, all students participate at some level of secondary education. In contrast, secondary-level enrolments 'plateaued' or fell in several regions within sub-Saharan Africa during the 1980s (Williams 1997:123). It remains to be seen whether this reversal of previous trends is temporary or indicative of more permanent changes in patterns of educational participation. In spite of this, education remains high on the political agenda in most developing countries and is invariably seen as the gateway to future economic prosperity (Papadopoulos 1995:493).

In South Africa the term *Further Education and Training* (FET) is used for the phase which follows the primary or basic school phase. FET is defined as a band of programmes between levels 2 and 4 on the National Qualification Framework (NQF). The FET is a band which allows for more specialisation than general education and offers multiple entry and exit points. What makes FET distinct from the old secondary system of schooling is that its training should prepare learners for both higher education and the world of work (Sedibe 1998:276). The organisational structure of schooling, however, has not changed and two years of the general education band, namely grade 8 and 9, are usually offered in high schools together with grades 10, 11 and 12 (or levels 2, 3 and 4 of the NQF).

4.3 School types

Every democracy allows parents to choose alternatives to the government-operated schools their children would otherwise attend. In most cases this entails additional tuition fees. Parents choosing alternative schools for their children usually do so on the basis of preference for a form of pedagogy, a religious or other world-view, or a cultural or language emphasis. The amount of supervision of non-state schools by the state differs. Sweden, for example, requires that the values taught in private schools correspond to those in state schools, while France, the Netherlands and Spain recognise as fundamental the right of a private school to determine its distinctive character (Glenn 1994:5192).

According to Cooper (1994:260) private or alternative schools fall into three sectors:

- *Independent*. Most alternative schools are independent, not being sponsored by established education, religious or government institutions.
- *Religiously affiliated*. These schools are related to a faith or confessional group, but may be operated outside its traditional structures.
- *Government-run schools*. In several countries, alternative schools are appearing within the state-run system, acknowledging the usefulness of programme diversity and the strong demand among parents for these schools.

There are 1 265 independent or private schools in South Africa out of a total of 30 000 schools (Lewis & Bot 1998:7). Government subsidy cuts since 1998, however, have threatened several schools with closure. Hardest hit were schools belonging to the Catholic Institution of Education. As a result some poorer independent schools have applied to be converted to public schools.

The following serve as examples of private or alternative forms of schooling found throughout the world.

4.3.1 Progressive schools

The oldest types of alternative schools are the so-called progressive schools. Although dating back to the nineteenth century, these schools were also influenced by twentieth century philosophers such as Dewey, Montessori, Steiner and Reimer (Cooper 1994:262). Most progressive schools are characterised by an abiding faith in the natural curiosity and goodness of children. This obviously results in these schools being arranged differently from those where educationists subscribe to the view that children are naturally lazy, slow and undisciplined. Examples of progressive schools are the following:

Waldorf schools

Waldorf schools date back to 1919 when Rudolf Steiner established the first such school for the employees of the Waldorf-Astoria cigarette factory in Germany. Waldorf schools now number 500 in 22 different nations, with 65 000 pupils attending the schools in Germany alone (Cooper 1994:262).

In Waldorf schools, pupils remain with the same teacher for nine years, from preschool to grade 8 (ages five to fourteen), allowing close ties to develop. Waldorf schools consciously avoid technology, preferring more simple, human forms of teaching and learning.

Waldorf schools have been attacked as highly rigid, and accused of an anti-scientific bias, and of an almost mystical philosophy. On the other hand, the personal, caring, human and secure environments of these institutions appeal to many parents in the industrial world.

Montessori schools

Montessori schools are perhaps the best-known type of alternative and are found in more than 60 countries. The schools are based on the philosophy of Maria Montessori, who aimed to help children from disadvantaged backgrounds in Rome (Cooper 1994:263). Like the Waldorf schools, the Montessori programmes believe that children are naturally curious, hard-working, and self-teaching. The importance of practical skills are stressed to learn competency, discipline and a desire to complete what is started. Because of this, Montessori classrooms are highly individualised, project-orientated and student-directed.

4.3.2 Religious schools

These schools originate from a conservative perspective in response to the perceived 'secular humanism', apparent godlessness and value 'relativism' of public schools. Each major religion – Christianity, Judaism and Islam – have produced schools that uphold the most traditional of their values.

Public policies have been adopted in many nations that support religious schooling on the basis of parental choice such as in Australia, Belgium and

Canada. This is similar to Israel, where parallel Orthodox Jewish schools exist within the state school system. In the Netherlands, Muslim and Hindu schools began to receive public subsidies in the late 1980s (Glenn 1994:5193).

One of the most significant developments in religious schools in recent years has been the decline in the number of 'religious' personnel who teach and administer in them (Cibulka 1988:210). Beginning in the 1950s, there was a decline in teachers belonging to religious orders and schools had to either close or be staffed by lay teachers. Today this is no longer a burning issue. It has proven possible to retain the religious emphasis and special character of most schools despite them being staffed by lay persons.

4.3.3 Alternative schools based on language, ethnicity or culture

This category of schools tends to reflect the language, ethnicity or culture of its students and parents, and may be started particularly because parents find the mainstream schools of the country oppressive, racist or simply of poor quality. An example of such schools are private black alternative schools established in the US as a response to perceived racism in the public school sector (Cooper 1994:264).

In some countries, parents are able to choose a school where a minority language is the primary language of instruction, with the national language also taught as a required subject and used to an increasing extent in the upper grades. Examples of this include the Basque and Catalonia regions of Spain as well as Friesland in the Netherlands. Turkish citizens of Bulgaria objected strongly when this form of choice was withdrawn under a policy of forced assimilation (Glenn 1994:5193).

4.3.4 Public and private alternatives to state schools

Many alternative schools throughout the world operate within the public school system; they are smaller, more focused, and enrol students who experience difficulty in integrating themselves into large, impersonal, and sometimes violent public schools (Cooper 1994:264). Often, these schools offer new 'experimental' programmes which may in future be used as models for larger efforts. Likewise, in many countries, such as the Netherlands, Denmark, England and Wales, parents are encouraged to start their own alternative schools, or take an existing state-run school and convert it into an independently managed, but government-financed, school (Cooper 1994:264). These schools are often referred to as 'magnet schools'.

In some countries, parents have opted for perhaps the oldest 'alternative' form of education: to teach their children themselves at home. So-called 'home-schooling' involves nearly a million children in the US (Cooper 1994:265), many of whom as fundamentalist Christians elect family education for religious reasons.

The National Coalition of Home Schools in South Africa estimates that there are 3 000 children being educated at home in the country (Shindler 1998:9).

4.3.5 Summary

Reactions to school choice proposals and experiments have been mixed. Advocates of school choice claim that this encourages parental involvement, promotes diversity, improves the curriculum and expands educational opportunities for underprivileged children. Opponents of choice argue that it violates civil liberties and democratic principles through the support of religiously affiliated schools, and fails to increase the educational opportunities of the poor who lack information about alternative schools and who are constrained by transportation difficulties and a family structure that makes attendance at the neighbourhood school more convenient and practical.

Likewise, public aid to private schools remains controversial. The main arguments in favour of aid are that the present situation imposes unfair financial hardship on parents by forcing them to support public schools through taxation as well as paying fees at a private school. In contrast, the general public enjoys a reduced tax burden by being relieved of the responsibility for the private school segment of the population (Cibulka 1988:211). In South Africa it has been proposed that independent schools should receive subsidies at the discretion of the provincial Member of the Executive Council. Criteria to grant funding will include whether the school is registered, has a proven record, a matric pass rate above 50% and does not compete with a nearby public school (Vally 1998:9). Subsidy levels will also favour schools charging lower fees.

Critics of private school aid also argue that the growth of private schools would drain off the most talented and highly motivated pupils from public education and would increase separatism. This is already happening in many townships in South Africa where parents, disenchanted with the state's failure to uplift their local disadvantaged schools, are choosing to send their children to former Model C (independent, state-sponsored) schools. The flight from township schools is causing some intakes to drop by 40 to 60% a year (Lewis & Bot 1998:6). The migration of learners from their communities also means that parents take their capacity and expertise elsewhere which decreases parental support and community involvement in the local schools. Likewise, parents are unlikely to establish close contact with their children's new schools because of the distances between these and their homes. This spells disaster for the concept of democratic governance as laid out in the South African Schools Act of 1996.

4.4 District characteristics

Schools situated in a particular district or area often reflect the characteristics of the area. This frequently necessitates coping with the problems of the communities these schools serve.

4.4.1 Rural schools

It is difficult to define what is meant by 'rural'. The United States census, for example, defines rural population as comprising persons living outside urbanised areas in the open country or in communities of fewer than 2 500 inhabitants (Muse 1988:214). This is criticised by some as being too simplistic and the point is made that an area with few inhabitants, but with a sophisticated infrastructure and high levels of employment, should not be classified as rural. Likewise, others suggest that the degree of isolation from an urbanised area is also important in determining how 'rural' a place is (Khattri, Riley & Kane 1997:81). However, all agree that schools found within rural areas differ from those found in urban areas.

Khattri et al. (1997:89-91) list the following characteristics of rural schools within developed countries:

- *Size*. Due to isolation and low population density in rural communities, rural schools are typically small compared to schools in more populated communities. This is seen by many as the main strength of rural schools.
- *Location*. In sparsely populated rural areas, pupils often travel long distances to attend school. This transportation is often costly and time-consuming, and could contribute to a student's decision to drop out of school.
- *Budgets*. Several researchers suggest that rural budgets are small and do not adequately cover the considerable costs of operation. This could lead to limited curricular and programme offerings, and a lack of resources.
- *Course offerings*. Many small rural schools are unable to provide the types of courses needed to prepare learners for further studies. Likewise, low career aspirations may be a factor in indicating that fewer rural graduates prepare for and enrol in post-secondary education.
- *Availability of special programmes and technological resources*. Programmes and extra-curricular activities offered in rural schools are limited, affecting pupils' opportunities to learn. Likewise, most rural schools do not have access to technological resources.
- *Staff qualifications and preparedness*. Teacher experience and the recruitment and training of teachers are frequently cited as major problems in rural areas. In the US, for example, 24% of teachers who teach in rural schools are typically younger, less experienced and less likely to have a master's degree than their counterparts in urban and suburban schools (Reaves & Larmer 1996:29).

Smith and Martin (1997:15) add that in rural areas there are higher poverty rates, a higher percentage of poor school districts, and fewer dropouts who return to finish high school as compared to urban areas. On the other hand, small class size, personable atmosphere and a nurturing environment are seen as strengths. Thus the potential of becoming a highly effective school exists in most rural areas.

The above, however, is true only of schools in developed or industrial countries. In the developing world the high population growth, the lack of infrastructure and resources, and the overcrowded classrooms typically found in rural areas place a severe strain on educational provision. As Hodgkinson, in Khattri et al. (1997:85), observes: '... rural poverty is not urban poverty in a different setting', implying that structures and processes are distinct from those in urban or suburban settings. Students in rural areas in general, and in poor rural areas in particular, may face a unique mix of obstacles to gaining a sound education.

4.4.2 Urban schools

In technologically advanced countries cities have evolved in ways that have greatly complicated the tasks of urban educators. The flight of the middle class from inner city areas has left many cities with a high concentration of 'dependent' individuals who have extraordinary needs. This is reflected by high poverty rates, unemployment and low per-capita income growth found in inner city areas. In Great Britain, for example, most inner cities are populated by the elderly, the very young, the incompetent, and the immigrant populations. In some developing countries, such as China, the large number of urban poor reflect the traditional migration of rural poor to the cities in search of a better life (Cibulka 1994:6552). This is also true of South Africa, although people migrating from rural areas tend to settle in 'squatter camps' (informal housing) on the fringes of the bigger cities and towns.

Schools in urban, particularly inner-city, areas of the world face tremendous challenges in providing successful schooling experiences for the culturally, ethnically, racially, economically and socially diverse students they serve. Moreover, students who attend inner-city schools are disproportionately poor and minority-group members. They have few positive role models who demonstrate the link between excellence in academic performance and personal fulfilment, gainful employment and career opportunities (Reed 1994:6559). Thus most schools found in inner-city areas are constant reminders of our failure to provide equal opportunities for all citizens.

According to Lightfoot (1988:146) problems faced by inner-city schools include the following:

They have the

- oldest facilities
- highest number of students per school

- highest numbers of newly qualified teachers
- largest teacher and administrator turnover
- tendency to place the greatest demand on teachers' time and energies in terms of discipline, instruction, lesson planning and class sizes
- highest absentee rates among school personnel of any urban schools
- larger share of substitute teachers
- greatest amount of teacher 'burnout' than any other type of school.

In addition, many of the problems that plague city schools stem from the cities themselves; the full solution lies outside the schools as well as in them (Fullan 1998:225). Some policy-makers go as far as to suggest that it is pointless to work on school reform without prior community-building efforts. The best strategy is probably to work on both. In other words, building the infrastructure of the school must explicitly include the development of, and relationships among, all those adults who can potentially affect the motivation, support and learning of students.

Reform initiatives in urban schools

A variety of programmes or interventions have been advocated to improve the performance of poor minority children in urban schools. In the United States one of the most successful interventions for students in urban schools is the developmental programme designed by James Comer (Comer 1980; Comer, Haynes & Joyner 1996). This programme calls for school-based teams of teachers, parents, psychologists, social workers, special education teachers, counsellors and other related support service staff who together focus on school planning and management, mental health and parental involvement.

Another intervention programme, 'accelerated school' advocated by Levin (1987), is built on the premise that the traditional school curriculum fails to recognise the strengths of minority and poor urban students and thus does not challenge them in ways that encourage active learning. These schools, therefore, provide for advanced subject matter to be introduced earlier through an enriched curriculum, higher levels of teacher expectations and the involvement of parents in the school.

In the United States of America it is also argued that the implementation of school-based governance models will improve urban schools. Such governing bodies are able to make decisions regarding curriculum, staff selection and budgeting. The school-based management approach is important for large urban districts, where excessive system-level bureaucracy and a lack of neighbourhood or community control are frequent complaints. This approach is also being followed in South Africa where the South African Schools Act of 1996 provides for the institution of governing bodies in all schools in the country, thereby making greater community participation in schools possible.

4.5 School and classroom issues

There are a number of issues within schools and classrooms which are universally recognised as influencing education. In the following section some of these issues are briefly discussed.

4.5.1 Class size and teacher-pupil ratio

Few issues rouse stronger feelings among educators than class size, and few have more direct implications for school policy and practice. Teachers believe that the quality of their teaching and their interactions with learners decline with an increase in the size of the class. Administrators argue that per-pupil costs increase markedly as class size falls below 25 pupils. Both arguments are valid.

Research indicates that teachers experience more *positive attitudes* to students and their work when teaching smaller classes (Sindelar & Vail 1988:58). However, teachers' perceptions that smaller classes result in more individual interaction and stronger rapport with learners are not supported by research. Likewise, the link between learner achievement and class size has not yielded the results attributed to it. In general, student achievement in small classes (fewer than 15) will exceed achievement in both average-size classes (about 25) and large classes (more than 30). However, in classes of 25 students achievement is only marginally better than the achievement of students in bigger classes.

A decision to decrease class size significantly, therefore, needs to take the following into consideration: on the one hand a decrease in class size will increase per-pupil costs by approximately 25%; on the other hand teachers teaching smaller groups of students are more likely to feel satisfied with their jobs and believe that they are doing better work. In reality, their teaching may not change and nor are students' attitudes toward school likely to change. Student achievement will improve, but not substantially so. A country or district that adopts a policy of reduced class size should, therefore, first train its teachers to take advantage of this initiative as effective teaching is largely unrelated to class size, at least within the range that encompasses typical class size and realistic reductions.

In developing countries teachers often have to cope with extremely large classes. Moreover, budgetary restraints make reductions virtually impossible. One possible solution could be to make use of para-professionals who need not be paid a teacher's salary to help cope with large classes. Teachers can also consider recruiting volunteer parents, grandparents, or retired persons to serve in their classrooms as instructional aides.

In South Africa the optimum pupil-teacher ratio in primary schools has been set at 40:1 and in secondary schools at 35:1 (Bot 1995:9). However, in practice, the real ratio is higher as a number of teachers such as principals, deputy principals, heads of departments and librarians, all of whom have limited teaching duties, are included in the equation. Lewis and Bot (1998:7) also report that nationally grade 1 is over-enrolled with underaged learners, while grades 8, 11 and 12 are also over-enrolled with over-age learners due to high failure rates.

4.5.2 Measuring student performance

The most commonly used measure of school performance is scores on standardised achievement tests, which are those constructed, administered, scored, reported and interpreted in a consistent fashion to provide for the measurement of individual differences in as unambiguous a way as possible (Lockheed & Hanushek 1994:1782). Properly treated, standardised tests provide consistent information across schools, as well as indications of performance differences among children within the same school.

At primary school levels, standardised tests provide good indicators regarding student attainment of educational objectives such as functional literacy and numeracy. In later grades, where other objectives of schooling increase in importance, standardised tests covering the entire curriculum are more difficult to construct.

The instruments of evaluation and assessment of students have, over the years, undergone gradual but radical change. Formative and continuous assessment have become common. Norm-referenced assessment has often made place for criterion-referenced assessment. In many countries external assessment is complemented by internal assessment (Kallen 1997:11). In South Africa the move is also toward continuous assessment of learners; examinations take place at the end of grade 9 with the completion of the general certificate and at the end of grade 12 with the completion of schooling.

A problem associated with assessment is that unsuccessful students have to repeat a grade. Repetition rates are generally highest in poorer countries. However, statistics of repetition rates are often misleading. For example, countries like Sudan, Korea, Zimbabwe and Malaysia now practise automatic promotion. If a public examination is included at the end of schooling the failure rate in such instances is usually very high. In contrast many states in the US have ended social promotion in response to concern over standards, making the country's annual repetition rate comparable to such low-income countries as Kenya (Kelly 1994:5225). In South Africa the failure rate of matriculants (grade 12) is high with only 47,4% of learners who sat for the 1997 examinations passing (Vally 1998:18).

4.6 Student issues

Many issues relating to students can be identified as problematic within the schooling system of countries. The following section deals with some of them.

4.6.1 Student absenteeism and truancy

Since the institution of compulsory schooling in many countries student absenteeism and truancy continue to be lingering problems for school administrators. In order to address the problem of truancy, a working, acceptable definition is needed. Absenteeism tends to be used to describe younger (under 12 years of age), non-school attenders. Truancy, on the other hand, tends to be used to describe more systematic, deliberate and often prolonged absenteeism for young people in a higher age bracket (Nyangoni 1988:249).

The reported rates of truancy vary widely as do the methods to determine such rates. Because of the latter it is difficult to compare rates from different systems or countries. Moreover, school attendance records may be inflated both because teachers and students tend to protect students from the negative consequences of being absent and because school attendance may be systematically exaggerated to protect the school's resources when such resources are based on measures of average daily attendance (Natriello 1994:1603).

According to available data, causes of chronic absenteeism and truancy can be placed into two broad categories: external-related causes and school-related causes. The former include financial and economic problems, familial obligations, peer-group pressures, and sociocultural and environmental factors. The latter include irrelevant curriculum and/or poor instructional methods, inflexible school schedules, insensitive, uncaring teachers, administrators and other school personnel, and poor academic or social skills.

One of the dangers of truancy is that the student will eventually drop out of school.

4.6.2 School dropouts

Much of the research on students who fail to complete school can be divided into two imperfect theories. The dominant theory conceives of early school leaving as *dropping out* and lists it as an individual act, signifying individual, or perhaps family or cultural, failure. The other theory conceives of non-completers as *pushouts*, and focuses on unequal economic, political and social structures, and certain school practices like tracking and expulsion that serve to stigmatise, discourage and exclude children (Kelly 1994:5225). Thus the term 'dropout' puts inordinate blame on the individual, while the term 'pushout' puts inordinate blame on the institution. The latest tendency is, therefore, to rather use the term 'disengagement' – emphasising that early school leaving is a mutual process of rejection.

Measuring school disengagement can be difficult to document because it occurs over time and may not always be observable (i.e. passive resistance to learning) or may be open to different interpretations. Moreover, statistics on dropout rates could differ depending on:

- the differences in the definition of 'dropout' between school districts (or countries)
- the time periods during the school year when dropout data are collected
- differences in the method of data collection
- differences in procedures for tracking youth no longer in school to determine if they completed their education elsewhere
- differences in the methods used to calculate the dropout rates (Natriello 1994:1604).

In general, primary school dropout rates are low in industrial countries such as Europe, North America, Japan, New Zealand and Australia. On the other hand 40% of students who enrolled in primary school in low-income countries such as Haiti and Mali dropped out or were pushed out before the terminal year of that cycle. Moreover, primary school completion rates declined over the 1980s in the poorest countries (Kelly 1994:5225).

Students at risk of dropping out

The following key variables help to explain why certain students are at risk of dropping out of school:

- *Socioeconomic status*. Children living in poverty are less likely to complete school. Some families cannot afford to pay for school fees, books and supplies, transportation and uniforms. Some children apparently drop out because of shame at their relative poverty, reflected in their clothes or lack of lunch (Kelly 1994:5226).
- *Race and ethnicity*. Research shows that groups that have been disadvantaged historically tend to leave school early. In a study performed in Canada, most First Nations (aboriginal) people who left school without completing it said racism, including discriminatory practices and attitudes on the part of teachers and peers, had affected their decision to leave (Kelly 1994:226). In the US ethnicity is often cited as a factor putting students at risk of educational failure. For example, African American and Hispanic students attain significantly lower proficiency scores on test subjects than do white students. Many reasons have been sought for this, including linking it to poverty, lack of English language proficiency, and lower expectations by teachers of students belonging to these groups (Khattri, Riley & Kane 1997:87).
- *Gender*. The sex role division of labour within the family and society influences the persistence in school by gender. In some regions boys drop

out more often and earlier to herd grazing animals and do other tasks. But more often girls – particularly in low-income and rural families – are needed at home to care for the younger siblings and to do housework and agricultural tasks. It is also common for schools around the world to exclude girls who become pregnant or get married.

- *Single-parent households*. Students who live in single-parent households tend to have lower achievement rates and higher school dropout rates than do students from more traditional two-parent households. Lack of time of single parents (90% of whom are mothers) to spend with children, coupled with increased economic burdens from a single source of income, produce less-than-desirable household conditions and, in turn, affect student outcomes (Khattri et al. 1997:87-88).

- *Limited proficiency in language of instruction*. Students with limited English proficiency (LEP) – if this is the language of instruction – are often at risk of educational failure due to the classroom challenges they face, particularly where bilingual curricula or English-as-a-second-language (ESL) programmes are not readily available.

- *Educational attainment of parents*. Literature on the subject indicates that low educational attainment of parents, especially mothers, has a negative effect on student achievement. Parents' own educational experiences also shape the expectations they themselves hold for their children (Khattri et al. 1997:88).

- *Community type*. Rural residents, especially in developing countries, drop out more frequently than their urban counterparts. Lack of schools, large distances between school and home, lack of flexible scheduling of classes and the school year to meet the local population's needs are some of the reasons cited. However, in the US and other highly industrialised countries, dropouts and pushouts more often live in the urban areas where schools are typically overcrowded, underfunded and bureaucratically run.

- *Student behaviours*. Certain student behaviours put them at risk of dropping out. These include:

  ○ Substance abuse. Teens in rural areas seem to prefer alc
  youth in urban communities display higher rates of drug

  ○ Absenteeism. Student absenteeism from classes is often cite   ..ctor
  strongly associated with low educational attainment and dropping out of school.

  ○ Teenage pregnancy. Approximately 40% of young women who drop out of school in the US do so because of pregnancy or marriage, suggesting an association between teenage pregnancy and educational failure.

- *School characteristics*. One of the most basic school characteristics affecting school attendance is the availability of a school. This has been demonstrated in developing countries where a school within the village tends to have a positive effect on the years of schooling completed. Dropping out has also been linked to features of school organisation and student experience within schools, such as a lack of a climate of caring and support which has been shown to increase the likelihood of students dropping out.

- *Environmental aspects*. Schooling may be perceived as less relevant when students see no connection between the curriculum of the school and the culture of their families and neighbourhoods, when the values presented and demanded by the school are at variance with those of their peer groups, and when they see no connection between their academic work in schools and their future economic prospects (Natriello 1994:1604-5). Likewise, conditions outside school may fail to provide support for students to attend regularly and continue in school. These include community problems such as teenage pregnancy, alcohol and drug abuse, delinquent gang membership, family violence and child abuse, family social and financial needs requiring students to be at home or at work, and socially disorganised communities with high rates of crime (Natriello 1994:1604-5).

In South Africa only an insignificantly small minority of young dropouts, if queried, give 'distance to school' as a reason for dropping out. The real tragedy in South Africa seems to be the fact that the youth who are in school, investing more than 12 years of their lives, have only a 1:4 or 1:3 chance of ever obtaining a matric pass (Crouch & Mabogoane 1997:25). It is perhaps because there is so little hope of achieving success that some of our youth leave school.

The consequences of dropping out of school

In some societies dropping out does not automatically foreclose the possibility of continuing one's education; in others such opportunities are limited. In addition, in some economies there are numerous opportunities for those who have not completed formal basic schooling; in others those opportunities are more restricted. However, most people agree that early school leavers will increasingly be at a disadvantage in the job market as economies develop. Natriello (1994:1605-6) lists the following consequences of dropping out of school:

- *Cognitive consequences*. Although not much research has been done in this field, it has been found that the cognitive skills of youngsters who stayed in school improved more than those of dropouts.

- *Economic and social consequences*. The lower levels of cognitive growth experienced by dropouts result in less success in the job market. Not only are early leavers more likely to be unemployed than those who complete their schooling, they are also likely to earn less when they are employed. Moreover, individuals who leave school early are more likely to engage in criminal activity, have poor health and lower rates of political participation, and require more government services such as welfare and health-care assistance.

With these consequences in mind it becomes important that ways of dealing with the problem of dropouts is found.

Dealing with the problems of dropouts

Most researchers, including Smith and Martin (1997:16), support the notion that successful programmes for at-risk youth include seven components:

- early identification and intervention
- intensive individualised attention
- personal and social skills training – which could include workshops on self-esteem, handling stress, self-responsibility and getting along with others
- attention to training – which includes subject-specific assistance as well as issues such as problem-solving and decision-making skills
- engagement of peers – where at-risk youth learn how to teach self-esteem activities, for example, to younger students
- involvement of parents – where opportunities are provided for parents and children to communicate, and parents are taught about life skills and ways in which they can support their children
- links to the world of work.

To summarise, it is suggested that students should focus on interactive skills like self-concept, locus of control, communication, social skills, problem-solving, decision-making and preparation for the world of work. These areas of individual and social competence, often referred to as 'life skills', appear to be particularly important in rural areas where young people have lower aspiration levels than their urban counterparts.

4.6.3 Violence in schools

School violence, in a real sense, mirrors the violence of the society which shapes the schools. Some students growing up in a violent society tend to perceive violence as a legitimate vehicle for conflict resolution. Because of the prevalence of crime and violence in and around many schools across the world an atmosphere of anxiety and apprehension of being criminally victimised often exists. This may result in bringing weapons to school, joining gangs for protection, truancy and dropping out (Stephens 1988:306).

However, the issue is not the degree of school crime, but rather the impact it has on the quality of children's education. Learners are missing school because they fear for their personal safety. Teachers are leaving the profession because they are tired of dealing with discipline problems. Education quality is diminishing in a climate of violence and fear.

Unfortunately, violence is not unknown to South African youth. During the liberation struggle many children were subject to an atmosphere of terror and intimidation. Far from being protected on account of their youth, children were targets of the political struggle, thereby being denied the opportunity of growing up in a safe environment. Although the country now has a democratically elected government, violence is still prevalent. Even teachers at times are guilty of violence – children continue to be caned or physically abused in spite of the fact that corporal punishment has been abolished for a number of years (Vally 1998:12). Sexual violence is also endemic. One principal in the Newlands area of Durban estimated that 30% of the girls in his schools had been raped or sexually molested. These assaults are carried out by teachers, fellow pupils and family members. Clearly schools in South Africa cannot improve until communities improve. This change requires a committed partnership effort between schools, parents, learners and community leaders.

4.7 Reforming schools

School reform is based on the belief that schools can teach essentially all students, rich or poor, to high levels of performance. This leads one to question how teaching and the nature of the school environment can be improved in order to provide high-level outcomes for all learners, irrespective of their backgrounds. The findings that some schools can and do teach essentially all their students to high levels of performance demonstrates that this is indeed possible.

School reform since the 1960s can be broadly divided into two main streams: the school effectiveness movement and the school quality movement.

4.7.1 School effectiveness movement

Most commentators on effective schools trace the origins of the subject to the 1966 study by Coleman and his colleagues, the so-called *Equality of Educational Opportunities* (Jansen 1995:181). In essence this report and similar ones at the time stated that schools had little effect on students' achievement when compared to the effects of family background and socioeconomic status. Researchers opposed to this view set about listing and researching the characteristics of effective schools. The assumption was that by identifying the salient characteristics, these could be transferred and replicated to other contexts in a relatively unproblematic manner. Edmonds' research, as set out by Jansen (1995:185), lists five factors attributed to effective schools:

- strong administrative leadership
- school climate conducive to learning
- high expectations for student achievement
- clear instructional objectives for monitoring student performance

- emphasis on basic skills instruction.

This list was not shared by all and many variations were offered in an attempt to distinguish between effective and ineffective teaching.

During this 'first wave' of effective school research much of the emphasis fell on determining the correlation between school *inputs* and *outcomes* (often in the form of student achievement). In other words, attention was paid to what *resources* were available to the school rather than to how these resources were organised or used (Jansen 1995:182).

In general the school effectiveness movement utilises large-scale statistical methods to determine the relative effects of different 'inputs' on achievement. The most common 'output' measures used include counts of students, enrolment rates, continuation rates or dropout rates at specific ages or grades, and a repetition or completion rate by grade or level. Few studies employed measures pertaining to the social, personal and vocational goals of schooling (Willms & Raudenbush 1994:1934). Thus the goal of the research was to discover whether schools vary in their *outcomes* after taking account of ability and background and, if so, whether particular school policies and practices account for these differences. The problem arising here is that it often treated many complex schooling processes as uni-dimensional concepts and examined only their direct effects on outcomes.

Today, the tendency is to research the complexities of what happens inside the classrooms rather than the simple input-output analysis associated with earlier approaches.

4.7.2 School quality movement

School effectiveness research placed great emphasis on the study of a set of *inputs* (i.e. textbooks) on a specific *output* (i.e. student achievement). This *production functional model* characteristic of school effectiveness research was gradually replaced by a model where the emphasis fell on changes in the *educational process*. This change in emphasis in school reform became known as the school quality movement. In this 'second wave' of research, *progress* rather than *achievement* as an estimate of school effectiveness was used.

Jansen (1995:194) lists the following as being characteristic of the school quality movement:

The research

- is influenced in part by anthropology, and uses descriptive procedures
- studies school and classroom-level processes and their interactions, and the impact on achievement
- uses ethnographic instruments (i.e. interviews, observation) adapted for particular contexts

- results are generally specific for particular schools or classrooms, though generalisations are also sought across schools and classrooms.

What soon became apparent in both schools effectiveness and quality research was that that which was effective in one setting or contributed to quality schooling would not invariably have the same effect in all settings and schools.

How to address contextual differences between schools has become one of the greatest challenges for school improvement. Different change strategies, leadership styles and communications networks may be required to effect change in a school that is struggling from one that is already relatively effective, but wants to become even more so (Fink & Stoll 1998:307). This is seen only too clearly when a principal moves to a new school, attempts to implement what worked well in her previous school and finds that, because of different culture, community, and micro-politics, the strategy is ineffective. Since no two schools are the same, there would appear to be no single best way to approach school improvement. This can be terribly frustrating for those who seek simple solutions.

4.8 Conclusion

The modern school is perhaps the most pervasive institution of modernity. A traveller to almost any village or town in the world is likely to find a clearly recognisable school, regardless of the country, the particulars of history, culture, language, religion, ethnic composition or legal framework. Often differences among schools reflect not those in national contexts or in clientele but those in the ability of the state to provide adequate schooling for its citizens (Williams 1997:119). This is a problem difficult to solve and is likely to perpetuate the divide between the developed and developing world for many years to come.

References

Ahmed, M; Ming, CK; Jalalubbin, AK and Ramachandran, K (1991) *Basic education and national development. Lessons from China and India.* New York: UNICEF.

Bennet, J (1994) Preschool education: worldwide trends. In T Husén and TN Postlethwaite (eds) *The international encyclopedia of education Vol 8.* Oxford: Pergamon Press.

Benson, CS (1994) Educational financing. In T Husén and TN Postlethwaite (eds) *The international encyclopedia of education Vol 3.* Oxford: Pergamon Press.

Bot, M (1996) Teachers. *EduSource Data News, No 12,* April:1-6.

Brookover, WB (1988) School improvement and effectiveness movement. In RA Gorton, GT Schneider and JC Fisher (eds) *Encyclopedia of school administration and supervision.* Phoenix: Oryx.

Cibulka, JG (1988) Religious schools. In RA Gorton, GT Schneider and JC Fisher (eds) *Encyclopedia of school administration and supervision.* Phoenix: Oryx.

Cibulka, JG (1994) Urban education: changing ecology, politics and reform. In T Husén and TN Postlethwaite (eds) *The international encyclopedia of education Vol 11.* Oxford: Pergamon Press.

Comer, JP (1980) *School power: implications of an intervention project.* New York: The Free Press.

Comer, JP; Haynes, NM and Joyner, ET (1996) The School Development Program. In JP Comer, NM Haynes, ET Joyner and M Ben-Avie (eds) *Rallying the whole village: the Comer process for reforming education.* New York: Teachers' College Press.

Cooper, BS (1994) Alternative schools and programs. In T Husén and TN Postlethwaite (eds) *The international encyclopedia of education Vol 1.* Oxford: Pergamon Press.

Crouch, L and Mabogoane, T (1997) Aspects of internal efficiency indicators in South African schools: analysis of historical and current data. *EduSource Data News,* No 19, December:1-3.

Cummings, WK (1997) Patterns of modern education. In WK Cummings and NF McGinn (eds) *International handbook of education and development: preparing schools, students and nations for the twenty-first century.* Oxford: Pergamon Press.

Fink, D and Stoll, L (1998) Educational change: easier said than done. In A Hargreaves, A Lieberman, M Fullan and D Hopkins (eds) *International handbook of educational change.* Dordrecht: Kluwer.

Führ, C (1997-1998) Seventy-five years. The German primary school. *European Education,* 29(4) winter:5-10.

Fullan, M (1998) The meaning of change: a quarter of a century of learning. In A Hargreaves, A Lieberman, M Fullan, and D Hopkins (eds) *International handbook of educational change.* Dordrecht: Kluwer.

Glenn, CL (1994) School choice and privatization. In T Husén and TN Postlethwaite (eds) *The international encyclopedia of education Vol 9.* Oxford: Pergamon Press.

Jansen, JD (1995) Effective schools? *Comparative Education,* 31(2):181-200.

Kallen, D (1997) Editorial. *European Journal of Education,* 32(1):3-13.

Khattri, N; Riley, KW and Kane, MB (1997) Students at risk in poor, rural areas: a review of the research. *Journal of Research in Rural Education,* 13 (2):79-100.

Kelly, DM (1994) School dropouts. In T Husén and TN Postlethwaite (eds) *The international encyclopedia of education Vol 9*. Oxford: Pergamon Press.

Levin, HM (1987) Accelerated schools for disadvantaged students. *Educational Leadership*, March:19-21.

Lewis, C and Bot, M (1998) Provincialisation of education: a review (May-October 1998). *EduSource Data News*, No 23, December:1-10.

Lightfoot, A (1988) Inner city schools. In RA Gorton, GT Schneider and JC Fisher (eds) *Encyclopedia of school administration and supervision*. Phoenix: Oryx.

Lingens, HG (1997-1998) Primary education. Changes and strategies. *European Education*, 29(4) winter:3-4.

Lockheed, ME and Hanushek, EA (1994) Educational efficiency and effectiveness, concepts of. In T Husén and TN Postlethwaite (eds) *The international encyclopedia of education Vol 3*. Oxford: Pergamon Press.

Muse, ID (1988) Rural school districts. In RA Gorton, GT Schneider and JC Fisher (eds) *Encyclopedia of school administration and supervision*. Phoenix: Oryx.

Natriello, G (1994) Dropouts, school leavers, and truancy. In T Husén and TN Postlethwaite (eds) (1994) *The international encyclopedia of education Vol 3*. Oxford: Pergamon Press.

Nyangoni, BW (1988) Student absenteeism and truancy. In RA Gorton, GT Schneider and JC Fisher (eds) *Encyclopedia of school administration and supervision*. Phoenix: Oryx.

Owens, RG (1988) High schools. In RA Gorton, GT Schneider and JC Fisher (eds) *Encyclopedia of school administration and supervision*. Phoenix: Oryx.

Papadopoulos, G (1995) Looking ahead: an educational agenda for the 21st century. *European Journal of Education*, 30(4):493-506.

Reaves, WE and Larmer, WG (1996) The effective school project: school improvement in rural settings through collaborative professional development. *Rural Educator*, 18(1):29-33.

Reed, RJ (1994) Urban schools. In T Husén and TN Postlethwaite (eds) *The international encyclopedia of education Vol 11*. Oxford: Pergamon Press.

Sedibe, K (1998) Dismantling apartheid education: an overview of change. *Cambridge Journal of Education*, 8(3):269-282.

Shindler, J (1998) Provincialisation of education: a review (June 1997-April 1998). *EduSource Data News*, No 21, July:1-10.

Sindelar, PT and Vail, CO (1988) Class size. In RA Gorton, GT Schneider and JC Fisher (eds) *Encyclopedia of school administration and supervision*. Phoenix: Oryx.

Stephens, RD (1988) Violence in schools. In RA Gorton, GT Schneider and

JC Fisher (eds) *Encyclopedia of school administration and supervision.* Phoenix: Oryx.

Smith, M and Martin, SS (1997) Parent involvement in a program for rural youth at risk: an exploratory study. *Rural Educator,* 19(2):15-29.

Spodek, B (1988) Preschool education. In RA Gorton, GT Schneider and JC Fisher (eds) *Encyclopedia of school administration and supervision.* Phoenix: Oryx.

Vally, S (1998) *Quarterly Review of Education and Training in South Africa.* Education Policy Unit, Wits, Vol 5(4), August.

Wickremasinghe, W (1992) *Handbook of world education: A comparative guide to higher education and educational systems of the world.* Houston: American Collegiate Service.

Williams, JH (1997) The diffusion of the modern school. In WK Cummings and NF McGinn (eds) *International handbook of education and development: preparing schools, students and nations for the twenty-first century.* Oxford: Pergamon Press.

Willms, JD and Raudenbush, SW (1994) Effective school research: methodological issues. In T Husén and TN Postlethwaite (eds) *The international encyclopedia of education Vol 4.* Oxford: Pergamon Press.

Woodhead, M and Weikart, DP (1988) Comparative studies in preschool education. In TN Postlethwaite (ed) *The encyclopedia of Comparative Education and national systems of education.* Oxford: Pergamon Press.

CHAPTER 5

CURRICULUM

 Prof Monica Jacobs
University of Zululand

Table of contents

5.1 Introduction

There is a limit to what one can expect to learn from an introduction to a complex study field such as curriculum studies. A word of caution may be helpful. This chapter will *not* provide the reader with ready-made solutions to practical curriculum problems such as poor subject choices, out-dated syllabi, demotivated learners and so on. Curriculum sources proposing particular solutions to such problems often contain arguments aimed at arousing public opinion and at promoting the interests of certain political or economic groups. The measures proposed by authors of such sources are sometimes based on a rudimentary view of the curriculum; consequently, their ideas tend to be prescriptive, superficial, one-sided and short-lived. A more profitable way to tackle curriculum problems is to first gain a deeper understanding of curriculum issues as seen by a variety of curriculum specialists before proposing solutions.

Recent growth in the area of curriculum theory has shown that solutions to curriculum problems are more likely to be effective when they are underpinned by an eclectic understanding of *different views* and *alternative perspectives* than by a single ideology. The aim of this chapter, therefore, is not to suggest ways to 'improve' curricula, but to guide the reader to a deeper, multi-dimensional understanding of curriculum issues. The chapter ends with a case study in which the recent introduction of outcomes-based education in South Africa is discussed as an example of curriculum reform.

5.2 Perceptions of what constitutes a curriculum

The word 'curriculum' comes from the Latin verb *currere* which means 'the running of a race'. Its root meaning can therefore be described as 'a course to be run'. A notable feature of this description is that it emphasises the role of the individual, that is, the personal experiences of an individual as he or she runs the race of life. To run the race successfully, it is believed that one needs a certain type of knowledge described as 'desirable knowledge'. For example, when parents wrestle with decisions about what they wish their children to learn – e.g. values such as honesty and good manners, knowledge needed for a career, social skills, mathematical skills and so on – they are deliberating about desirable knowledge. In the same way curriculum planners, teachers, politicians and others involved in curriculum issues constantly deliberate about the nature of the desirable knowledge they believe students should learn.

The phrase 'desirable knowledge' naturally gives rise to the question: 'Desirable for what?' Responses to this question by different people are so numerous, diverse and contradictory that they have led to various perceptions and definitions of the term 'curriculum'. Of the many diverse views expressed in this regard, the most prevalent standpoints describe a curriculum as:

- *Subject matter*. People often equate a curriculum with the subjects being taught at schools and other learning institutions. For example, people speak about the *high school curriculum* or the *Bachelor of Arts curriculum*, meaning the subjects students need to study to obtain a certain qualification. To supporters of this definition desirable knowledge is knowledge obtained by studying suitable subjects.

- *Content*. This perception of the curriculum focuses on course content as it appears in written documents. For example, the syllabus of subjects such as Geography or Accountancy is sometimes viewed as the curriculum of that particular subject. To supporters of this definition desirable knowledge is knowledge obtained by studying suitable content.

- *Planned activities*. This perception embraces all activities planned for students aimed at enabling them to complete a course of studies. Supporters of this view believe that desirable knowledge is much more than content; desirable knowledge can only be obtained if suitable content is learned using appropriate teaching methods, lesson plans, evaluation procedures and other planned activities. Therefore all these actions form part of their definition of 'curriculum'.

- *School-directed experiences*. According to this definition, the curriculum includes not only planned classroom experiences, but also unplanned school-related experiences, both inside and outside the school. It encompasses the hidden curriculum. People who agree with this perception reject the idea that the curriculum consists only of desirable knowledge. They regard the curriculum as including all experiences directed by school personnel (e.g. experiences on the playground, sports field, school concerts, in the community and so on), regardless of whether these experiences are desirable or not.

- *Individual experiences*. People who favour this interpretation perceive the curriculum as that which a particular learner *actually experiences* as a result of schooling i.e. both desirable and undesirable experiences. For example, two learners from the same class studying the same subjects follow two different curricula because each one's actual experiences are entirely different.

- *Transfer of culture*. Some contend that the curriculum is the transfer of the existing knowledge, skills and values of a particular culture to each succeeding generation. To them desirable knowledge is current knowledge identified by representatives of society like government agents or community leaders as being suitable for transmission to the next generation.

- *Social reform*. This perception assumes that the curriculum should consist of content and experiences that will equip the next generation to improve society. This *cultural reconstructivist* view favours school systems in which desirable knowledge is determined by students and/or teachers who support the establishment of a new social order.

The definition of curriculum as used in this chapter is the one proposed by Marsh (1997:5): 'Curriculum is an interrelated set of plans and experiences which a student completes under the guidance of the school'.

5.3 The field of Curriculum Studies

Curriculum Studies is a field of study at many universities, teacher education colleges and other tertiary institutions where students learn various aspects of the curriculum, often within the larger study field of education. A substantial part of Curriculum Studies revolves around *what* and *how* individuals learn or should learn in formal institutions. It would, however, be unrealistic to assert that Curriculum Studies consists only of technical descriptions and analyses of well-known curriculum constructs like objectives, subject units, academic programmes and the like.

Below the level of structured courses in Curriculum Studies, curriculum specialists deal with significant philosophical questions such as:

● What is knowledge?

● Which types of knowledge transform people from passive to active human beings?

● How does one teach a child to feel love for all creatures?

● What elements of knowledge enable individuals to rise to great heights of wisdom?

● To what extent should one person control another's destiny?

● What causes the growth of human beings?

According to curriculum theorist Schubert (1986:8):

> We are not merely dealing with choices among textbooks or learning packages ... What we are addressing is as profound and serious an issue as humankind can address: the fate of our children and youth and what it means to turn their lives toward greater growth, goodness and enlightenment.

It is against the backdrop of philosophical reflections of this kind that the surface structures of Curriculum Studies manifest themselves.

In the continuous struggle to make curricula more effective, curriculum specialists reflect on various aspects of the curriculum, depending on their area of interest. Some researchers are interested in the *historical aspect*, i.e. they explore past curriculum developments and the belief systems that guided these developments. Theorists are engaged in the *theoretical aspect* which entails the critical examination of an ever-growing body of curriculum theories. Planners study the *design aspect* – the construction of teaching programmes, the preparation of curriculum materials, the planning of assessment requirements and so on. Other authorities specialise in the *value aspect*, i.e. the moral and ethical elements of the curriculum. Political analysts work on the *political aspect,* i.e. they analyse the political impact of the curriculum as well as unpopular facets of it. Some researchers focus on the *negotiation aspect* by investigating negotiation impediments and formulating guidelines for successful curriculum negotiations. Many curriculum experts in the public service study the *framework aspect* by working out groupings of school subjects or themes according to prescriptions emanating from government policies. Other specialists concentrate on the *implementation aspect* by checking on the delivery process and reporting on the extent to which curriculum policies are being implemented. Finally, some researchers work on the *reform aspect* which requires research into existing curricula and an ability to propose creative, innovative ideas to improve them.

In developed countries continuous activities in all these areas of Curriculum Studies provide systematic analyses of ongoing curriculum developments.

5.4 Prominent curriculum theories

Curriculum theories that gained prominence during the twentieth century can be divided into two broad categories: the traditional paradigm and the inquiry paradigm.

5.4.1 The traditional paradigm

The traditional paradigm is characterised by theories that tend to be prescriptive and exclusive in the sense that each one resembles a definite 'package'. Among the large number of traditional curriculum theories, the three most deeply embedded in curriculum thinking are:

- *The liberal theory*. According to this theory, the main purpose of the curriculum should be to develop students' minds in such a way that they gain substantial insight into the great ideals of life such as truth, beauty, goodness, liberty, equality and justice (Adler 1981). The content of the curriculum should consist of the great works produced through the ages such as famous books of poetry, prose, history, mathematics, philosophy, science and other fields of inquiry, as well as renowned pieces of art and music. In terms of this theory 'curriculum' is seen as being synonymous with 'content'. The teacher is regarded as the chief policy maker. Liberalists are against detailed planning of the curriculum and prescriptions given to teachers on what and how they should teach. Theorists who advocate this paradigm include Whitehead (1929), Hutchins (1936), Highet (1950), Ulich (1955), Broudy (1961), Phenix (1964) and Adler (1982).

- *The experiential theory*. The central argument in this theory expounded by John Dewey is that students can only acquire knowledge through personal experiences. Since each student's experiences are different – in school as well as in the outside world – the purpose of the curriculum should be to facilitate personal growth by exposing students to as many relevant real-life experiences as possible. Supporters of this theory believe intensely in equality and justice. Some experientialists go as far as to propose that students should be equipped to create a new social order that is more democratic and egalitarian than the present one. Experientialists hold the view that the separation of students and teachers into two groups is superficial since both learn continuously from each other. They also believe that one cannot place curriculum components (content, methods, evaluation and so on) in neat little boxes because all these components are intricately interwoven. Furthermore, the curriculum should focus on the students' interests, and not necessarily on material prescribed by the state. Dewey (1902, 1916, 1938) is the chief proponent of this theory but his views are advocated by numerous followers such as Ashton-Warner (1963), Holt (1964), Kozol (1967), Kohl (1968), Dennison (1969), Rosenblatt (1983) and Garrison (1994).

- *The behaviourist theory*. Given the well-attested fact that this theory is the most popular and influential of this century, it is no exaggeration to state that all other theories constitute a combined force which opposes it. According to behaviourist theories each lesson in the curriculum should result in a desirable change in the behaviour of the student. To this end the curriculum should be divided into definitive components and sections as determined by bureaucracies appointed to implement state policy, and teachers should then proceed to implement this prescribed curriculum in a systematic, logical and value-neutral fashion. The chief initiator of this theory was Ralph Tyler (1949) who built his theory around four fundamental questions, each one of which led, in due time, to the development of a perennial curriculum component as illustrated in Figure 5.1. (The perennial components are explained in the section on curriculum design – see page 105.)

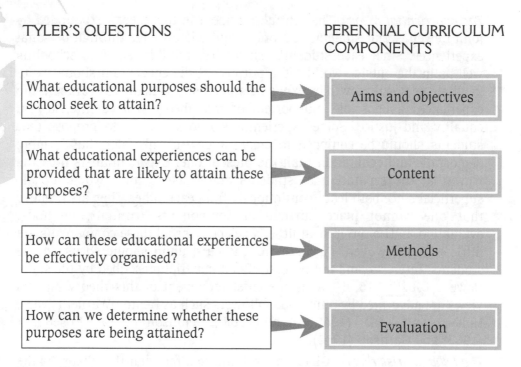

TYLER'S QUESTIONS — PERENNIAL CURRICULUM COMPONENTS

What educational purposes should the school seek to attain? → Aims and objectives

What educational experiences can be provided that are likely to attain these purposes? → Content

How can these educational experiences be effectively organised? → Methods

How can we determine whether these purposes are being attained? → Evaluation

Figure 5.1: Links between Tyler's Rationale and perennial components

During the past few decades the Tyler Rationale has led to multiple variations and applications of the curriculum. Objectives became the standards teachers use to select classroom activities and timeframes aimed at changing students' behaviour. Large-scale scientific studies are conducted on subjects, subject choices and subject content. The curriculum came to be seen as an agglomeration of operationally designed skills, curriculum packages, instructional techniques and scientific evaluation procedures, often implemented through the use of innovative high-tech equipment. Behaviourist approaches to learning are often equated with 'technical rationality', i.e. linear processes of cause and effect which are measurable, rationally controlled and informed by myriad studies on youth needs, principles of learning and subject-matter experts. Some of the most influential authors who propound the behaviourist theory are Bobbit (1918), Bloom (1956), Taba (1962), Mager (1962), Popham and Baker (1970), Gagne (1977), Gage (1978) and Beauchamp (1981).

5.4.2 The inquiry paradigm

One of the distinctive developments in the latter half of the twentieth century is the rise of the inquiry paradigm. Traditional theories are closed systems in the sense that they tend to be prescriptive: they prescribe how the curriculum 'should' be. Inquiry theories, on the other hand, are more open, descriptive, critical and eclectic. Instead of focusing exclusively on how things 'should' be done, their point of departure is how things *are* being done, i.e. that which is actually happening in schools. Cutting across all traditional theories, inquiry analysts question many current practices, political motives and ideologies underlying curriculum developments. They use the results of their inquiries to propose new theories. The difference between the two paradigms is illustrated in Figure 5.2, where traditional theories are conceptualised as self-contained 'boxes', necessitating a distinct choice between each theory. Inquiry theorists, on the other hand, tend to select different features from various traditional theories to structure their own theories.

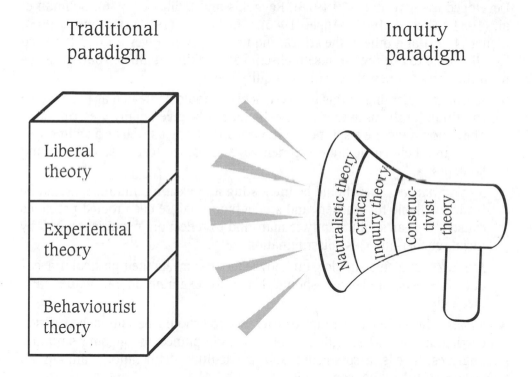

Figure 5.2: Inquiry theories cast their light over self-contained traditional theories

Three of the most important inquiry curriculum theories are the naturalistic, critical inquiry and constructivist theories:

The naturalistic theory

The naturalistic theory was designed by Walker (1971) and further developed by authors such as Goodlad and Klein (1970), Rudd (1973), Richardson (1973), Pinar (1980), Roby (1985), Reid (1978) and Mulder (1991).

Walker's theory consists of a three-step sequence of curriculum reform:

- the formation of a *platform* consisting of members of the school community who agree on beliefs, theories, aims and procedures on which the curriculum at their school rests
- the *deliberation* stage involving the assessment of actual states of affairs, problems and alternative solutions
- the *design* stage during which the school community decides how each problem will be addressed.

The critical inquiry theory

Developed by Schwab (1970,1978), Reynolds and Skilbeck (1976), Soliman et al. (1981), Greene (1986), Apple (1986), Van Manen (1991), Huebner (1993), Eisner (1994) and others, the critical inquiry theory revolves around the need for all people to acquire and use their critical thinking abilities. Four variables form the cornerstones of the critical inquiry theory:

- *Teachers*. According to this theory, teachers should be treated as people who can think for themselves (i.e. they should not be given many prescriptions). They should radiate a spirit of joyfulness and caring as well as a willingness to share their curriculum experiences with other teachers, parents and students.
- *Subject matter*. This should be interesting and exciting and time should be made available for teachers and students to analyse deep-rooted problems caused by 'man's inhumanity to man' and to reflect on inequities caused by racial, gender and class discrimination.
- *Students*. Students should gain knowledge that meets their particular needs and interests, and they should learn to examine moral values and ideologies.
- *Milieu*. The *milieu* or culture of each school should be entrenched in the curriculum of that specific school and underpinned by ongoing situation analyses, needs assessments and curriculum deliberations among all sectors of the school community.

The constructivist theory

This theory – sometimes referred to as socio-constructivism – is an eclectic theory in which elements from various other curriculum theories are combined. Constructivists redefined many curriculum concepts using 'constructivist' terminology. They have ignited a new burst of enthusiasm for Dewey's experiential theory and also reasserted the importance of *meaning-making*:

Traditionally, learning has been thought to be a 'mimetic' activity – a process that involves students in repeating, or miming, newly presented information. Brooks and Brooks (1993:15) state that 'constructivist teaching practices help learners to internalize and reshape, or transform, new information'.

Constructivism is based on the belief that learners should be helped to construct knowledge that is meaningful and useful in their own lives. What is important is not so much *what* learners learn, but *how* they learn. Once learners have acquired effective learning skills such as research, excursions, interviews and group discussions, they can use these skills to learn whatever they wish to learn. Constructivists agree with most of the ideas propagated in the critical inquiry theory, but develop them in greater detail, especially their application in real-life learning classrooms. Well-known authors who promote constructivism include Harris (1991), Noddings (1992), Snyder et al. (1992), Brooks and Brooks (1993), Cohen et al. (1993), Spector (1993), Aspin (1994) and Henderson and Hawthorne (1995).

5.5 Curriculum design

Curriculum design can be broadly defined as a planned programme of studies which may include anything from a five-year course to a thirty-minute lesson. On a *macro-level* curriculum design deals with planning which occurs on a national scale; on a *meso-level* it deals with planning within a particular school and its immediate environment, but outside individual lessons; and on a *micro-level* it refers to the planning of individual lessons or units (Krüger & Müller 1988:6).

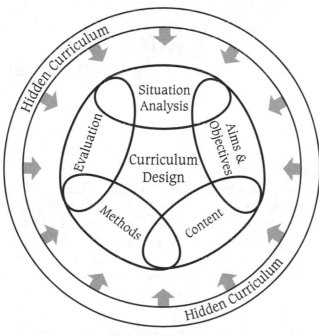

Figure 5.3: Conceptual framework of curriculum design using perennial components

When curriculum planners design a curriculum, they find it more systematic and manageable to build their planning around a frame of reference that is accepted by most educationists. The framework in Figure 5.3 on page 116 meets this requirement. It consists of five perennial curriculum components acknowledged by the majority of teachers and curriculum specialists: situation analysis, aims and objectives, content, methods and evaluation. The perennial components are tightly intertwined and only on an abstract level do they function as separate entities. In real-life teaching situations all five components manifest themselves simultaneously and continuously.

In everyday teaching the five perennial components function together. For example, when a teacher shows a group of students how to conduct literary research for an assignment on Ghana, he or she constantly bears in mind all five components:

- the background of the students and the school (situation analysis)
- the purpose of the assignment (aims and objectives)
- the topic, Ghana, which is being investigated (content)
- the steps students can follow while they search for information on Ghana (methods)
- the way in which the assignments will be assessed.

During the design process, however, the planner focuses on each perennial component in turn for purposes of clarity, especially if the final design must be presented in document form:

- *Situation analysis*. This is that aspect of the design in which the planner analyses the *context* in which the curriculum will be implemented and the process of how contextual factors will be *incorporated* and applied when the curriculum is put into practice. Typical situational factors that are analysed are the background of the targeted students, teachers and school, the facilities/resources available, the nature of the surrounding community, the size of classes and time-table constraints.
- *Aims and objectives*. These are the specifications of the goals of the curriculum. Aims are the long-term goals and the general expectations of the planners for the intended course. For example, in a course on Market Gardening, one aim of the curriculum may be 'to supply fresh vegetables to

people living in the surrounding area'. Objectives are the more detailed, short-term curricular goals, for example 'to sell fresh tomatoes, potatoes, onions and carrots at a roadside stand for six hours'.

- *Content*. This is the subject matter, themes or topics that will be studied in the curriculum. Each subject has its own unique set of elements which forms the learning content. The content of a school Psychology curriculum, for example, may include topics such as learning, motivation, perception, personality, the nervous system, social behaviour and so on.

- *Methods*. These are the special activities that will be used to help students acquire the desirable knowledge described in the content. Examples are group discussion, the project method, simulation games, role-play, problem-solving and experimentation. Effective methods are regarded as those which lead to productive interaction between participants and to the achievement of specific curriculum objectives. Included in this component are the design, production and use of teaching media.

- *Evaluation*. This is the procedure that will be employed to assess the learning gain of students, the effectiveness of the teacher and the curriculum as a whole. A well-designed curriculum contains guidelines on evaluation criteria and assessment methods that should be applied to judge student progress, maintain desirable standards, assess the teaching and determine the efficacy of the curriculum.

5.6 The hidden curriculum

The hidden curriculum relates to a wide variety of planned as well as unplanned experiences which students and teachers have at schools but which are not stipulated in specific syllabi.

Educationists interested in the hidden curriculum often focus their debates on the hidden *macro-curriculum*, that is, on covert school experiences that take place on a national level, often as a result of governmental and political influences. A government has complete control over the vast amount of state money available for education in a country and it sometimes uses that economic power to create a hidden curriculum which helps it to achieve certain political goals (Chalufu 1996:98). The hidden macro-curriculum, therefore, tends to be related to politics.

In most countries the hidden macro-curriculum has characteristics which obstruct equal educational opportunities for all. Problematic aspects of the current hidden macro-curriculum in South Africa, for example, include the following:

- Élitism continues to exist because richer parents are able to pay for better facilities, private schools, education abroad and so on (Christie 1985:126; Bergh 1993:477).

- Students who pass Science and Mathematics are given better educational and career opportunities than pupils studying other subjects (Apple 1978:64).

- Throughout the school system there is discrimination against girls such as limitations in subject choice, bias in classroom interaction, sexual harassment, rape and unwanted pregnancies (Lemmer 1993:21-22).

- Mother-tongue instruction at primary schools causes divisions between the various language groups (Christie 1985:125).

However, it would be a mistake to think that the hidden curriculum always exerts a *negative* influence on students. Important *positive* influences also flow from the hidden curriculum. As stated in the definition given earlier, the hidden curriculum encompasses all school-related experiences which are not described in syllabi and directives issued by educational authorities. Of the many factors that make up the hidden curriculum, there are, *inter alia*, the social skills students learn, the friends they make, the many student-student relationships, all the pleasant and unpleasant student-teacher relationships, the numerous verbal and non-verbal interactions, the school facilities and atmosphere, the types of sport, hobbies and cultural activities students encounter and so on. Moreover, the hidden curriculum influences teachers as much as students. For example, most teachers learn daily how to relate to different types of students more effectively and continuously improve their teaching. In fact, the hidden curriculum covers such a wide scope that it is difficult to disentangle the web of possible factors that form part of it. For examples of the hidden curriculum, see Table 5.1.

Macro-level	Meso-level	Micro-level
Part of a country's hidden curriculum may be to encourage students to wear school uniform. By eliminating the possibility of students perceiving clothing as a status symbol, this custom reduces competition and promotes equity between rich and poor students.	The hidden curriculum at one school raised the achievement of all students when teachers started teaching better after the students' parents sponsored in-service courses for teachers, upgraded the staff room and installed a well-equipped computer room.	The hidden curriculum changed Wendy Mkhize's life. When she was in Grade 8, an enthusiastic Art teacher helped to develop her talent for drawing colourful patterns. Today Wendy is a qualified carpet designer, enjoys a high degree of job satisfaction and earns a good salary.

Table 5.1: Examples of the hidden curriculum

5.7 Controversial aspects of the curriculum

The curriculum field is riddled with controversies. To provide an insight into the complexity of these ongoing disputes, three examples of controversial aspects of the curriculum are discussed below.

5.7.1 Values: whose values?

People involved in the development and implementation of a curriculum recognise that educational practices are inextricably linked to human values and the creation of a 'good' society. A 'good' society is generally seen as one that provides a sense of caring, compassion and justice to all its members. Curriculum specialists agree that the curriculum needs to promote two types of liberation: individual and social.

Individual liberation refers to the ability to develop the mental and emotional tenacity to encounter and deal with 'the great events and mysteries of life: birth, death, love, tradition, society and the crowd, success and failure, salvation, and anxiety' (Ulich 1955:255).

The curriculum should therefore cultivate personal values like positive self-esteem, independence, motivation, responsibility and self-realisation.

Social liberation, on the other hand, advocates a society that provides equal access to goods and services for all its members – a society in which there is no discrimination against people simply because they belong to certain racial, ethnic, gender, age, disability or economic groups.

About these general aims of the curriculum there is not much dispute. What are hotly disputed are questions such as the following:

- How does the school curriculum help students to realise the goals of individual and social liberation?
- Which subjects should be taught?
- Should the curriculum be culture-centred or vocationally-centred?
- Should liberal arts such as Art, Drama and Music be taught?
- What should the content of the chosen subjects be?
- Which teaching methods should be used?
- Should religious values be taught?

Conflicts about these issues can become so vehement that all school learning comes to a standstill. To prevent such a catastrophe from occurring, merely because people have conflicting opinions about the *what* and the *how* of teaching students values, states create *educational policies*.

An educational policy constitutes legal statements of the state's mission, purposes and governing procedures regarding education in that country. It includes extensive regulations and guidelines on how schools should function to instill specific values prescribed by the state. Whereas a policy is imperative to reduce large-scale conflicts about values, it also has a downside: instead of criticising each other, citizens begin to criticise the state. In a democratic country, such criticism automatically moves issues concerning the teaching of values into the political arena.

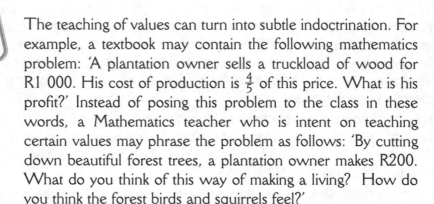

The teaching of values can turn into subtle indoctrination. For example, a textbook may contain the following mathematics problem: 'A plantation owner sells a truckload of wood for R1 000. His cost of production is $\frac{4}{5}$ of this price. What is his profit?' Instead of posing this problem to the class in these words, a Mathematics teacher who is intent on teaching certain values may phrase the problem as follows: 'By cutting down beautiful forest trees, a plantation owner makes R200. What do you think of this way of making a living? How do you think the forest birds and squirrels feel?'

One formidable obstacle in efforts to resolve disagreements about the role of values in the curriculum is the constant tug-of-war that takes place between various policy makers. Among the more important policy makers are politicians, administrators, educationists, curriculum experts, teachers, parents and community leaders. The challenge to overcome criticism of 'policy' frequently causes inter- and intra-group conflicts, especially on governmental committees where uneasy compromises are sometimes made. If countervailing powers fail to resolve conflicts, controversies about values become power struggles which can destabilise or stagnate curriculum development.

5.7.2 Structure: centralised or decentralised?

Another controversial aspect of the curriculum is whether the curriculum should be centralised or decentralised.

Centralised curriculum development is controlled by a central education department, either on a national or a provincial level. In a centrally-controlled curriculum decisions about what is to be taught, how it is to be taught and how it is to be assessed are made by senior politicians and administrators of the department (Marsh 1997:139). The main advantages of a centralised system are that it creates uniformity of curricula and standards, promotes continuity of policy, allows teams of experts to work out the curriculum and ensures that high-quality materials are produced.

A decentralised system is one in which control over the curriculum is shared by the department, teachers, students and the local community. Although decentralised structures vary in their division of powers, at least 50% of decision-making powers are vested in the teachers and students of each particular school. For this reason decentralised systems are often described as 'School-based Curriculum Development' (SBDC). Advantages of decentralisation are that it provides:

- closer links between the curriculum and local conditions
- increased efficiency through the avoidance of bureaucratic procedures
- greater enthusiasm and motivation among participants
- a fairer distribution of national resources.

5.7.3 School subjects: separate or integrated?

School subjects are groupings of study fields and intellectual thought that broadly represent the response of educational authorities to the question: 'Which knowledge should students acquire through the curriculum?' Traditionally, subjects have been taught as separate entities because this enables students to gain systematic, in-depth knowledge of selected study fields in preparation for future careers and personal development. Separate subjects make the curriculum more manageable. For example, knowledge can be arranged in logical hierarchies that coincide with the developmental stages of students and teachers can specialise in certain subjects.

Recently, however, many voices have questioned the feasibility of the separate subject approach, forwarding arguments such as:

- … schooling contributes to atomization and alienation (Miller 1988)
- … students will have a fragmented approach to problems … Each subject comes in its own box, its own wrapper, is evaluated by its own test and usually has nothing to do with anything else the student is studying (Eisner 1991:11)
- … it reflects a Euro-centric view of knowledge organization (Marsh 1997:95).

Writers who are against a separate subject curriculum argue that integrated curricula:

- enable teachers to concentrate on several skills (e.g. communication skills) which are often disregarded in single-subject teaching
- help teachers to teach the 'whole child'
- result in the curriculum revolving more pertinently around students' interests.

They propose that, instead of teaching subjects separately, teachers can organise the curriculum around themes that lend themselves to multidisciplinary approaches, e.g. Egypt, Plants, War, Relationships, Discoveries and so on. The themes can be chosen by teachers or students, resulting in their becoming more involved and motivated. Another way to integrate subjects is to create broad fields, i.e. related subjects are grouped together to form a single broad field. For example, a broad field named 'Natural Sciences' may be created by removing the subject boundaries of related subjects such as Physics, Biology, Chemistry, Environmental Science, Botany and Technology. When this approach is adopted, teachers teaching these subjects can work as a team to structure their curricula around themes.

While arguments for an integrated curriculum are persuasive, opinions differ on whether they are practical. The main drawback of integration is that it goes against the grain of tradition. Although researchers have proved that integrated subjects can be beneficial in primary schools, efforts to introduce this in secondary schools have met with worldwide resistance from teachers. The separate-subject curriculum is deeply entrenched in secondary school teachers' belief systems and attempts to force an integrated curriculum on them may prove to be a tall order. Therefore, the organisation of school subjects is likely to remain a controversial issue in the foreseeable future.

5.8 Curriculum negotiation

The interplay of ideologies in formal discussions of the curriculum means that an increasing demand for successful curriculum negotiation is being generated. Among the various forums where curriculum negotiation regularly takes place are: national policy meetings, provincial curriculum committees, teacher-teacher discussions, meetings of educators involved in school-based curriculum development, discussions related to policy implementation and many other curriculum forums. Parallel to the growth of curriculum negotiations there developed a body of literature and research with respect to curriculum negotiations. A look at these sources reveals interesting information about the reasons why some negotiations are unsatisfactory and others are successful.

Curriculum negotiation is unsatisfactory when:

● the final product lowers the quality of the curriculum instead of raising it.

● the new arrangement is not cost-effective

● the negotiation process alienates the people involved instead of uniting them.

Several factors can combine to make curriculum negotiation outcomes unsatisfactory. Three common causes of unsuccessful negotiations, identified through research, are:

● *Stress*. Studies by Anderson (1976), Keinan (1987) and others revealed that stress is caused by fear of yielding too much or too little, coupled with pressure produced by deadlines. People under stress tend to narrow their vision and overlook alternative solutions, leading to ineffectual decisions.

- *Intolerance of uncertainty*. Educators who are unable to tolerate uncertainty become impatient and make weak decisions rather than make no decision at all (McCutcheon 1995:19).
- *A rush-to-solutions tendency*. This is probably the most common reason why curriculum negotiations sometimes fail. Roby (1985) identified six undesirable manifestations of this tendency:
  - pet solutions wherein vested interests are protected at the cost of progress
  - a global mentality in terms of which participants believe that nothing can be solved without changing the whole system
  - either/or thinking implying that only two extreme solutions are discussed instead of many alternatives
  - the Lone Ranger approach meaning that the most domineering member imposes his or her ready-made solution on the group
  - crisis consciousness in terms of which people only start negotiations when the problem has reached crisis proportions
  - Utopian anticipations wherein the team comes up with idealistic solutions based on wishful thinking.

At the empirical level it was found that there are at least five factors that increase the chances of successful negotiations. According to McCutcheon (1995:23-28):

- An experienced, neutral mediator should be appointed who is fully *au fait* with negotiation techniques.
- The governing body who initiates the negotiation should organise a short in-service course so that negotiators can become familiar with the pitfalls of curriculum negotiation.
- High-quality time should be set aside for the negotiation (preferably week-day mornings when people feel fresh).
- If the negotiation *adds* to the workload of participants, they should be offered compensation or incentives.
- A time schedule should be agreed upon at the beginning of the negotiation process to prevent directionlessness, but if additional time is later requested, the request should be treated leniently.

5.9 Curriculum implementation

Below the level of theories, designs and negotiations, there is the level of operating culture and day-to-day teaching. Key curriculum questions are:

- What is happening on the ground?
- Are policies, plans and regulations being put into practice?

113

An important stage in curriculum development, therefore, is to investigate and assess existing conditions and practices in schools. It is commonly found that what is planned is not necessarily what happens, and what teachers are instructed to do is not necessarily what they practise: 'The teachers started by doing it and only then looked for an explanation of why they were doing it ... in the end it was what worked that survived' (Goodson 1994:118).

A leading researcher on implementation, McLaughlin (1987), identified four factors that have a decisive influence on the success or failure of curriculum implementation:

- *Local capacity*. Implementation is more likely to succeed if support is provided in the form of finances and teacher training, on condition that the support is substantial and continues over a period of years.
- *Motivation and commitment*. Although attitudinal changes among teachers and administrators are difficult to achieve, such changes do occur if local leaders show commitment to the project and convey a sense of enthusiasm to school staff.
- *Internal institutional conditions*. The school climate must be conducive to change, especially in terms of good staff relationships and democratic leadership.
- *Balance between pressure and support*. Pressure is needed to concentrate attention on a specific innovation, but it must be balanced by support in the form of expert assistance and finance.

On close analysis researchers found that a primary reason why teachers frequently resist the implementation of curriculum reforms is that when new curricula are prescribed, they are accompanied by the directive that they be put into practice by *all* teachers in *all* schools and no choice is available (Goodson 1994:118). Teachers are not given alternatives and their views are not taken into account. When this happens, teachers experience the change as nothing more than some new-fangled innovation imposed on them by authorities which are out of touch with real problems and real conditions in schools.

The problem of non-implementation is often caused by school authorities which dictate previously agreed-upon approaches to teachers, instead of including teachers in the bargaining process *before* the innovation is decided upon. Teachers tend to balk at changes which they neither understand nor support. When teachers are disenfranchised in this manner, an interesting but lamentable power game founded on pretence tends to ensue. The teachers pretend to implement the change, yet continue with traditional practices, realising that they have tremendous power over everyday teaching which the bureaucracy cannot control. Educational authorities, on the other hand, play their own pretence game: they pretend that they have the power to force teachers to change their teaching practices. Goodson (1994:112) refers to this scenario as 'the mystique of central control' and 'the myth of prescription':

To continue to exist, teachers' day-to-day power must remain unspoken and unrecorded. This is one price of complicity: day-to-day power and autonomy for schools and for teachers are dependent on continuing to accept the fundamental lie.

An obvious way to overcome this problem is to acknowledge the pathological pretence scenario and expose it for what it is, followed by actions to genuinely involve the teachers of each school during the negotiating and planning of innovations. Studies have shown that teachers do have a desire to reduce the gap between current and preferred practices, but they will only become involved in implementing reforms if they perceive a dysfunction (Leithwood 1981; Marsh 1997:156).

5.10 Curriculum reform

Curriculum reform refers to the improvement of the curriculum by removing flaws and weaknesses. It is associated with planned innovation, adoption, change and departure from established practices.

5.10.1 Reasons for curriculum reform

Broadly speaking, there are three reasons why governments or communities embark on curriculum reform:

- *Social reconstruction*. At the core of the reason for reform is a belief that schools should provide students with knowledge and values that will enable them to build a new social order that is more humane, just and egalitarian (Counts 1932; Freire 1970; Giroux 1983). Proponents of this belief advocate curriculum reforms in which students are taught critical thinking skills through incisive and sometimes disturbing inquiries into existing social practices. While it is true that many reforms have undertones of social reconstruction, the theory is opposed by critics who maintain that schools are not powerful enough to bring about major social changes and that this type of social engineering is a form of indoctrination.

- *Politics*. There is no doubt that politicians play a leading role in curriculum reform. Consider, for example, the major reforms in American education instigated by political commissions, e.g. the reforms of the Commission on the Reorganization of Secondary Education (1918), The Purposes of Education in American Democracy (1938) and the Elementary and Secondary Education Act of 1965 (Schubert 1986:145-146). Because of the power politicians can wield, they normally have the financial clout to breathe new life into the national curriculum.

- *Academic concerns*. The battle to reform is often led by educationists who are concerned about alleged deficiencies in the curriculum, each according to his or her own theoretical persuasion. To address these concerns, they promote diverse post-modern reform measures ch as the application of autobiographical reflection, collaborative interpretation, multicultural debates, ecological sustainability and others (Marsh 1997:304-307). One reform model which became popular in the 1980s and 1990s is Outcomes-based Education which emphasises an outcome-defined curriculum, self-directed learning, interpersonal competence and skills to deal with Information Age issues.

5.10.2 Change dynamics

A well-known scheme reflecting the process of changing the curriculum has been formulated by Fullan (1982). It consists of four phases:

- *The orientation/needs phase.* One or more persons become perturbed about a weakness in the curriculum and start discussing these concerns. The person or group reflects about the need for change and whether they would like to take steps to solve the problem.

- *The initiation/adoption phase.* A specific activity or programme is initiated and facilitated by an individual or group aimed at solving the problem. They work out practical ways in which the activity or programme can be implemented. This is a phase of uncertainty and gathering more information.

- *The implementation/initial use phase.* Teachers attempt to implement the activity or programme. The attempt may be a complete failure, but if it is moderately successful, the teachers gradually discover better ways to apply the innovation. They assist each other and develop a certain expertise. They also begin to assess the effect that the innovation has on students.

- *The institutionalisation/continuation phase.* Measures are taken to entrench the new activity or programme into the curriculum and to ensure that teachers will continue implementing it. This usually requires appointing a teacher or community leader to monitor the operation over a period of time.

When reform is in progress, all four phases intermingle and become indistinct.

5.10.3 School evaluation

A crucial aspect of curriculum reform is school evaluation to assess the implementation of reform. School evaluation is a process of collecting information from school premises, administrators, teachers, students and parents for the purpose of making informed judgements about the functioning of the school. A wide spectrum of techniques are used including:

- time-on-task analysis
- interviews with teachers, students and parents
- audio and video tapes of lessons and meetings

- students' books and files
- checklists of resources
- questionnaires of attitudes and opinions.

5.11 South African case study o

During the period 1990-2000 the South Afri
stormiest reform years in its history. These r
the end of the post-colonial era and the dram
in the 1990s.

5.11.1 Background of the South African curriculum ..

Most attempts to change the curriculum hinged on problems caused by
apartheid: racism, poverty and a negative school climate. In 1990 apartheid
structures were still in place. There were no less than 18 departments of
education. In that year of the government budget allocated an amount of
R3 018 per white student and R853 per black student (Jacobs 1992:103). Large
disparities between white and black education led to immense shortages of
black schools, teachers, classrooms and all other resources needed within
formal education. This contributed to a situation in which approximately six
million young blacks aged 15-30 were unemployed and unemployable, while
the education of whites surpassed the standards of most First World countries
(Collins et al. 1993:34-35). In addition to these frustrations, political turmoil in
the country once again affected black schools.

During the 1980s and early 1990s school children took centre stage in the
struggle for liberation. Numerous uprisings and incidents of violence occurred
in black schools. In KwaZulu-Natal, for example, some 6 000 young people
under the age of 25 were killed during the period 1988-1994, and dozens of
schools were burnt down in the low-key civil war between the ANC and Inkatha.
Although the violence in KwaZulu-Natal was arguably worse than in other
parts of South Africa, there was continuous political upheaval in black schools
in all the regions.

In an attempt to control the turmoil in schools, there was a flurry of activity on
the curriculum front in the early 1990s. As a last-gasp action, the white
government produced a curriculum model for education that contained some
reform elements but still emphasised general education rather than
vocationally-orientated education (Committee of Heads of Education
Departments 1991). The ANC, on the other hand, propagated a single
department of education and favoured People's Education – a model based on
social reconstructionism. However, in the course of the six major publications
on education produced by the ANC during 1991-1996, the party moved away
from People's Education towards a technocratic, employment-orientated

996 the new government published the South African Schools
ned the way for a new curriculum to be designed.

period 1991-1997 a new curriculum was designed by nine task
nder the auspices of the National Training Board – an organisation
by the Department of Manpower. The National Training Board worked
ose collaboration with the trade union, COSATU and representatives from
arious governmental institutions such as Transnet, Escom, Technikons, the
National Education Department and Industrial Training Boards to construct a
curriculum that would prepare students more pertinently for the world of work
(National Training Board 1994).

5.11.2 The new curriculum

In March 1997 the government announced plans for the introduction of
Curriculum 2005, based on Outcomes-Based Education. Outcomes-Based
Education (OBE) is a theory that branched out of competency-based teaching
and mastery learning which, in turn, are rooted in behaviourist theory. The
notion that teachers should focus on intended learning outcomes instead of
aims and objectives was first broached by Johnson (1977) and further
developed by Posner (1982), Spady (1982, 1994), Daggett (1991) and others. As
the theory developed, some of its supporters incorporated elements from other
theories, especially those of constructivist theory. Since OBE supporters believe
that ends are more important than means, the purpose of Curriculum 2005 is
to be explicit and defensible regarding what is offered to students.

Curriculum 2005 is the South African government's curriculum framework
which it intended to be implemented from Grades 1 to 9 by the year 2005. In
accordance with OBE, it is seen to be a design-down process which was
developed to completely overhaul the previous education system by introducing
the National Qualifications Framework (NQF). (See Figure 5.4 on page 119.)
The NQF is controlled by the South African Qualifications Authority which
formulated seven critical outcomes plus five 'nice-to-have' outcomes. These 12
outcomes are broad, cross-curricular outcomes that underpin all school
programmes. Subjects are replaced by eight learning areas and, for each
learning area, a list of compulsory specific outcomes are prescribed. Programme
designers are expected to specify a large number of exit outcomes divided into
programmes, performance categories, modules, units and sessions.

Curriculum 2005 is described as a curriculum that will:

- prepare all learners to become effective in the workplace
- focus on the results or outcomes that are expected at the end of each
  learning process
- integrate knowledge so that learning is relevant and related to real-life
  situations

- be learner-centred
- bring success to all learners, although some may take longer to achieve this than others
- allow teachers to act as facilitators rather than information-givers
- involve parents, guardians and community leaders in the curriculum
- provide ongoing assessment of learners' skills in critical thinking, reasoning and action
- result in equal opportunities and equity for all.

SCHOOL GRADES	NQF LEVEL	BAND	TYPES OF QUALIFICATIONS AND CERTIFICATES	
	8	Higher Education and Training	Doctorates Further research degrees	
	7		Degrees, diplomas and certificates	
	6			
	5			
Further Education and Training Certificates				
12	4	Further Education and Training	School/College/NGOs Training certificates, mix of units	
11	3		School/College/NGOs Training certificates, mix of units	
10	2		School/College/NGOs Training certificates, mix of units	
General Education and Training Certificates				
9 8 7	1	General Education and Training	Senior Phase	ABET 4
6 5 4			Intermediate Phase	ABET 3
3 2 1			Foundation Phase	ABET 2
R			Pre-school	ABET 1

Figure 5.4: National Qualifications Framework

5.11.3 Preliminary analysis of the new curriculum

The struggle for curriculum reform in South Africa, as in most other countries, can be viewed as a political contest. An obvious dilemma of the government in 1997 was how to improve education and create jobs for the masses, without having sufficient revenue to do either. Faced with the impossibility of providing the staggering number of facilities, schools, teachers, resources, materials and teacher-training facilities needed to bring black schools on a par with historically white schools, it seems to have created Curriculum 2005 as a red herring to appease the voters until more satisfactory solutions can be found for the educational and unemployment problems in the country. This is an essential aspect to bear in mind when one examines the new curriculum.

From a theoretical perspective the merits of Curriculum 2005 are the same as those of the so-called 'objectives' models of Tyler (1949) and Bloom (1956): central authorities choose the critical and specific outcomes deemed most desirable, thus creating a uniform system to be implemented throughout the country. The outcomes can become the standards that teachers will use to select or create learning activities, select materials, allocate time and develop assessment methods. These are positive features of the new curriculum.

On the other hand, the OBE approach is nothing new. It rests on behaviourist theory, and therefore carries much of the baggage of behaviourism. Based on an industrial model of learning, OBE is suitable to use in training students to perform industrial-related tasks such as mechanics, word-processing and technical skills. But for teaching disciplines like Art, Mathematics, Humanities, Science and Literature, a much broader conceptual framework is required (McKernan 1999:1). People who accept the liberal, experiential or naturalistic curriculum theories argue that OBE treats knowledge as instrumental, i.e. knowledge is used merely as a means to learn job-related skills, lists of performances and observable behaviours. This view is simplistic because the acquisition of knowledge also has intrinsic value, namely that knowledge is often an end in itself, for example when we seek knowledge merely to satisfy our curiosity. Knowledge is, therefore, far more complex in nature than the way OBE defines it. Knowledge can never be reduced to sequential lists of goals and exit outcomes. True knowledge and understanding lead students to unforeseeable pathways, unexplored meanings and high standards of sensitivity, judgement and creativity. Since such learning is unpredictable and unintentional, not all outcomes can be stated beforehand. What is needed in certain teaching situations are aims or non-behavioural objectives and – according to Huebner (1993:11) – a curriculum that focuses on 'developing an imagination that has room for the spiritual'.

The following quote illustrates this:

> Imagine a student of *Macbeth* purchasing a text that includes all the possible interpretations and understandings of that play. If we teachers

possessed all the answers, we could publish such a text – surely an absurd scenario. The educated mind will always achieve unique and novel interpretations because knowledge is a tool to think with. To cite the significant outcomes in advance of teaching and learning is absurd. (McKernan 1999:3)

Another disturbing feature of Curriculum 2005 is that it aims to achieve equality at the cost of excellence. OBE revolves around three basic principles:

- All students can learn and succeed (but not at the same rate).
- Success in school breeds further success.
- Schools control the conditions of success (Spady & Marshal 1991:67).

While the advisability of all three premises can be called into question, the first one has attracted the most criticism. Opponents of OBE contend that Curriculum 2005 will teach students that failure is acceptable and that is contrary to conditions in the real world: 'In the real world, repeated failure results in discipline, not rewards. Repeated failure gets you fired' (*Kossor Education Newsletter 1996:7*).

In addition, the emphasis on peer teaching and equal success could result in the 'dumbing down' of standards and prevent higher-achieving students from excelling. There is also a widespread feeling that Curriculum 2005 contains such a preponderance of radical changes to traditional school practices – integrated subjects, time-table conversion, new terminology and labour-intensive assessment methods – that Curriculum 2005 may create more problems than it solves.

Regarding the third premise ('Schools control the conditions of success'), there is some perplexity. One of the basic maxims of Curriculum 2005 is that parents, guardians and community leaders will be involved in constructing the curriculum. Teachers were also reassured that they would have much say in the curriculum. Yet, from the outset, the new curriculum was centrally-controlled, accompanied by prescriptions from the state. Who, then, controls the curriculum – the schools, the community or the state? Two years after the reform was announced, this question still elicits nothing more than bland denials or blank faces. Implementation will be more likely to occur if clearer indications are given about the decision-making powers of different stakeholders.

The most crucial question regarding Curriculum 2005 is: To what extent will it be implemented? It would appear that mechanisms have not been created to monitor and evaluate its implementation. As mentioned earlier, reform denotes the *improvement* of the curriculum by removing flaws and weaknesses. If the definitions of 'curriculum' and 'curriculum reform' previously proposed in this chapter are to be accepted, reform must be experienced (i.e. implemented) and shown to be an improvement for it to be considered a reform. Since this case study, written five years before Curriculum 2005, is intended to be fully functional, judgement regarding its success or failure has to be reserved until the year 2005.

5.12 Conclusion

The purpose of this chapter was to sketch with broad strokes the vast array of theoretical, political, social, technical, financial and personal factors that influence the curriculum. Over the years, the curriculum needs to be continually adjusted and updated to ensure that the quality of life for most people continues to improve. One of the distinctive developments in recent years is the integration of post-modern trends into the curriculum. It is clear, for example, that the needs for multicultural education, gender equity awareness, AIDS prevention and knowledge of information systems are transforming many people's perceptions of what constitutes the desirable knowledge the next generation will need. One can expect that the tug-of-war between people with clashing values and belief systems will continue to perpetuate the thrust and counter-thrust movements which lead to curriculum change, increasingly correlating the curriculum with both social priorities and the growth of wisdom.

References

Adler, MJ (1981) *Six great ideas*. New York: Macmillan.

Adler, MJ (1982) *The paideia proposal: an educational manifesto*. New York: Macmillan.

Anderson, NH (1976) Coping behaviours as intervening mechanisms in the inverted-U stress-performance relationship. *Journal of Applied Psychology*, 61:30-34.

Apple, MW (1978) Ideology, reproduction and educational reform. *Comparative Education Review*, 22(3):16-21.

Apple, M (1986) *Teachers and texts*. London: Routledge and Kegan Paul.

Ashton-Warner, S (1963) *Teacher*. New York: Simon and Schuster.

Aspin, DN (1994) *Knowledge and the curriculum: a pragmatic approach*. Paper read at the Faculty of Education Research Seminar, University of the Witwatersrand, September 1994.

Beauchamp, GA (1981) *Curriculum theory*. Fourth edition. Illinois: FE Peacock Publishers.

Bergh, A (1993) Curriculum reform and reconstruction in Africa and Latin America. In EI Dekker and EM Lemmer (eds) *Critical issues in modern education*. Durban: Butterworths.

Bloom, BS (ed) (1956) *Taxonomy of educational objectives: cognitive domain.* New York: David McKay.

Bobbit, F (1918) *The curriculum.* Boston: Houghton Mifflin.

Brooks, JG and Brooks, MG (1993) *In search of understanding: the case for constructivist classrooms.* Alexandria, VA: Association for Supervision and Curriculum Development.

Broudy, HS (1961) *Building a philosophy of education.* Englewood Cliffs, NJ: Prentice-Hall.

Chalufu, N (1996) Curriculum Design. In M Jacobs and N Gawe (eds) *Teaching-learning dynamics: a participative approach.* Johannesburg: Heinemann.

Cohen, DK; McLaughlin, MW and Talbert, JE (1993) *Teaching for understanding: challenges for policy and practice.* San Francisco: Jossey-Bass.

Christie, P (1985) *The right to learn: the struggle for education in South Africa.* Braamfontein: Ravan Press.

Collins; Colin, B; Gillespie, and Roselyn, R (1993) Educational renewal strategies for South Africa in a post-apartheid society. *International Journal of Educational Development,* 3(1):33-44.

Committee of Heads of Education Departments (1991) A curriculum model for education in South Africa: discussion document. Pretoria: Department of National Education.

Counts, GS (1932) *Dare the school build a new social order?* New York: John Day.

Daggett, WR (1991) *Identifying the skills students need for success in the workplace: implications for curriculum and assessment.* Paper presented at the Outcomes-Based Education Conference Project, East Greenville, North Carolina: November 1991.

Dennison, G (1969) *The lives of children.* New York: Random House.

Dewey, J (1902) *The child and the curriculum.* Chicago: University of Chicago Press.

Dewey, J (1916) *Democracy and education.* New York: Macmillan.

Dewey, J (1938) *Experience and education.* New York: Macmillan.

Eisner, EW (1994) *The educational imagination: on the design and evaluation of school programs.* Third edition. New York: Macmillan.

Freire, P (1970) *Pedagogy of the oppressed.* New York: Seabury.

Fullan, M (1982) *The meaning of educational change.* New York: Teachers' College Press.

Gage, NL (1978) *The scientific basis of the art of teaching.* New York: Teachers' College Press.

Gagne, RM (1977) *The conditions of learning.* New York: Holt, Rinehart and Winston.

Garrison, J (1994) Realism, Deweyan pragmatism and educational research. *Educational Researcher,* 23(1):5-14.

Giroux, HA (1983) *Theory and resistance in education: a pedagogy for the opposition.* South Hadley, MA: Bergin and Garvey.

Goodlad, JI and Klein, MF (1970) *Behind the classroom door.* Worthington, Ohio: Charles A Jones.

Goodson, Ivor F (1994) *Studying Curriculum: cases and methods.* New York: Teachers' College.

Greene, M (1986) Philosophy and teaching. In MC Wittrock (ed) *Handbook of research on teaching.* Third edition. New York: Macmillan.

Harris, I (1991) Deliberative inquiry: the art of planning. In EC Short (ed) *Forms of curriculum inquiry.* Albany, New York: SUNY Press, 289-307.

Henderson, JG and Hawthorne, RD (1995) *Transformative curriculum leadership.* Englewood Cliffs, NJ: Merrill, an imprint of Prentice Hall.

Highet, G (1950) *The art of teaching.* New York: Knopf.

Holt, J (1964) *How children fail.* New York: Delta.

Huebner, D (1993) Education and spirituality. Unpublished manuscript. New Haven, CT: Yale University, The Divinity School.

Hutchins, RM (1936) *The higher learning in America.* New Haven, CT: Yale University Press.

Jacobs, M (1992) *A statistical overview of education in KwaZulu-Natal 1990.* Johannesburg: Education Foundation.

Johnson, M (1977) *Intentionality in education.* New York: Center for Curriculum Research and Services.

Keinan, G (1987) Decision-making under stress: scanning of alternatives under controllable and uncontrollable threats. *Journal of Personality and Social Psychology,* 52:639-644.

Kohl, HR (1968) *36 children.* New York: Signet.

Kossor Education Newsletter (1996) Vol 1(1).

Kozol, J (1967) *Death at an early age.* Boston: Houghton Mifflin.

Krüger, RA and Müller, ECC (1988) *Lesson structure and teaching success.* Johannesburg: RAU Press.

Leithwood, KA (1981) Managing the implementation of curriculum innovations. *Knowledge, creation, diffusion, utilization,* 2(3):238-251.

Lemmer, EM (1993) Gender issues in education. In El Dekker and EM Lemmer (eds) *Critical issues in modern education.* Durban: Butterworths.

Mager, RF (1962) *Preparing instructional objectives*. Palo Alto, California: Fearon Publishers.

Marsh, CC (1997) *Planning, management and ideology: key concepts for understanding Curriculum 2*. London: The Falmer Press.

McCutcheon, G (1995) *Developing the curriculum: solo and group deliberation*. New York: Longman Publishers.

McKernan, J (1999) *Perspectives and imperatives: some limitations of Outcomes-Based Education*. Http:/enc.org/reform/journals/ENC2373.html

McLaughlin, MW (1987) Learning from experience: lessons from policy implementation. *Educational Evaluation and Policy Analysis*, 9(2):171-178.

Miller, JP (1988) *The holistic curriculum*. Toronto: OISE Press.

Mulder, M (1991) Deliberation in curriculum conferences. *Journal of Curriculum and Supervision*, 6(4):325-339.

National Training Board (1994) *National training strategy initiative*. Pretoria: National Training Board.

Noddings, N (1992) *The challenge to care in schools: an alternative approach to education*. New York: Teachers' College Press.

Phenix, PH (1964) *Realms of meaning: a philosophy of the curriculum for general education*. New York: McGraw-Hill.

Pinar, WF (1980) Life history and educational experience. *The Journal of Curriculum Theorizing*, 2(2):159-212.

Popham, JW and Baker, EL (1970) *Systematic instruction*. Englewood Cliffs, NJ: Prentice-Hall.

Posner, GJ (1982) A cognitive science conception of curriculum and instruction. *Journal of Curriculum Studies*, 14(4):343-351.

Reid, W (1978) *Thinking about the curriculum*. London: Routledge and Kegan Paul.

Reynolds, J and Skilbeck, M (1976) *Culture in the classroom*. London: Open Books.

Richardson, E (1973) *The teacher, the school and the task of management*. London: Heinemann.

Roby, T (1985) Habits impeding deliberation. *Journal of Curriculum Studies*, 17(1):17-35.

Rosenblatt, LM (1983) *Literature as explanation*. Fourth edition. New York: Modern Language Association.

Rudd, A (1973) Local curriculum development. In R Watkins (ed) *In-service training: structure and content*. London: Ward Lock Educational.

Schubert, WH (1986) *Curriculum: perspective, paradigm, and possibility*. New York: Macmillan.

Schwab, JJ (1970) *The practical: a language for curriculum*. Washington DC: National Education Association.

Schwab, JJ (1978) *Science, curriculum and liberal education: selected essays*. Chicago: University of Chicago Press.

Snyder, J; Bolin, E and Zumwalt, K (1992) Curriculum implementation. In PW Jackson (ed), *Handbook of research on curriculum*. New York: Macmillan, 402-435.

Soliman, I; Dawes, L; Gough, J and Maxwell, T (1981) *A model for school-based curriculum development*. Canberra: CDC.

Spady, WG (1982) Outcomes-based instructional management: its sociological implications. *Australian Journal of Education*, 26(2):123-143.

Spady, WG (1994) *Outcomes-based education: critical issues and answers*. Virginia: American Association of School Administrators.

Spady, WG and Marshal, KJ (1991) Beyond traditional outcomes-based education. *Educational Leadership*, 49:67-72.

Spector, BS (1993) Order out of chaos: restructuring schooling to reflect society's paradigm shift. *School Science and Mathematics*, 93(1):34-47.

Taba, H (1962) *Curriculum development: theory and practice*. New York: Harcourt, Brace and World.

Tyler, RW (1949) *Basic principles of curriculum and instruction*. Chicago: University of Chicago Press.

Ulich, R (1955) Comments on Ralph Harper's essay. In NB Henry (ed) *Modern philosophies of education*, Forty-fifth Yearbook (Part 1) of the National Society for the Study of Education (254-257). Chicago: University of Chicago Press.

Van Manen, M (1991) *The tact of teaching: the meaning of pedagogical thoughtfulness*. Albany, NY: State University of New York Press.

Walker, DF (1971) A naturalistic model for curriculum development. *School Review*, 80(1):51-69.

Whitehead, AN (1929) *The aims of education and other essays*. New York: Macmillan.

CHAPTER 6

GOVERNANCE OF EDUCATION

 Prof Joan Squelch
Rand Afrikaans University

Table of contents

6.1 Introduction

Education systems worldwide are subject to ongoing change and reform. As societies develop, the various societal structures respond in kind to the mutable contextual realities in which they operate. Moreover, throughout the world, reform in education ultimately aims to improve education through the ongoing evaluation of existing structures, policies and processes. A major feature of education reform agendas has always been education governance and, more specifically, the decentralisation of education governance to the local school level. In a number of countries, some of which are discussed in this chapter, various reform initiatives have been implemented to devolve more authority over education matters and decisions to individual schools, and to strengthen the parents' position and role on school governing bodies (Levin 1998:132-133).

This approach to governance assumes that decentralised decision-making authority is the key to improving schools and raising students' performance levels. Major shifts have taken place in governance and there is widespread support for decentralised education governance. Nevertheless, its successful implementation remains a challenge. As Guskey and Peterson (1996:10) note: 'the road to classroom change through school-based decision-making obviously has more potholes than its proponents originally thought'.

In this chapter, we travel the road of reform towards decentralised governance examining along the way the underlying assumptions, tracing some of the developments that have occurred in various countries, including South Africa, flagging the emerging 'potholes' that have challenged the implementers and suggesting a number of conditions that need to exist if decentralised school governance is going to work in South Africa.

6.2 The nature of and rationale for decentralised school governance

Traditionally, in South Africa and elsewhere, school governance and management have been hierarchical and authoritarian in nature. Locus of control and decision-making powers have resided mainly in the school principal with minimal participation from teachers, parents or students. The principal viewed the school as his or her domain, organising and managing it according to his or her particular frame of reference and leadership style. Holt and Murphy (1993:175) observe that school leaders in most countries in the past have been 'lords in their own education fiefdoms'. Moreover, although school governing bodies have played an important role in school management, this role has been of a supportive nature, with limited decision-making powers. In contrast to this centralised, authoritarian and non-participative approach, is the decentralised, co-operative (participative) approach, which has gained increasing favour over many decades. In practice, the myriad of policies and practices that make up the operations of a school will shift between these two approaches along a continuum.

Decentralised school governance (also referred to in the literature as site-based management and school-based management) is considered to be a more effective and appropriate form of governance, especially in this day and age. The efficacy of decentralised school governance is based on a few important assumptions:

First, decentralised school governance presupposes a *devolvement* of power from the central level down through the system to the local level. Hanson (1998:112) describes the following three major forms of decentralisation:

- *Deconcentration*. The simplest form of decentralisation, this involves the transfer of certain tasks and work, but not authority, to other units in an organisation.

- *Delegation*. This entails the transfer of decision-making authority from higher to lower hierarchical units, but the authority can be withdrawn at the discretion of the delegating unit.

- *Devolution*. This refers to the transfer of authority to a unit that can act independently, or without first asking permission. Thus the unit functions in its own name and accepts far greater responsibility for its actions.

The degree to which authority is transferred varies greatly in education systems. In schools where authority has been transferred (e.g. grant-maintained schools in England), governing bodies are able to act independently. However, this implies that far greater responsibility and accountability rest with the school's 'corporate body'. Decentralising power is thus also aimed at reducing centralised bureaucratic control over schools that often prevents them from responding to change and transforming their environments in order to meet the needs of the community they service. In practice, authority over school affairs and governance is seldom transferred by education authorities *in toto* to the local level, but there should be at least a balance of power and authority between state departments and local schools. Therefore, it is not a question of centralised or decentralised control; all decisions should retain a degree of centralised and decentralised input.

Second, decentralised school governance is also a *democratic* form of governance based on the principles of representation, equity and participation. In other words, structures of school governance are representative of the school community and such representatives (i.e. governors) are elected according to fair, democratic procedures.

Third, it further rests on the principle of *shared decision-making*, which presupposes open communication, consultation and a willingness to negotiate. This raises the question of who should participate in decision-making and how.

David (1995:7) states that participatory decision-making does not mean that everyone decides everything – some decisions are best left to the professionals and some to parents. Nor does it mean that all decisions must be made at local level. Moreover, sharing does not necessarily mean that everyone participates equally or that a particular group needs to have the most dominant voice (Shields & Knapp 1997:292). Decisions are made on all levels of the education system that directly and indirectly affect schools.

Fourth, it requires *active participation* of all stakeholders who have a vested interest in the school. This implies creating the necessary climate, structures and support mechanisms for engendering genuine participation and involvement. This is essential if all stakeholders are to be involved in raising the quality of education. More often than not, the participation of teachers, parents, students and other external groups (e.g. business) is tokenistic and piecemeal. Thus the illusion of decentralised school governance is created without it being realised in practice.

Fifth, this governance is considered to be a more effective means of *improving standards* of teaching and *creating effective* schools because it is more inclusive and seeks to meet the collective needs and aspirations of the community. The assumption is made that through a redistribution of authority that brings about changes in aspects such as organisation, governance and curriculum control, improved educational quality will follow (Hanson 1998:123). This is one of the most overriding objectives of decentralised school governance, believed to be more effective than centralised control because it empowers those closest to the students. The result will be decisions better tailored to the particular needs of students and improved school performance (Wohlstetter & Briggs 1994). It is also based on the belief that governors, teachers and parents are the ones who best understand the contexts and cultures of the school (Guskey & Peterson 1996:11). And as David (1995:16) comments, '… let the education professional make the important professional decisions'.

However, the correlation between participation in governance and an increase in student performance is not to be assumed and evidence to support this theory is scant.

Sixth, the governance under discussion displays *adaptability*. Schools can be more responsive to the demands of their communities and the changing social environment. Here school governors should be free to make their own decisions, especially about financial affairs. The assumption is that by allocating funds to schools and allowing school governing bodies to control these, they can meet the needs of the community and finance aspects such as staff development, instructional material, equipment and student bursaries.

The democratisation of education systems and the trend towards decentralising school governance and management have taken on various forms in other countries with varying degrees of success. However, while there is wide consensus on the advantages of democratic school governance, the practical consequences and successful implementation thereof are subject to ongoing debate. In practical terms, it is possible to distinguish between strong and weak approaches to realising the concept of this kind of governance. Strong decentralised governance is essentially characterised by active participation of stakeholders, genuine shared decision-making and a palpable shift in the way in which schools are governed, while in weak approaches only lip-service is paid to the principles and implementation of the governance.

6.3 Comparative and international trends in decentralised school governance

The philosophy of decentralised (democratic), participative governance is not new. The movement towards decentralised school governance is a global phenomenon. Over several decades, many countries have implemented a process of decentralisation aimed at creating more effective schools, those which are flexible and responsive to rapidly changing environments (Sharpe 1994:4-5). As has been noted, while the principle is considered sound, there is disagreement about the practice. In this section, a few examples are cited to illustrate some of the initiatives that have been taken to decentralise school governance and to create democratic, participative structures.

6.3.1 The Chicago School Reform Programme

Perhaps one of the best-known initiatives of decentralised governance is the Chicago School Reform Programme, spearheaded in the late 1980s and precipitated by the steady decline in education standards in the US. In 1987, the US Secretary of Education, William Bennett, declared the Chicago public school system 'the worst in the nation' (Walberg & Niemiec 1994:713). The poor performance of the Chicago schools was ascribed to '... a bloated, uncaring central office bureaucracy that had ill-defined, often overlapping job descriptions' (Walberg & Niemiec 1994:713).

In response to the education crisis in Chicago, the Illinois General Assembly adopted the Chicago School Reform Act of 1988 with the specific mandate to improve the quality of education and student achievement. The reform legislation was explicitly required to raise achievement, attendance and graduation rates to national norms within five years of enactment.

At the heart of this reform legislation was the transfer of considerable power and decision-making authority from the central office to local school councils. According to Walberg and Niemiec (1994:714), the rationale for the transfer was simply that local citizens and school personnel know their schools best and, if given the chance, are in the best position to solve most of the problems experienced by the schools (i.e. local solutions to local problems). The newly

131

formed school councils had considerable decision-making power over budgets, the curriculum and the 'hiring and firing' of teachers and principals. The councils were also mandated to set policy and formulate improvement plans.

The local school councils, charged with the duty of implementing the reform legislation and achieving the aforementioned goals, consist of 11 members: the principal, two teachers, six parents and two community members. Their peers elect all members except the principal. Notably, the parents form the majority and there is no student representation. This has not gone unchallenged. In 1994, for example, the Chicago Principals' Association challenged the composition of the school bodies on the basis that parents were vested with too much power and authority, which seriously undermined their positions. The principals lost the court case, but the question of excessive parent power remains a contentious issue (Walsh 1996:1).

Almost four years after the devolution of powers to the local school councils, Walberg and Niemiec (1994:714) assessed the success of this school-based control in terms of school achievement, attendance rates and graduation. The conclusion was that, on the three outcomes specified in the reform legislation, the Chicago public schools had shown little improvement, even though the councils thought well of their accomplishments. According to Walberg and Niemiec (1994:715):

> ... despite radical reform legislation and transfer of considerable power to local school councils, there has scarcely been any demonstrable progress on outcome goals. Chicago schools continue to rank very low by national standards.

According to the research conducted by Walberg and Niemiec (1994:714-715), the reform effort had not been successful in raising student achievements or increasing student attendance, and student dropout rates remained the same.

6.3.2 The Kentucky initiative

Kentucky, like Chicago, is one of the few states in America to legislate the establishment of decentralised, democratic school governance. The move towards this governance began in 1990 when the state legislature passed the Kentucky Education Reform Act of 1990 (KERA), which, *inter alia*, introduced radical reform measures to school governance. This followed a landmark decision by the Kentucky Supreme Court in 1989 declaring the public education system unconstitutional and giving its opinion on essential characteristics of an efficient system of common schools. In terms of KERA, the establishment of School-Based Decision-Making Councils (SBDM) in every public school was made mandatory. By 1996, every school in Kentucky was supposed to have a new council in place. The aim of this provision was to strengthen individual schools' decision-making authority by locating it at school level. The SBDMs allocated this authority to 16 areas of operation and policy, including appointing the school principal, selecting instructional material, choosing textbooks and managing their own institutional finances. The school councils also had ultimate responsibility for the following eight policy areas: the curriculum, staff assignments, students' assignments, school schedule, instructional practice, discipline, extra-curricular programmes and the alignment with state standards (Lindle 1996:20).

In contrast to the Chicago Programme, the school councils consist of the principal, three teacher representatives and two parent representatives, but there is no representation by students and non-teaching staff. Teachers elect each other and the local PTA elects the parent representatives. Although high schools often include students as non-voting members, student governors are not officially provided for in the legislation. In 1994, in order to address the issues of diversity and representation, the Kentucky Legislature mandated that any school with 8% or greater minority enrolment elect a minority member to the SBDM, if one had not already been elected (Lindle 1996:21). The fact that there are fewer parents on the councils has drawn some criticism, and the Kentucky PTA's proposal to add a parent to the school councils was debated by lawmakers during the 1996 legislative session, but did not produce a result. This proposal was not supported by the Kentucky Education Association, the state's largest teachers' union, who wants teachers to maintain a majority on the councils because of their expertise.

According to Lindle (1996:20), due to the move to decentralised school governance and the creation of school-based decision-making councils, schools have encountered a few obstacles – members are concerned about being involved in more meetings, more work and more conflict. Decentralised decision-making is more time-consuming and the fact that there are more constituencies involved in the process creates the potential for conflict. As Lindle (1996:22) points out, decentralisation has upset the status quo because teachers and principals no longer dominate the decision-making process; other groups are now represented in councils. However, notwithstanding such issues, Lindle (1996:20) argues that school councils are able to make decisions and work effectively if there is supportive leadership, a collegial climate and a respect for the democratic process that is contentious and time-consuming.

6.3.3 Decentralised school governance in England

The legislative developments in England over the past few decades provide another interesting example of the movement towards decentralised and self-governance. According to Deem (1994:58-60), as far back as 1967, the Plowden Report emphasised the importance of parent involvement in education and called for greater representation. However, it was the Taylor Report of 1977 *(A new partnership for our schools)* that provided the most detailed recommendations for the restructuring of school governing bodies and the decentralisation of decision-making powers. It called for all schools to have their own representative governing body that exercised full authority and had full decision-making powers regarding the way the school operates. In terms of representation, the Taylor Report favoured a structure which would offer equal representation of different groups (teachers, parents, older students, Local Education Authorities (LEAs) and community representatives). However, following the Taylor Report, only a few LEAs experimented with student governors, a practice which was later prohibited under the Education Act of 1986. The Act established the structure of governing bodies and set out their basic functions, thus following the Taylor recommendations very closely. The governing body is composed of five parent governors, one but not more than two teachers, the head teacher and a number of foundation or first governors. There are no student governors. Since 1988, parents and co-opted governors have achieved numerical dominance on school governing bodies.

The Education Reform Act of 1988 paved the way for further decentralisation by providing for the local governance of schools (LMS). The Act devolved more power and responsibility for decision-making, particularly over financial and personnel matters, from the LEAs to the earlier reconstructed school governing bodies under the 1983 Act (Williams 1995:12). The LEAs, who funded the schools and thus had considerable authority over them, found themselves in a position of greatly diminished authority and control. The Education Act required LEAs to allocate a budget to all its schools to cover almost all of their running expenses, over which schools would have full control. School governing bodies became responsible for managing the budget, and appointing, disciplining and dismissing staff (Levacic 1995:8). The local governance of schools provided the opportunity to control their own financial affairs and to be more self-sufficient and independent of the LEAs.

Another particularly significant development in the establishment of self-governance was the introduction of grant-maintained (GM) schools under the Education Reform Act of 1988 and reinforced by the Education Act of 1993. In terms of the new education laws, GM schools could 'opt out' of the LEAs and receive their funding directly from central government. This meant that from the beginning GM schools received larger financial allocations than those remaining within the LEA sector (Williams 1995:15). In grant-maintained schools, governors have total responsibility for every aspect of the running and functioning of those schools. The governing body is equivalent to the executive board in a commercial business. Although the introduction of GM schools met with mixed reaction, and research and reports on their success paint varying pictures, there are success stories of schools that have elected to opt out and flourished under their new status and independence (Beatie 1995; Cotter 1995).

6.3.4 Decentralised school governance in Australia

In Australia, the term 'devolution' has been used to describe the process of restructuring and decentralisation in education during the 1980s and 1990s. The process was typically driven by issues such as quality, effectiveness, accountability and flexibility (Sharpe 1994). However, the beginnings of decentralisation can be traced back to 1948 when New South Wales became the first Australian state to initiate decentralisation (Gamage 1994:38-40).

Sharpe (1994:5) defines 'devolution' as:

> ... a process through which an agency (such as a government) deliberately relinquishes aspects of control over the organisations for which it is responsible, thus moving along the continuum in the direction of total self-management.

The devolution of power and authority to school communities has been effected through the establishment of school councils (akin to our school governing bodies). This was not mandatory for school systems, however. Although all states and territories are engaged in devolution, the Victoria initiative and devolution project has been cited as one of the most advanced and a model example for other states (Gamage 1994; Sharpe 1994). The Education Act of 1958 was amended in 1983 enabling a Victorian school council to determine the general education policy of the school. The amendments emphasised the importance of local responsibility and shared decision-making on educational policy. The powers given to the councils were extensive. School councils were empowered to be responsible for the general education policy of the school, buildings and grounds including maintenance, the selection of principals and deputy principals, employment of ancillary staff, maintenance of accounts, general budget planning and effecting auditing (Gamage, Sipple & Partridge 1996:26). At the same time, the councils and their members were protected from having to meet costs arising from any action for damages while performing their legal functions. Councils consist of the principal and elected parents, teachers, community members and, in secondary schools, the students. The membership may vary, subject to the proviso that parents should be in the majority.

6.3.5 Decentralised school governance in New Zealand

Like Australia and other countries, New Zealand also embarked on a process of transforming and restructuring the education system in the 1980s with a view to bringing about greater decentralisation. The Picot Committee recommended a system that was more efficient, promoted equity and fairness and encouraged greater local decision-making (Williams, Harold, Robertson & Southworth 1997:627). In 1989 the new Education Act came into being and provided for schools to take over their own governance. In the place of regional education boards, schools could establish their own boards of trustees consisting of a three to five parent representative body, the principal, a staff representative and, in secondary schools, a student representative (Wylie 1995:54). The school boards are responsible for appointing and dismissing staff, maintaining buildings and grounds, staff development and the school's general performance. The Ministry of Education provides the funding for all state schools, sets broad guidelines for the curriculum and determines standardised assessment tasks for all primary schools (Wylie 1995:55).

A survey of research on decentralised school management in various countries points to a number of positive initiatives and shows a general consensus on the reasons for and benefits of decentralised, participative decision-making. Although variations are to be found in different countries, in all the examples looked at, an important part of the reform process has been the establishment of representative, democratically elected governing bodies or councils. A common feature of governing bodies is the strong position accorded to parents. In all the examples, parents form the majority of governors, thereby exercising considerable influence. Similarities are also found in the areas of responsibility and authority that governing bodies have acquired regarding the budget and other financial matters, use and management of physical resources, staffing, student affairs, school policy and matters regarding the curriculum.

Decentralised school governance is not without its problems, however. For instance, the roles of principals, teachers and parents have changed; there is often tension between governors and principals, and between parents and school authorities; teachers do not necessarily want the extra responsibility and work that accompanies devolution; and parent involvement is not necessarily as extensive as it should be (mainly because they do not have the skills or the time). In other words, what is advocated in theory and underpinned by sound arguments is not always easy to achieve in practice, even when it is mandated from higher authorities.

6.4 Decentralised school governance in South African schools

Prior to the legislation of the 1990s, governing schools was a much less demanding activity. Governing bodies or management councils played a supportive role with restricted powers and functions. They did not make fundamental policy decisions; nor did they shape management policies to any great extent. For the most part, school governors tended to have symbolic powers rather than actual authority. Moreover, the majority of black schools (hence the majority of schools in SA) did not have governing bodies *per se*.

During the 1990s legislative developments resulted in governing bodies gaining more power and responsibilities. In 1992, with the establishment of Model C (state-aided) schools, the powers of governing bodies were extended widely in two particular areas: first, they could determine their own admission policy and, second, they could levy compulsory school fees. The overall effect was that school governing bodies became more responsible for the governance and management of schools. The supportive, advisory role of school governing bodies was beginning to change.

Following the General Elections of 1994, the adoption of a new constitutional dispensation and the phasing in of new education legislation under the new government, a new system of education has been created based on the fundamental principles of democracy, unity, non-discrimination, equity and equality. The most important aim of transforming the apartheid education system was to create a system of education that 'open[ed] the doors of learning and culture to all' and that would 'benefit the country as a whole and all its people' (*White Paper on Education and Training* 1995:17). Moreover, the aim was to develop a democratic system that provided for the participation of all stakeholders with a vested interest in education. According to the first *White Paper on Education and Training* (1995:22):

> ... the principle of democratic governance should be increasingly reflected in every level of the system, by the involvement in consultation and appropriate forms of decision making of elected representatives of the main stakeholders, interest groups and role-players.

Therefore, in keeping with international trends, South African schools have subsequently moved towards greater decentralised school governance. The South African Schools Act 84 of 1996 (hereafter called the Schools Act) has mandated the establishment of democratic structures of school governance which provide the basis for decentralised governance between education authorities and the school community. The rationale for the establishment of representative school governing bodies is essentially to ensure that teachers, parents, learners and non-teaching staff will actively *participate* in the governance and management of their schools with a view to providing better teaching and learning environments.

6.4.1 The legal status of school governing bodies

With the introduction of the Schools Act, the legal status of public schools has changed considerably. Public schools are now categorised as juristic persons (Section 15 of the Schools Act). A juristic person is an abstract legal entity, such as a church, bank and university, which stands apart from the people who are members of it. A juristic person can in itself have rights and duties that have nothing to do with its members. Therefore, a juristic person can engage in legal activities in its own name. However, a juristic person is not a natural person (i.e. human being) so it cannot perform the functions of a human being. Thus, it participates in legal activities through its organs or functionaries, who act on its behalf. But, unlike a natural person, a juristic person continues to exist as a legal entity despite any changes to any of its organs.

A school operates as a juristic person through its governing body in which school governance is vested (Section 16). For example, the governing body acts on behalf of the school when it suspends a learner in terms of Section 9 of the Schools Act. The action taken against the learner is taken in the name of the school and the school (not the governing body or disciplinary committee) is legally responsible for its conduct. Therefore, a school may sue and be sued in its own name. However, this does not mean that school governors and educators cannot be sued in their personal capacity. If a teacher administers corporal punishment to a learner in contravention of Section 10 of the Schools Act, the parents may sue the school and the teacher. The school, through its governing body, functions in both the private and public sphere of law. For example, the school, as a separate legal entity, may enter into a private contract with a firm to purchase computers. The contractual relationship is called the 'private law relationship'. However, as a public organ of state, a school operates mainly in the public law sphere.

The Schools Act also states that the governing body *stands in a position of trust* towards the school (Section 16). To be in a position of trust means that the governing body must:

- act in good faith
- carry out its duties and functions in the best interests of the school
- not disclose confidential information that might harm the school
- not engage in any unlawful conduct
- not compete with the school's interests and activities.

6.4.2 Composition of school governing bodies

The Schools Act prescribes the composition of school governing bodies of ordinary public schools. These bodies are made up of the school principal, as an *ex officio* member, elected members and co-opted members. Elected members of the governing body comprise parents, educators at the school, members of staff who are not educators and learners in the eighth grade or higher.

The Schools Act states that parents must form the majority of membership on the governing body. Therefore, there must be one more parent on the governing body than the combined total of the other members with voting rights. A parent who is elected to the governing body must have a child or children at the school and *may not* be employed at the school. So a parent who has a child at a school and is employed at the school as an administrator may not serve as a parent governor. When interpreting and applying this provision, the word 'parent' must be read as it is defined in Chapter 1 of the Schools Act. In other words, the definition includes a person who is the learner's guardian, or is legally entitled to custody of the learner, or who has undertaken to fulfil the obligations of a parent or guardian towards the learner's education. Only a parent who is not employed at the school may be the chairperson of the governing body. In other words, the school principal or a teacher may not be the chairperson.

This provision is particularly important because it ensures that all major role players in the school are represented on the governing body, including learners. Note that learner representation on governing bodies applies to high schools and that principals do not have a choice in this regard. Although learner representatives have voting rights and are full, active members of the governing body, minors (i.e. learners under the age of 18) may not contract on behalf of the governing body or vote on resolutions which impose liabilities on third parties or on the school. A minor also cannot incur personal liability for any consequence of his or her membership.

A governing body may also co-opt members from the community to serve on it. This enables the governing body to draw on people with certain skills and expertise. Co-opted members have no voting rights, however. If the school is situated on private property, the governing body may also co-opt the owner of the property, or a representative of the owner.

The governing body of an ordinary public school that provides education to learners with special educational needs must, where practically possible, co-opt a person or persons with expert knowledge on the needs of such learners. This is a *positive obligation* and a school must take reasonable steps to co-opt such a person.

6.4.3 Participative decision-making

An important aim of decentralised governance is to reduce bureaucratic control and enhance shared decision-making at local school level. A major consequence of the new Schools Act is that the new structure of governing bodies does allow for considerable parent involvement on substantive issues that extend beyond the traditional fund-raising activities and tuck-shop duties. Parents are now placed in a powerful position and, effectively, have the authority to influence decisions on very fundamental issues, for example the school budget, language policy and discipline. Principals no longer play the role of primary decision-maker. They now find themselves as members of governing bodies which are dominated by parents and 'non-educationists'. Despite this position, the primary locus of power, authority and decision-making often remains with the principal because he or she is the key educational leader in a school and responsible for its day-to-day running. Although principals' decision-making authority has been curtailed to some extent and although they may not serve as chairpersons, strong governing bodies require strong leadership from principals.

The nature of decision-making that school governors are engaged in also raises the question of whether governors should participate in substantive issues. It is common for governors to deal with less important issues that have little impact on improving education, for example school maintenance matters and school uniform issues. More substantial issues that have a direct bearing on learner performance, for example matters regarding the curriculum and personnel evaluation, are left to the principal and staff. This is largely because teaching personnel believe that parents are not equipped to participate in such matters and should not interfere in the professional and academic side of school life. However, the Schools Act empowers parents and makes specific provision for parents to participate in substantive issues, which principals and teachers cannot ignore. For example, Section 8 of the Schools Act requires the governing body to adopt a code of conduct after consulting with parents, teachers and leaders. Section 39 also stipulates that school fees at public schools may be charged only if the majority of parents vote on a resolution to do so. In other words, the Schools Act confers certain responsibilities on the school *governing body* which is obliged to consult with the parents on matters which require full participation in the decision-making process. But, for fair consultation and decision-making to take place, the necessary processes and procedures need to be determined and put in place, lest the governing body acts merely as a rubber stamp.

6.4.4 Functions of school governing bodies

The powers, functions and duties of governing bodies are set out in sections 20 and 21 of the Schools Act. Section 20 lists the prescribed functions of all governing bodies. According to this section, the governing body of a public school *must*:

- promote the best interests of the school and strive to ensure its development
- adopt a constitution
- adopt the mission statement of the school
- adopt a code of conduct for learners at the school
- support the principal, educators and other staff in performing their professional functions
- determine times of the school day consistent with any applicable conditions of employment of staff at the school
- administer and control the school's property, buildings and grounds which include school hostels
- encourage parents, learners, educators and other staff at the school to render voluntary services to the school
- recommend to the head of department the appointment of educators at the school

- at the request of the head of department, allow the reasonable use under fair conditions of the facilities for educational programmes not conducted by the school
- discharge all other functions given to the governing body by the Schools Act
- discharge functions that are set out by the member of the executive council in the *Provincial Gazette*.

Section 21 includes a list of functions that may be allocated to a governing body by the head of department. According to Section 21, a governing body may apply in writing to the head of department to be allocated any of the following functions:

- to maintain and improve the school's property, buildings and grounds
- to determine the extra-curriculum of the school and the choice of subject options according to the provincial curriculum policy
- to buy textbooks, educational materials or equipment for the school
- to pay for services to the school
- other functions consistent with this Act and any applicable law.

As in the case of the various countries surveyed, South African school governing bodies have been given more control over a number of school matters. Typically, site-based councils or governing bodies are given greater control over financial matters, school buildings and general school policy and school improvement. However, compared with other countries, South African school governing bodies do not have the power to hire and fire teachers and principals unless they are specifically governing-body-appointed teachers. Moreover, decisions concerning the choice of textbooks and instructional matter fall under Section 21 which means that not all governing bodies have been allocated these powers.

6.4.5 Accountability of school governing bodies

Decentralised decision-making and authority place a greater responsibility and accountability on school governing bodies. If a governing body does not perform its functions properly, the head of department may withdraw it on *reasonable grounds* and provided that he or she follows correct procedures. In cases where the governing body fails to perform its functions properly, the head of department may appoint a person to act in the place of the governing body. However, the head of department may not take action against a governing body unless he or she has informed the governing body of his or her decision to withdraw its functions, granted the governing body reasonable opportunity to prepare its case and make representations relating to such, and given due consideration to any such representations. The governing body is also entitled to be given reasons for any actions that are taken by the MEC. The Schools Act makes it possible for anybody who is unhappy or disagrees with the decision of the head of department to withdraw the functions of the governing body to appeal to the MEC.

6.5 Making decentralised school governance work: lessons from abroad

Although decentralised school governance (site-based management) has existed for a long time, it has been implemented with varying degrees of success. In all the countries that were discussed above, the following common issues have presented themselves:

6.5.1 The power factor

The successful functioning of site-based councils/governing bodies depends to a large extent on the political structure of a school. Decentralised control inevitably results in a redistribution of power and authority. Principals are, supposedly, no longer in a dominant position whereby they can manage schools in an autocratic, top-down manner. The establishment of democratically elected and representative councils or governing bodies has changed the political structure of schools and the nature of decision-making. Under a democratic model of governance, schools do not function according to a hierarchy of authority whereby decisions are made by a few. However, in practice, principals are sometimes reluctant to relinquish or even share their power and authority. Moreover, councils/governing bodies often 'delegate' authority back to the principal, thus preserving the status quo (Lindle 1996:20). Schools are still strongly influenced and regulated by national policy. Experience in other countries shows that national policy making, from which people in schools are largely excluded, continues to play a significant role in what happens in those schools. Therefore, the tension between schools and their sources of funding does not end with decentralised decision-making; it merely changes form (Wylie 1995:58).

6.5.2 The expertise factor

A common problem experienced by many school councils or governing bodies is the lack of or inadequate expertise. Not all governing bodies have the good fortune to be served by skilled professionals. And even if there are professional parents or governors on the governing body it does not mean they are familiar with or knowledgeable about complex educational matters. Therefore, although school councils may be given extensive decision-making authority over educational matters, many governors are reluctant to make a contribution in this area because they feel they lack the relevant knowledge and experience. The problem is compounded by the fact that school governors, many of whom are already overloaded with work, do not have the time to develop expertise or

142

keep up to date with new developments and research in education. Thus, Guskey and Peterson (1996:12) observed that some school councils avoid, ignore or neglect issues related to teaching and learning.

6.5.3 The time and workload factor

In all the countries visited, the time and workload factor emerged as another major issue. Decentralised governance is a time-consuming enterprise, placing enormous demands on principals' and governors' time. According to Guskey and Peterson (1996:11), this is inevitable because 'meaningful discussions and carefully reasoned decisions about complex issues require considerable time'. However, in practice, principals, teachers and parent governors do not have the necessary time to devote to regular council meetings, especially lengthy ones. Meetings are held infrequently and they seldom leave time for in-depth discussions on crucial issues.

6.5.4 The training and development factor

Another common problem encountered in all the above countries is the lack of or insufficient training and development. The shift to decentralised, site-based management requires principals and teachers to develop a wide range of skills and capacities to deal with the complex issues and tasks of decentralised decision making, for example problem-solving skills, conflict resolution, time management, change management and financial planning. However, insufficient investment in training opportunities has not fully prepared teachers and principals for their new roles and responsibilities.

6.6 Implications for South African governing bodies

Compared with other countries, South African education is still fairly centralised and the implementation of decentralised school governance in terms of the Schools Act is still in its infancy. Moreover, the effective and efficient functioning of school governing bodies varies greatly between schools and school districts. In spite of legislative reform, the successful implementation of decentralised governance will depend on a number of factors:

6.6.1 Enabling leadership

Leadership plays a pivotal role in nurturing any kind of change (Lindle 1996:22). Whether or not decentralised governance works will, to a great extent, depend on leaders who are able to develop decision-making structures and processes that promote rather than hinder meaningful participation and collaboration. Although it is assumed that teachers and parents want to and are eager to participate in decision-making processes and to serve on governance structures, experience and research suggest that teachers and parents do not necessarily jump at the opportunity. In practice, the number of parents and teachers running for councils and voting in elections remains small. Moreover, teachers are often reluctant to participate because it means assuming more responsibility and devoting more work and time to governance issues which adds to a schedule that is already overloaded. Therefore, to succeed, schools need to have strong leaders (principals) who are prepared to share their power and authority and who can initiate and manage change. Furthermore, a principal, as the key leader in a school, should be able to plan, organise, motivate and direct people towards achieving the common goals that are aimed at genuine transformation and school improvement.

6.6.2 Collaborative or team approach

A school's organisational culture or school climate directly affects the establishment of an atmosphere that is conducive to participative decision-making and collaboration. Shields and Knapp (1997:292) suggest that school improvement is more likely to happen when a collaborative professional culture is developed among the staff so that they act as a team rather than a loose collection of individuals. In their research they found that in schools with more promising types of decentralised governance, there was a shift away from staff working as individuals towards a staff that worked together as a team to improve the entire school. However, staff members need the skills and commitment to work collaboratively as a team. Strategies also need to be devised to provide staff with the time and opportunity to work together. For example, some schools arrange common planning sessions so that teachers can work together at times and not always in isolation.

6.6.3 Opportunity for professional development

One of the most important concerns about the implementation of decentralised school governance in South African schools is the issue of expertise and the availability of parents. Governing bodies are made up of individuals who have different levels of expertise and experience and who have different reasons for being a school governor. Schools who can draw on the particular expert knowledge of parents and community members (e.g. lawyers and accountants) as co-opted members are at a distinct advantage over schools who do not have this resource. Therefore, schools need to invest in training and development to ensure that school governors have the opportunity to develop skills and knowledge that will enable them to participate more meaningfully in transforming and improving schools.

6.6.4 Access to resources

Access to resources and information is a further prerequisite for effective and efficient decentralised governance and management. According to Guskey and Peterson (1996:13), council members must ensure that they make decisions based on valid evidence rather than persuasive opinion. This means that council members will need ready access to knowledgeable and reliable sources. Principals, in collaboration with education departments and resource units, need to ensure that relevant information is collected and disseminated so that people are kept up to date with developments and issues and are in a better position to make informed decisions.

6.7 Conclusion

The shift towards greater site-based governance and management is not confined to South Africa nor is it a recent phenomenon. In both the international and local contexts, there has been considerable movement towards decentralised governance and self-management. The rationale for the establishment of this kind of governance is in essence a desire to make schools more efficient and effective, to improve the quality of education and raise levels of student performance, and to be able to respond to the needs of learners. However, research and experience show that decentralised school governance does not necessarily bring about the radical change that is desired, and legislative mandates will not guarantee that democratic, decentralised governance structures will function in practice. Decentralised school governance will require more than legislative mandates. As Fullan (1993:7) points out, while mandates are important, 'you can't mandate what's important' and 'systems do not change themselves, people change them'. The success of democratic, decentralised governance will depend on various factors, not least of which are the individuals involved and their commitment to shared decision-making, the structures and processes created to help governors operate, the resources (financial and human) available and the training opportunities provided.

References

Beatie, B (1995) Burntwood School's transition to GM status: an illustration of the complexities of choice and diversity. In V Williams (ed) *Towards self-managing schools*. London: Cassell.

Cotter, P (1995) Tewkesbury School: the road to GM status. In V Williams (ed) *Towards self-managing schools*. London: Cassell.

David, JL (1995) The who, what and why of site-based management. *Educational Leadership*, 53(5):4-9.

Deem, R (1994) School governing bodies: public concerns and private interests. In D Scott (ed) *Accountability and control in educational settings*. London: Cassell.

Fullan, M (1993) *Change forces: probing the depths of educational reform*. London: Falmer Press.

Gamage, DT (1994) The evolution of school councils in Australia. *The Practising Administrator*, 1:38-41.

Gamage, DT; Sipple, P and Partridge, P (1996) Research on school-based management in Victoria. *Journal of Educational Administration*, 34(1):24-30.

Guskey, T and Peterson, K (1996) The road to classroom change. *Educational Leadership*, 53(4):10-14.

Hanson, EM (1998) Strategies of educational decentralisation: key questions and issues. *Journal of Educational Administration*, 36(2):111-113.

Holt, A and Murphy, PJ (1993) School effectiveness in the future: the empowerment factor. *School Organisation*, 13(2):175-186.

Levacic, R (1995) *Local management of schools*. Buckingham: Open University Press.

Levin, B (1998) An epidemic of education policy: can we learn from each other? *Comparative Education*, 34(2):131-141.

Lindle, JC (1996) Lessons from Kentucky about school-based decision-making. *Educational Leadership*, 53(4):20-23.

Sharpe, FG (1994) Devolution. Where are we now? How far should we go? *The Practising Administrator*, 1:4-8.

Shields, PM and Knapp, MS (1997) The promise and limits of school-based reform. A national snapshot. *Phi Delta Kappan*, 79(4):288-294.

South African Schools Act 84 of 1996.

Walberg, HJ and Niemiec, RP (1994) Is Chicago school reform working? *Phi Delta Kappan*, 75(9):713-715.

Walsh, M (1996) Court rejects appeal in Chicago-Council case. *Education Week*, 19 June. Internet URL: <http://www.edweek.com/htbin/fastweb. Accessed 06/03/1998.

White Paper on Education and Training (1995) *Government Gazette*, 15 March. Pretoria: Government Printer.

Williams, V (1995) The context of development. In V Williams (ed) *Towards self-managing schools*. London: Cassell.

Williams, RC; Harold, B; Robertson, J and Southworth, G (1997) Sweeping decentralisation in educational decision-making authority. Lessons from England and New Zealand. *Phi Delta Kappan*, 79(4):626-631.

Wohlstetter, P and Briggs, K (1994) The principal's role in school-based management. *Principal*, 74(2):14-18.

Wylie, C (1995) Finessing site-based management with balancing acts. *Educational Leadership*, 53(4):54-59.

CHAPTER 7

PARTNERSHIPS IN EDUCATION

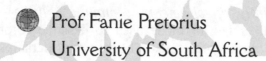

Prof Fanie Pretorius
University of South Africa

Table of contents

7.1 Introduction

An extensive body of literature exists concerning co-operation between schools, as well as other educational institutions, and the *'world' outside of the educational environment*. This body of literature is also expanding rapidly. Various names have been given to this co-operation, which comprises a rich variety of characteristics, and to its range. In some countries it is generally referred to as *partnerships* in education, but terms such as *school-community connections, stakeholder participation, networks, compacts, coalitions, alliances, community involvement, community links,* and *role-player involvement* are but a few of those used to describe co-operation between education and community structures. The term 'partnerships' is used here as an umbrella term for all types of co-operation.

From the rich literature available, it is clear that it is almost impossible to compile a comprehensive list of the various types of collaboration; neither is an orderly classification possible. This collaboration can occur between schools and higher educational institutions such as colleges and universities, but can also involve the parent community, industries, businesses, other work providers, the media, libraries and community organisations such as social services and police services. Collaboration projects can develop on a small scale, as between an individual educator and a business contact, but may also be extended to larger and more formally organised agreements between schools and various employers in a specific area.

Co-operation can also be aimed at meeting various goals. Examples include partnerships between schools and higher educational institutions or other institutions concerned with further education and training of teachers where more effective management of schools may be the long-term objective. Other partnerships may be aimed at serving special educational needs, environmental education, technological education, or mathematical and scientific education. Other approaches may be aimed at improved understanding between educators and learners regarding the world of work; yet others are aimed at employers gaining greater understanding of the problems of educational provision. More effective vocational training may be the aim of some programmes, while others may strive for higher standards and relevance in education in general. The goals depend on the type of institution or community structure involved.

The nature of collaboration can also depend on a variety of other factors. These may involve a country's economic development, the political order, the nature of centralisation or decentralisation applied in a country, the attitudes and norms of the prevailing culture, approaches regarding curriculum formation and reform and the nature of the vocational environment. It is also influenced by the urban or rural context in which it occurs.

The following section is an attempt to interpret the extensive and amorphous field of co-operation between education and its partners. It is an introduction as a basis for further and more advanced studies. The questions guiding the discussion are the following:

- What are the origins of the movement towards greater collaboration between education and the outside world?
- What is the meaning of an educational partnership?
- Who are the partners?
- What are the benefits of educational partnerships?
- What are the key issues concerning partnerships and the essentials for a successful partnership?

It should be noted that the literature concerning partnerships is dominated by the relationship between schools and business and industry. Within this concept of a partnership much attention is also given to the parent community as partner and to parent involvement in education. However, this chapter examines an educational partnership from a broader perspective which includes 'new' as well as fundamental partners of the school in the debate concerning partnership in education.

7.2 The origins of the partnership movement

A 1992 report of the Organisation for Economic Co-operation and Development (OECD) discussing the partnership phenomenon in OECD countries indicates that this movement had its origin in the supposed *failures* of education systems funded and governed entirely by the state. During the twentieth century, the power which has overwhelmingly exerted the greatest influence on education has been the state. This led to the view that education was an insular activity. Although, until recently, the state has been viewed in many countries as being a satisfactory vehicle for transmitting society's priorities to the education system, there has been, especially during the decades of the 1970s and 1980s, a stronger movement in the direction of recognising the *need to utilise outside influences in education* and ending educational isolation (OECD 1992:9).

An entire series of international developments has led to the perception that state intervention in education should be tempered and that outside influences should be allowed to assert themselves. A key consideration in this respect is the *intense economic competition* raging among leading global economies. The stronger a country's economy, the better its chances of offering its citizens a more prosperous life. Another significant reason for this change of attitude is rapid *technological change*. Technology directs the ability of developed societies to be economically competitive. It is critically important for countries to keep abreast of technological inventions which enable them to produce high-quality products more cost effectively and to deliver them more conveniently and within delivery deadlines.

Economic competition and technological inventions have exerted an immense impact on the world of work during the last two decades. Organisations of today are compelled to manage themselves in a different manner than they did two decades ago. This includes decreasing the hierarchical levels of management, with greater responsibilities and accountability being passed on to the front-line workers. Workers should be able to handle the available technology themselves and be able to train themselves in order to keep abreast with the rapid expansion of knowledge and technological change. This implies that they should be lifelong learners. They should also be competent problem-solvers, be able to work as part of a team, be good communicators with good interpersonal skills, be creative, have good foundations in basic skills such as reading and writing, and should be capable of insight into corporate objectives. Whereas reasoning capacity was formerly the responsibility of management and workers simply carried out instructions, the contemporary work situation requires much higher thinking skills from all employees.

Economic competitiveness, technological advances and changes in the functioning of work organisations have inevitably brought state-controlled education into the limelight. According to the OECD report (1992:23-24), education has been placed in the firing line for three reasons:

- The insular nature of education in the past created an academic emphasis and neglected an emphasis on vocational training; consequently the relevance of the outcomes of the education system were not brought into line with the needs of a changing workforce.

- The perception exists that educational standards have actually declined, specifically at a time when they should have been on the rise.

- Schools have not succeeded in establishing among learners some of the life skills required in the world outside the school.

The concern that education should be provided in a different way from what has been the case in state-isolated schools emerged clearly by the 1980s and 1990s and led to large-scale educational reform in the USA, Britain, New Zealand, Australia, Canada, Japan, Hong Kong, as well as in other countries. Whereas a 'first wave' of reform attempted to standardise education and training by centralised control, a 'second wave' was initiated which focused on educator professionalism and *decentralised decision-making*. Examples of second-wave reform initiatives are teacher teaming, school-based management and parental-choice initiatives (Merz & Furman 1997:47). A core consciousness developed that schools alone cannot provide community requirements regarding education and that the community as a whole should accept a shared responsibility for educating children (Kochhar & Erickson 1993:1). What is obviously needed is a *co-operative venture* where home, school and community work together (Decker & Decker 1991:xi). As Prescott (in OECD 1992:49) says:

'Education is too important to be left to the educators. The more people who are involved in changing it, the better'.

Apart from incisive change and the standardisation of school curricula and emphases, one of the key trends of worldwide reform thus far is *greater devolution of power to the local communities*; this includes the responsibility and accountability for educational provision. Where central authorities are moved to the background, the principle of maintaining standards of excellence is situated in the communities involved. With the launch of educational reform in the US in the 1990s, the president in office at the time described this trend as follows:

> Education depends on committed communities determined to be places where learning will flourish; committed teachers, free from the non-educational burdens; committed parents, determined to support excellence; committed students, excited about school and learning (Bush 1991:3).

In line with this viewpoint, Finlay (1998:6-8) refers to a participatory educational environment and the creation of a participative democracy. On the agenda is the empowerment of all stakeholders in order to involve them in the decision-making process and, in so doing, to enable educational institutions to respond more appropriately to the requirements of the world outside the school.

The trends are clearly visible. The importance of high standards in educational provision are being realised anew. Education should be provided in a fundamentally different way from what has been the case up to now. It should be more skills and vocationally orientated and should address the needs of the economy more effectively. In addition to that provided by the state, the input and contributions of all interested parties and stakeholders should be obtained. Committed societies are essential. The ideal is the co-operative action of communities in partnership with educational provision, which leads us to the question: what is the meaning of an educational partnership and who are the partners?

7.3 Defining educational partnership

Although a lengthy discussion is not possible here, it is necessary to consider the nature of an educational partnership in order to identify key elements without trying to provide rigid definitions.

Swap (1993:47) has the following view:

> Envision a school where children are working hard, succeeding academically, and feeling good about themselves; where teachers are working enthusiastically with each other, with administrators, and with other resource persons to figure out even better ways to reach all the

children; where parents and grandparents are champions of the school and committed to working with educators toward a common mission; where community resources enrich the school's curriculum and provide support to the staff.

According to Swap this vision is a reality in some American schools. It is dependent upon strong relationships among parents, students, educators and community personnel working collaboratively to achieve a *common mission*. Swap's model (1993:57-58) is a partnership model focused specifically on school-home relationships and is built on four elements:

- the creation of two-way communication
- the enhancement of learning at home and at school
- the provision of mutual support
- joint decision-making.

Another significant view is that of Bastiani (1993:105). After reviewing various definitions of the term *partnership*, he describes his view of an educational partnership as one in which the following essential characteristics are present:

- sharing of power, responsibility and ownership – although not necessarily equally
- a degree of mutuality, which begins with the process of listening to each other and which incorporates responsive dialogue and 'give and take' on both sides
- shared aims and goals, based on common ground, but which also acknowledge important differences
- a commitment to joint action, in which parents, pupils and professionals work together to get things done.

Swap and Bastiani's views depict fairly accurately the meaning of an educational partnership. First, learning success is central to the partnership. Second, all parties concerned are clearly identified – learners, parents, educators and the broader community. Third, the principles on which such a partnership is founded are clearly indicated including, among others, the following:

- shared aims, goals and mission based on common ground
- 'ownership' by the partners/community of educational endeavours
- a management style of participatory decision-making
- a commitment to success
- joint action
- mutuality
- good communication (a constant dialogue among partners).

7.4 The most fundamental partnerships: those within the internal school environment

7.4.1 Teachers and learners as partners

Swap's reference to learners that are 'working hard' and Bastiani's inclusion of learners 'in joint action ... to get things done' are significant in the debate concerning partnerships in education. In previous discussions of partnership education it has not been customary to refer to learners as partners in education. As was stated earlier in the introduction, the collaboration discourse has been dominated by business and industrial involvement or by parental or community concerns. However, a new development is to recognise learners as stakeholders in education. Stakeholders are described by Finlay (1998:6) as 'all groups or individuals who can influence, or who are affected by, the organisation's actions.' There is no doubt that learners are stakeholders according to this definition.

That learners are also partners in education should be taken for granted. In fact, Westwood (1995) argues that the most fundamental partnership of all, as far as positive learning outcomes goes, is that between learner and teacher. If there is any reference to 'sharing of ownership', 'mutuality', 'listening to each other', 'shared aims and goals, based on common grounds' and 'joint action', how could learners possibly be excluded?

The traditional role of educators was that of providers of information (Glasgow 1996:13). In this context learners were passive listeners into which knowledge 'was poured as into empty vessels'. According to this viewpoint, the better the discipline in schools and the quieter the learners in the educational situation, the more effective the education that was taking place. There was little or no question of positive relationships or of a *teacher-learner partnership*. The following anecdote described by Tribus (1996:97) is an apt illustration of this outdated paradigm: 'You know, last Wednesday I taught my dog to whistle. I really did. I taught him to whistle. It was hard work. I really went at it very hard. But I taught him to whistle. Of course, he didn't learn, but I *taught*.'

Coinciding with the reforms referred to earlier, there has emerged a general belief that *learning* rather than *teaching* is the central issue in schools. The new paradigm makes provision for the teacher as a mediator or facilitator of learning. The accent falls on the learning process and how to improve the learner's learning process and how to improve the learner's grasp of *how learner and teacher can work as a team* to understand the process of learning. In this regard the writings of Reuven Feuerstein are of special significance. Just as W Edwards Deming, the father of the Total Quality Management model, was instrumental in causing a paradigm shift in the management of organisations, so Feuerstein has been instrumental in changing views of education and learning.

In the new paradigm, in which learning is of central importance rather than teaching, the accent inevitably falls on a positive learner-teacher partnership – a partnership in which there is sharing of power, responsibility and ownership, and where there is mutuality, listening to each other, a dialogue, shared aims and a commitment to joint action. In such a partnership learners are not simply receivers of information; their potential to make diverse contributions to reach shared aims is recognised by resourceful teachers.

What can learners offer? Wagner (1992:56-59) lists some of the many contributions that can be made by learners towards this teacher-learner alliance including:

- Valuable feedback about the success of programmes from the learner's point of view – the best learner programmes in governance and collaboration involve every student.

- Connections forged by means of the learners' own personal networks – their parents and parents' friends may come from all walks of life and can offer valuable contributions to various facets of the learning process.

- Support for school policies – learners can influence adults outside the school system by their attitudes towards school policies.

- Involvement in school activities that help the school and the community – by means of community service, learners can be connected to the adult world by learning to wage battles against pollution, crime and corrupt government in their community.

Another partnership which does not normally receive enough attention in the partnership discourse is the one between educators and their peers. This partnership is discussed briefly in the following section.

7.4.2 Teachers and their peers as partners

The reform movement discussed earlier does not only focus on the role of the teachers in the learning process, but also on the way in which schools function internally. Until as recently as 1989 it was observed that teachers tend to work in isolation behind the classroom door:

> In too many schools, teaching is experienced as isolated and isolating work. Teachers just do not have very much to do with one another. The negotiations they should have among themselves take place with administrators – or not at all. ... Given no time in the school year or school day to talk to one another about their work, teachers find themselves hanging around one another's classrooms at the end of the day just to work out some of their concerns before they turn around and head home to the demands of their domestic lives and families (Grumet (1989:21-22).

The isolation of the educational situation which was largely controlled by the state did not only mean that external influences were excluded but, as a result of bureaucratic procedures and the view of teachers as subject specialists, teaching in schools has been seen as an insular activity. As early as 1986 Spady (1986:61) pleaded that the most incisive changes which should be brought about should be the operational definition and conviction of teachers as 'isolated (grade-level or subject matter) specialists to instructional delivery team members capable of contributing to a wide variety of instructional needs.'

According to this view, the accent falls on work done in teams, on joint action, on the use of wider expertise than that of a single teacher for a group of learners. The whole approach is about a style of consensus, of shared power and decision-making, of mutual responsibility. It is about accountability in a system where the onus of success at the local level becomes the responsibility of the teacher, with devolution of power to the person leading a class. It concerns the empowerment of teachers as creative facilitators of learning as a partnership in accountability for educational excellence, emphasising positive interdependence. It is:

> ... the perception that one is linked with others in a way that one cannot succeed unless they do (and vice versa), and that their work benefits you and your work benefits them. It is the belief that you 'sink or swim' together ... It promotes working together to maximise joint benefits, sharing resources, providing mutual support, and celebrating joint success (Johnson & Johnson in Thousand & Villa 1992:83).

The co-operation between teachers can take on a multiplicity of forms and labels. It is sometimes referred to as 'teachers' assistance teams', 'peer collaboration' or 'team teaching'. At other times teacher collaboration is referred to as a 'unified community' or 'school as a community'. The interaction and teamwork can comprise collaborative problem-solving or peer coaching. It can be classroom-specific or have school-wide significance.

What can such a school partnership based on mutual responsibility, shared aims and goals and a commitment to joint action by educators offer? The innumerable advantages include:

- Teachers feel more secure and can feel more free to experiment, as they are part of a team in which successes as well as failures are accredited to the team as a whole.

- Teachers' self-esteem is enhanced by the feeling that certain of their ideas and approaches that may have been suppressed in the past can now be applied in a team setting.

- Teachers are involved in a daily learning situation as they share ideas, experience the successful methods of others and evaluate each other's approaches.

- Learners reap the benefit of the increasing improvement in teachers' teaching abilities.

7.4.3 School managers and teachers as partners

Swap (1993:17) reflects as follows on traditional styles of management in schools: 'The traditional approach to managing schools emphasises hierarchy, individualism, and technology rather than dialogue, relationship, and reciprocity'. Because of this, according to Kidder (in Swap 1993:17), 'teaching has been and continues to be an isolated and isolating experience'.

This contributes to the situation where school connections with the 'outside world' are also governed by hierarchical and authoritarian principles. Therefore, before a positive partnership can be created with external partners, another fundamental partnership according to the principles of the new paradigm should be formed, namely that between school managers and partners.

As has been indicated before, one of the key trends in international reform movements (cf par 2) is the devolution of authority and decision-making to local levels. Within schools this gives rise to a change in the accountability structure. School management teams and teachers are equally accountable for successful learning in the school.

In conjunction with these developments, under the guidance of changes in management in organisations where the principles of W Edwards Deming exercised extensive influence, there has also been pressure on schools to implement changes in management which reflect the changes in the external environment. This approach proposes that schools be managed as decentralised bureaucratic structures and that the command-and-control hierarchical system and levels of control should be abandoned (Berry 1995:39).

The new style of management should be one where teachers are regarded as managers. They are management-level colleagues and therefore equal partners. Teachers, like other managers, are decision-makers (cf Streshly & Newcomer 1994:63). Within the partnership teachers' creativity becomes more important because group decisions are frequently better than those taken by any individual manager. In order to fully utilise this creativity of fellow partners, 'managers' lead by listening and in this way all members of the partnership are given the opportunity to voice innovative solutions to problems, some of which may not have been thought of by management. Thus members of staff take ownership of innovations and solutions that work which then stimulates a commitment to success by those who have to turn decisions taken into reality (cf Pretorius 1998:103-106).

In school partnerships where the new vision of the sharing of power, responsibility and ownership is made a reality and where there is a climate of positive interdependence, a true culture of teamwork exists. In addition to instructional delivery teams, Furman (1995:37) identifies a second type of team which she calls 'building core teams'. All facets of management are placed in the hands of these teams. Thus, there can be teams for financial management, for strategic planning, for sport organisation, public relations, the school programme, building/grounds management etc. In this way teamwork becomes a kind of accountability mechanism. The procedures and methods are not the issue, but the team in possession of the necessary expertise is accountable for high standards in the function allotted to it. 'Management' as facilitators of decisions taken play an active role in the work being done in teams.

The principles of power sharing, decreasing of hierarchical levels, division of the accountability structure among all members of an organisation and a true spirit of teamwork among professionals have proven to have many advantages worldwide. These include:

- The school management and staff extend the spirit of partnership so that it is on a healthy footing with the external community.
- School management members work together enthusiastically as a team – every member of the partnership has a distinctive contribution to make in reaching a common mission, namely the effective learning by learners.
- The unique creativity and ideas of each member of the partnership are used 'to work out even better ways to reach all children'. (cf Swap's definition on pp 151-2)
- The self-image of teachers is enhanced when they begin to perceive themselves as valued partners and as equal management-level colleagues.
- Everyone finds 'joy' in the organisation.
- Learners are seen to be working hard and succeeding academically.

7.4.4 Conclusion

The preceding discussion has shown that the idea of partnership in educational provision may also imply a partnership in the internal functioning of the school. At the same time, it is clear that the internal partnerships are the most fundamental as a lack of collaborative effort of this nature leads to hierarchical and authoritarian management styles and therefore to isolation. The latter destroys partnerships with the external environment because, where applicable, they also govern the relationship with parents and other interested parties.

In a new paradigm, learning rather than training is regarded as the focal point of educational enterprise as this is dependent on strong relationships between learner and teacher. Learners are also recognised as important partners in education. In addition, there is a trend to view education as less isolated than in the past. This also applies to the internal functioning of the school where, traditionally, individual teachers have worked behind closed doors. The ideal is a learning environment where teachers are members of an instructional delivery team working within a true culture of teamwork and of partnership, and being capable of contributing to a wide variety of instructional needs. Moreover, the internal partnership has a third dimension, namely between school managers and teachers. The scaling down of hierarchical levels in the management of schools implies a partnership between teachers and school managers where teachers are treated as equals and thus as management-level partners. Finally, Swap and Bastiani's views of the educational partnerships (cf par 3) also include strong relationships with the external school environment, inclusive of parents and other interested parties. The following section will focus on these aspects.

7.5 Building a learning community: schools in partnership with the external environment

7.5.1 Home-school partnerships

Parental involvement with education is nothing new. That this can lead to more effective learning has been apparent for some time. Ebersole (1979:v) wrote as follows:

> The ring of respect encircling students, teachers, and parents is an essential relationship for effective learning. A break anywhere in the circle results in a breakdown in student performance. If there is close communication, co-operation, sincere caring, however, there seems to be no limit to what might happen – students learn more, teachers feel more fulfilled, and parents feel better about their children and themselves.

More recently Swap (1993:1) has commented as follows regarding the essence of active involvement of parents with the education of their children:

> Home-school partnership is no longer a luxury. There is an urgent need for schools to find ways to support the success of all our children. One element that we know contributes to more successful children and more successful schools across all populations is parent involvement in children's education ... when families and educators work collaboratively, both experience new learning and an important source of support.

Both opinions cited in the preceding paragraphs cast no doubt on the fact that parent involvement has a positive influence on the learning process of learners. There is, however, an important distinction between the two viewpoints: the greater urgency expressed in the second opinion is closely connected to the reform movements of the 1980s and 1990s referred to earlier (cf par 2). An important aspect emphasised in global reform is that schools alone cannot resolve the supposed failures of the education system, but that it is the shared responsibility of communities. Co-operation – a joint effort from parents, educators and other community structures – is what is required. This is the reason for the urgent need for home-school partnerships.

Furthermore, the use of the term 'home-school partnership' in the second quotation is also relevant. 'Home-school partnership' or 'home-school collaboration' are terms that have only become popular since the 1990s. The use of these terms in preference to the term 'parent involvement', used freely up to the 1980s, is explained by Christenson, Rounds and Franklin (1992:21). Home-school collaboration is related to parent involvement, but is broader and more inclusive. Parent involvement focuses on the role of parents in their children's education. Home-school collaboration focuses on the relationship between home and school and how parents and educators can work together to promote the social and academic development of learners. Although home-school collaboration implies parent involvement, the reverse is not always true. Home-school collaboration implies that there should be a partnership between the two systems and that both systems work towards a common goal. The underlying philosophy of home-school collaboration is the recognition that the two systems can achieve more by working together than by functioning separately, although both may have legitimate respective roles. This underlying point of departure resembles the description of positive interdependence discussed previously (cf par 7.4.2). The two terms will nevertheless be used interchangeably in the following section.

From the above two quotations it follows that there are specific advantages to be derived from the two systems. In the first place, home-school partnerships lead to improved learning. Henderson (in Swap 1992:54) has no hesitation about this aspect: '... the evidence is now beyond dispute: parent involvement improves student achievement. When parents are involved, children do better in school, and they go to better schools'.

The international literature abounds with accounts of research indicating benefits for all involved: for learners, for parents and for educators. In addition to improved academic performance, these benefits include:

- improved learner attitudes, conduct and attendance
- improved classroom performance when parents tutored learners
- better understanding of learner needs by both parents and teachers
- increased self-confidence and personal satisfaction for particular parents
- active parental support of instructional programmes
- augmented instructional resources (Chrispeels 1996:302-303).

In spite of numerous research reports (cf Swap 1992:54; Swap 1993:11-12; Brand 1996:76; Merz & Furman 1997:60) which indicate that the home-school partnership has a positive influence on the academic performance of learners, it is apparent that this is an ideal that does not always become a reality.

According to Christenson et al. (1992:20) 'Although there is strong interest in partnerships, the field is characterised more by rhetoric than reality'.

Swap (1993:13) suggests that although research findings indicate that both parents and teachers are aware of the importance of parent involvement, it can be expected that programmes in this regard should be a reality in all schools: 'The paradox is that parent involvement in the schools is surprisingly minimal ... Despite the urgent need for partnership and the weight of supportive evidence, parents continue to be kept at a distance in most schools.' The reason for this, according to Bastiani (1993:113), is 'Partnership is easy to talk about, much more difficult to achieve in practice.'

What then are the barriers to the ideal of home-school partnerships becoming a reality? Swap (1993:14 and following) identifies the following:

- *Changing demographics*. Larger percentages of working mothers, divorces, single-parent families, second and third marriages, children having children; an increase in poverty, and increasing racial, language and ethnic diversity in classrooms are some of the relevant aspects in this regard.

- *School norms that do not support partnerships*. Hierarchical instead of collaborative organisation of schools, holding onto authoritarian principles, avoidance of conflict, fear of injury to the status of educators, as well as to the school culture are critical issues in this regard.

- *Limited resources to support parent involvement*. Time, as one of the school's most important resources, is not allocated for this purpose; neither is money because money is concentrated on essential personnel, programmes and supplies.

- *Lack of information about how to establish partnerships*. Inadequate training of teachers about possible problems in designing, implementing and evaluating partnerships is the order of the day, while positive leadership is essential in achieving good results.

- *Barriers from the parents' perspective*. Insufficient knowledge about how they may contribute to their children's schooling, increased diversity among the parent population, lack of time during the day and where their 'second-class' status is underlined are barriers mentioned by parents.

In another source, Swap (1992:56-57) adds the following aspects for consideration:

- a tradition of separation between home and school
- a tradition of blaming parents for children's difficulties, particularly when parents are poor and not consistently involved in school
- traditional and persistent patterns of interacting with 'outsiders' such as meetings in the mornings, short conferences and fundraising activities.

In spite of the barriers mentioned, there are many descriptions of home-school partnerships that deliver ample dividends. Christenson et al. (1992:20) writes that 'there are innumerable opportunities and challenges to change the rhetoric to reality'. It is clear that there is no one best or correct method of applying a partnership: 'What works is for parents to be involved in a variety of roles over a period of time' (Henderson in Swap 1992:54).

The various ways that parents and schools interact can be divided into five major categories:

- involvement in shared governance on mandated advisory committees
- communication between school and home, with most communications coming from the school
- parental support for the school in the form of fundraising, helping with field trips, or attending school events
- participation with teachers as assistants in the classroom
- provision of parents' education activities (usually at school) (Chrispeels 1996:302).

Much could probably be added to these categories mentioned. The most important matter is the role parents play in supporting learners' own work at home, especially with regard to homework, additional learning opportunities, the creation of a culture of learning at home, setting an example as lifelong learners and the encouragement of additional reading.

Regarding home-school partnerships, the following deductions can be made from the literature examined:

- There are many dimensions and facets to parent involvement. As mentioned previously, there is no one best or correct method.
- It seems as though home-school collaboration is an attitude, not an activity, which occurs when partners (parents and teachers) share common goals and responsibilities, are seen as equals and contribute to the collaborative process.
- Parent involvement is correlated with learner achievement. When parents are involved, learners achieve higher grades and test scores and better long-term academic success.
- Parent involvement influences non-cognitive behaviour: learner attendance, attitudes towards school, maturation, self-concept and behaviour improve when parents are involved.
- There are benefits for parents, teachers, communities and schools when parents are involved. More successful programmes and effective schools are the order of the day.
- All forms of parent involvement seem to be useful. However, those that are meaningful, well-planned, comprehensive and long-lasting offer more

options for parents to be involved and appear to be more effective.

- Achievement gains are most significant and long-lasting when parent involvement is begun at an early age.

7.5.2 The involvement of business and industry with education

Although there is reference in this subsection to business and industry, the discussion could just as well be applied to a wide variety of other employment sectors. Other collective terms that could be used are 'working world', 'world of work', 'work sector', 'commercial world', 'workplace', 'business world' and so forth.

Until as late as the 1970s, the idea of co-operation between education and business and industry was still virtually taboo (cf Cerych 1985:7). For a considerable period during the twentieth century it was considered equally vulgar to connect the educational priorities of a country with the needs of the economy. The belief that education could have a utilitarian aim and that the needs of technology and industry might be a priority was simply unacceptable in the best circles (McMillan 1989:6).

The 1980s and 1990s, however, brought about a large-scale shift in attitudes as well as increasing pressure to strengthen links between education and the economy. Because of a combination of worldwide developments described in section 7.2, it was claimed that schools should serve the needs of industry and commerce more directly and effectively. Moreover, schools cannot solve all the educational ills on their own. In addition, the realisation has dawned that the solution does not lie in mutual accusation. The task of business and industries extends beyond merely stating their objections to the relevance of schooling. The answer lies in mutual involvement in a variety of ways, because 'schools have as much to offer industry as industry has to offer schools' (Banham 1989:11).

So important has the relationship between education and industry become, that as early as 1985 Cerych (1985:7) stated 'there are currently only a few countries or international organisations which have not held seminars or conferences or conducted research on the subject'. The literature demonstrates that a partnership between education and industry has much to offer all parties involved.

Benefits for learners include:

- work experience
- stimulation in a subject/career using industrial resources
- academic work which relates to the demands of the working world
- motivation
- special events, e.g. competitions or business games

- joint education-industry training exercises
- joint education-industry curriculum projects.

Benefits for educators include:

- attending company training courses
- attending education-based courses with industrial contributions
- use of up-to-date material in classrooms
- developing and maintaining personal contacts
- expert assistance from business for policy-making, resource allocation and strategic management
- information about the needs of the workplace for the purpose of curriculum development
- use of experts from business and industry as part-time or temporary full-time teachers and trainers.

Benefits for business and industry include:

- educated and well-prepared workers
- use of facilities, equipment and other resources of educational institutions
- direct economic benefits arising from educational institutions buying goods and services from their local communities
- help in applying technology to improve business operations
- up-to-date information about developments and new approaches in education
- better understanding of problems in education provisioning (cf Pretorius 1993:130-131).

From the above it is clear that if links between education and the business world are well-planned and there is commitment to the principles of a positive partnership (cf par 3), the relationship holds benefits for all parties concerned.

It is evident from the international literature that the possibilities for co-operation between education and the working world are virtually limitless – from informal partnerships to highly structured formal agreements. These can include work-experience placements, visits to companies, work shadowing, teacher secondment, curriculum development projects, mini-enterprises, mentorships of learners, donation of equipment, coalitions, and compacts or programmes that reward innovation (cf OECD 1992:13-14). No single model can be accepted as suitable for all situations and countries. Education bodies and workplaces should co-operate in order to develop a relationship which suits specific needs. Although partnerships therefore have a great deal of variation, researchers have found that there does appear to be a gradual shift from broad, loosely defined relationships to more well-defined and sustained involvement of schools and businesses (Kochhar & Erickson 1993:2).

Various classification schemes of partnerships have been developed to describe the variety that exists. Rigden (in Kochhar & Erickson 1993:2) distinguishes the following three categories:

- *Adopt-a-school model*. This is where a single company selects a single school and provides resources and volunteers to support school activities. This model is useful as a first step in building a relationship. Businesses that are involved in this type of relationship are typically very generous, but they are not likely to challenge the school or tackle underlying problems.

- *Project-driven model*. This type of partnership is formed to address specific academic or social problems such as inadequate achievement of learners in science or mathematics. Businesses would offer to help schools to improve the content and instruction in science courses or support teachers in developing new curricula. Although this can change attitudes and practices in the classroom, school and school system, the shortcoming of this type of involvement is that it is relatively short-term and often isolated from the rest of the school activities. Corporate partners are normally unable to maintain a permanent programme. Once outside resources are withdrawn, the project is not continued. Another shortcoming is that there is often little transfer of the programme to other classrooms in the school or other schools in the district.

- *Reform model*. Partnerships of this kind are directed at challenging common practices in schools and districts and changing the education system itself. These partnerships are often developed after companies and educators find that their project-driven programmes have shown few positive results after years of co-operation. They then consider ways they can work with a school district to support broader reform or restructuring goals. As Taylor (1998:398) indicates, 'involvement becomes more strategic over time'.

According to Kochhar and Erickson (1993:2), the above classification distinguishes between partnerships that are developed solely to create linkages between schools and the workplace and those that are designed to create real change in teaching and learning environments and improve learner outcomes. Programmes designed may fall into one or a combination of the three categories.

A wide variety of obstacles appear to affect co-operation between education and the working world. The OECD report therefore argues: 'The 1990s will determine whether partnerships prove to be a passing fad, or whether they consolidate their position, to become a permanent, integral part of the education process'.

The following is a brief summary of a few obstacles mentioned in the literature:

Failure to communicate

Education and the world of work represent two different 'worlds'.

> For many decades, business and education preferred to keep each other at arm's length and viewed each other with mutual distrust. Many educators feared that business would take over schools if closer involvement were encouraged. In turn, business has looked at schools with an expectation of failure and has tended to view education as a purely social issue. (Northeast-Midwest Institute 1988:8)

The isolation resulting from the traditional state-funded education model broke down communication for a long time. It will take time before the necessary communication skills between the partnerships have developed to make fruitful communication possible.

Prejudice and misperceptions

Many misconceptions are mentioned which can obscure the relationship between education and the world of work, for example industries are only interested in making profits and that is their hidden agenda with their involvement in education. The profit motive often distorts people's principles. They are therefore not interested in the so-called higher purposes and principles of schooling. On the other hand, many people from industry are under the impression that educational institutions are always begging for money or that education is so unstructured that no project can be well-organised. In addition, educators have little experience in working effectively with other organisations.

Conflicts of aims and values

The business world is compelled to respect the demands of short-term deadlines, while education is geared towards a more long-term approach. The activities therefore differ in terms of tempo, time frames, aims and nature. Thus, for example, the training needs of business do not always fit in with the term or semester systems at schools.

Lack of flexibility in educational structures/rigidity/bureaucracy

Rigid regulations and procedures cause delays in the achievement of agreements. Approval for plans of action and projects is always applicable. In addition, schools are more often subject to inconvenient legislation and administrative measures which inhibit decision-making. Businesses therefore prefer more informal liaison.

Concerning the partnership between education and business and industry, the following conclusions may be drawn from what has been presented here:

- Co-operation between the two sectors – business and education – is essential and has advantages for all concerned.

- The possibilities for greater collaboration are virtually limitless and ought to develop in relation to the requirements of specific situations.

- In spite of the flexibility of partnerships, it is clear that partnerships that are more long-lasting and strategic in nature, aiming at a broader system reform and more substantial change will, in time, replace isolated co-operation and will attain more positive results.

- There are still obstacles to forming meaningful partnerships and during the 1990s it will become apparent to a greater extent whether business and industry involvement will have a more permanent place as part of the mainstream education provision process.

7.5.3 Partnerships with other educational institutions

There is much less discussion in the literature concerning partnerships between educational institutions than is the case with partnerships between parents and other structures in the community in general. There are various reasons for this. The isolation of education, as was the case in the traditional state-funded education model (cf par 2), was traditionally the cause of little or no contact between educational institutions. In the past, bureaucratic procedures prevented schools from having contact with other schools and with institutes for higher education which could lead to beneficial, long-lasting partnerships. This is still the case to some extent. Various other barriers also impede this kind of contact. Regarding partnerships between universities and schools, with a view to improving education, Higgins and Merickel (1997:173-174) indicate the following as a result of their research:

- *Partnership work conflicts with the university's reward system*. In terms of the culture of a research university, productivity, promotion and tenure are determined by research resulting in refereed publications, university courses taught, and service. Unless evaluated as service, which is the least important of the productivity, promotion and tenure measures, the time it takes to build trust with public school partners is not valued at the university. Decline in research productivity because of time spent on any other worthwhile activity is seen as a major barrier.

- *Establishing collaborative research agendas is difficult*. University faculty members were often not welcomed by schools. They therefore found it difficult to pursue any aspect of their personal research agendas in which they have developed expertise over years. Public school teachers seemed to be sceptical of the very term research because of the perception that academics would be visiting the school in order to perform research on it. The school climate therefore does not lend itself to systematic inquiry.

- *University faculty members must balance two worlds*. Partnership with schools require a lot of time. If they want to establish positive relationships, they need to visit the schools regularly and become involved in the day-to-day operations of schools. However, while they are busy at schools, their responsibilities at the universities continue: phones need answering, mail needs to be read and answered, e-mail keeps coming in, meetings go on, students need advising and classes need to be taught.

This perspective from the side of the university faculty members may very well be true, but it is a field where there are many possibilities. Imagine the following scenario: school X, involving all relevant stakeholders, plans specific strategies with a view to the continuous improvement of learning experiences offered to all learners at the school. One of the decisions made is to break the 'isolation' of the school and to enter into partnerships with outside organisations. Some of the identified requirements include the following:

- greater knowledge/expertise regarding educational law
- quality management
- quality assurance
- multicultural education
- continuous development of personnel
- technological education
- skills education
- curriculum development.

Those organising the liaison decide that the nearby higher educational institutions have the necessary expertise to help the school with the problem areas identified.

After discussions with various institutions for higher education, a partnership is entered into. Some of these partners are parents who would like to be associated with the school in any case. Others are researchers who would like to serve their own research agendas, researchers who would like to build their courses in educator training on relevant practical knowledge and specialists who would like to disseminate their knowledge and management teams to schools as part of their community service. Principles on which this partnership is built include the following:

- Improved learning by learners is central to this partnership.
- There should be shared aims and goals which also acknowledge important differences.
- There should be a commitment to working together, sharing resources and providing mutual support.
- Collaboration should benefit all members of the partnership – teachers and college or university faculty members.

The partnership starts on a small scale, but is extended over two or three years to co-operation benefiting both parties. University faculty members bring expertise to the school, which contributes to a higher quality of management. Quality assurance is built into all processes and this leads to improved achievement of learning outcomes. Teachers reach a better understanding of working with multicultural groups and, in addition, there is a new culture of learning. Teachers become more aware of exciting courses presented by institutes of higher learning and the school develops into 'a learning community'. University faculty members are no longer perceived as researchers whose 'ivory tower knowledge' has no practical value. In addition to these benefits, university faculty members and members of higher educational institutions become more aware of the actual problems in schools at grass-roots level: they have the opportunity of witnessing first-hand the realities of 'being in the trenches'. Their isolation from the public schools, for which they have to train their students, is lifted, bringing various new insights. They become more aware of teachers' frustrations, among others those of having to deal with large classes, the lack of additional educational resources and so on. New research problems are identified and they now have a much broader vision than the personal research agendas with which they have been occupied for a number of years. The partners become engrossed in team research projects and their refereed publications are doubled. Teachers and faculty members work together enthusiastically, all feeling good about their joint successes.

McLaughlin(1997:26) is of the opinion that 'valuable partnerships can also be built between one school and another'. He reports a number of resounding successes experienced with science projects involving high school and primary school learners. Whereas schools in the traditionally isolated situation only experienced incidental contact and co-operation, there was now no reason why partnerships could not be built up. We live in an era in which cost-effectiveness and productivity have become important principles in virtually all spheres of life. This trend obliges schools to share resources to a greater extent than was the case in the past. There is no reason why schools in the same region could not launch a number of research projects. For example, expertise can be exchanged regarding instructional programmes in, for example, mathematics or science or technology education. Buildings and staff can be shared for specific activities. In an article entitled *The Power of Partnering*, Bernauer (1996:71-77) reports a technology integration project and the establishment of an interactive technology lab in which various institutions, including universities, were involved. The final deduction was: 'Partnering breeds success'.

In future the application of technology in the learning process will play an increasingly important role. However, technology costs money. Individually, schools do not have the funds to implement expensive interactive technology labs. There is no reason why schools cannot establish communal facilities and

168

utilise these to optimise learning opportunities for all learners.

Once more, there is no one single best or correct method for partnering between schools. There are numerous possibilities depending on the region.

7.6 Conclusion

This section has attempted to establish greater understanding regarding the school and its relationship with the external environment. Three essential educational connections have been discussed briefly – those between parents, the employment sector and other educational institutions. Because of the limited scope of this chapter the possibility of a variety of other networks could not be explored, for example community structures such as neighbourhood groups, clubs, libraries, local government, police services, social services, health agencies and others who could influence the development of learners' understanding and knowledge.

The line running through all three relationships discussed is the realisation that schools alone cannot shoulder the enormous reform challenges confronting the education systems of the world. The community as a whole, including structures not discussed here, must accept the shared responsibility for educating children. We live in an era in which greater co-operation in most domains of life is the ideal. Joint action contributes to greater success than can be achieved by individuals and by isolated ventures. For this reason countries even strive towards economic co-operation with other countries to enable them to operate from greater power bases and thus face contemporary challenges. The same principle guides the reform movements of education systems.

However, there is another dimension to the idea of partnerships: unparalleled changes and progress in technology compel countries to let their workers keep on learning. This applies to the entire community. A community which stagnates in the continuous stream of development also regresses in the creation of a better life for all its citizens. The ideal is to create a community of lifelong learners. By ensuring the involvement of the entire community and by sharing the responsibility of educational provision for the children of the community, a culture of co-learners and of being a learning society is created:

> The goal of a learning society is to refocus education's mission, turning its emphasis from a conventional K through 12 educational time frame to lifelong learning; to a society that uses its educational resources, its family resources, and its community resources to educate people of all ages at all stages of their lives. (Decker & Decker 1991:vi)

7.7 Summary

Partnerships in education is a subject about which much has been written. The content of this chapter offers an interpretation of the movement, especially as

169

it has developed during the last two decades of the twentieth century. Content is therefore not based in a specific country, but offers a more general perspective endeavouring to interpret general world trends. There has been a particular focus on global considerations giving rise to the partnership movement.

The partnerships between education and parents and between education and business and industry predominate in the existing literature. However, in this chapter the movement has been argued from a broader perspective so as to include other key relationships. The opinion is held that the partnerships in the internal school environment are also essential in the discussion, and that these often influence the external environment negatively if they do not function in a beneficial manner. The conclusion is that educational provision is a shared responsibility of the total community, eventually standing in a central position with regard to the creation of a community of lifelong learners.

References

Banham, J (1989) Building a stronger partnership between business and secondary education. *British Journal of Educational Studies*, 37(1):5-16.

Bastiani, J (1993) Parents as partners: genuine progress or empty rhetoric? In P Munn (ed) *Parents and schools: customers, managers or partners?* London: Routledge.

Bernauer, JA (1996) The power of partnering. *T.H.E. Journal*, 24(3):71-73.

Berry, JE (1995) Reorganizing a district to support education outcomes. *The School Administrator*, 52(February):39.

Brand, S (1996) Making parent involvement a reality: helping teachers develop partnerships with parents. *Young Children*, 51(2)76-81.

Bush, G (1991) *America 2000: An education strategy (sourcebook) – 'making this land all that it should be'.* Washington: US Department of Education.

Cerych, L (1985) Collaboration between higher education and industry: an overview. *European Journal of Education*, 20(1):7-18.

Chrispeels, J (1996) Effective schools and home-school-community partnership roles: a framework for parent involvement. *School Effectiveness and School Improvement*, 7(4):297-323.

Christenson, SL; Rounds, T and Franklin, MJ (1992) Home-school collaboration: effects, issues, and opportunities. In SL Cristenson and JC Conoley (eds) *Home-school collaboration: enhancing children's academic and social competence.* Maryland: The National Association of School Psychologists.

Decker, LE and Decker, VA (1991) *Home/school/community involvement.* Virginia: American Association of School Administrators.

Ebersole, P (1979) Foreword. In RS Brandt (ed) *Partners: parents and schools*. Virginia: Association for Supervision and Curriculum Development.

Finlay, I (1998) Stakeholders, consensus, participation and democracy. In I Finlay, N Stuart and S Young (eds) *Changing vocational education and training: an international comparative perspective*. London: Routledge.

Furman, GC (1995) Administrators' perceptions of outcomes-based education: a case study. *International Journal of Educational Management*, 9(6):32-42.

Glasgow, NA (1996) *Taking the classroom into the community: a guidebook*. Thousand Oaks: Corwin Press.

Grumet, M (1989) Dinner at Abigail's: nurturing collaboration. *Real Professionalism*, January:20-25.

Higgins, KM and Merickel, ML (1997) The promise and the promises: partnerships from a university perspective. *Teacher Educator*, 3293:165-184.

Kochhar, CA and Erickson, MR (1993) *Business-education partnerships for the 21st century: a practical guide for school improvement*. Maryland: Aspen.

McLaughlin, CW (1997) School to school partnerships: create a communication connection between elementary and secondary schools. *Science and Children*, 34(5):26-29.

McMillan, CM (1989) The needs of a future education for the RSA: the needs of industry and how they can be met. *Transvaal Education News*, 85(4):6-8,18.

Merz, C and Furman, G (1997) *Communities and schools: promise and paradox*. New York: Teachers' College Press.

Northeast-Midwest Institute (1988) *Education incorporated: school-business co-operation for economic growth*. New York: Quorum Books.

Organisation for Economic Co-Operation and Development (OECD) (1992) *Schools and business: a new partnership*. Paris: OECD.

Pretorius, F (1998) Managing the change to an outcomes-based approach. In F Pretorius (ed) *Outcomes-based education in South Africa: policy and concepts; implementation; management; quality assurance*. Johannesburg: Hodder & Stoughton.

Pretorius, SG (1993) Business and industry involvement in education. In EI Dekker and EM Lemmer (eds) *Critical issues in modern education*. Durban: Butterworths.

Spady, WG (1986) The emerging paradigm of organisational excellence: success through planned adaptability. *Peabody Journal of Education*, 63(3):46-64.

Streshly, WA and Newcomer, L (1994) *Outcomes-based education: something old, something new, something needed*. Unpublished Paper. Eagle Colorado: The High Success Network, Inc.

Swap, SM (1992) Parent involvement and success for all children: what we know now. In SL Cristenson and JC Conoley (eds) *Home-school collaboration: enhancing children's academic and social competence*. Maryland: The National Association of School Psychologists.

Swap, SM (1993) *Developing home-school partnerships: from concepts to practice*. New York: Teachers' College Press.

Taylor, A (1998) 'Courting business': the rhetoric and practices of school-business partnerships. *Journal of Education Policy*,13(3):395-422.

Thousand, JS and Villa, RA (1992) Collaborative teams: a powerful tool in school restructuring. In RA Villa, JS Thousand, W Stainbock and S Stainbock (eds) *Restructuring for caring and effective education: an administrative guide to creating heterogenous schools*. Baltimore: Paul H Brookes Publishing Company.

Tribus, M (1996) Quality in education according to the teachings of Deming and Feuerstein. *School Psychology Journal*, 17(1):93-112.

Wagner, PJ (1992) *Building support networks for schools*. Santa Barbara: ABC-CLIO.

Westwood, P (1995) Learner and teacher: perhaps the most important partnership of all. *Australasian Journal of Special Education*, 19(1)5-16.

Additional reading

Finlay, I (1998) Stakeholders, consensus, participation and democracy. In I Finlay, N Stuart and S Young (eds) *Changing vocational education and training: an international comparative perspective*. London: Routledge.

McLaughlin, CW (1997) School to school partnerships: create a communication connection between elementary and secondary schools. *Science and Children*, 34(5):26-29.

Organisation for Economic Co-Operation and Development (OECD) 1992. *Schools and business: a new partnership*. Paris: OECD.

Swap, SM (1993) *Developing home-school partnerships: from concepts to practice*. New York: Teachers' College Press.

Thousand, JS and Villa, RA (1992) Collaborative teams: a powerful tool in school restructuring. In RA Villa, JS Thousand, W Stainbock and S Stainbock (eds) *Restructuring for caring and effective education: an administrative guide to creating heterogenous schools*. Baltimore: Paul H Brookes Publishing Company.

CHAPTER 8

HIGHER EDUCATION POLICY AND PRACTICE

 Prof Eleanor Lemmer
University of South Africa

Table of contents

8.1 Introduction

Since 1994 the restructuring of the racially fragmented system of higher education in South Africa has been set in motion. The National Commission on Higher Education (NCHE) was established by President Mandela in February 1995 with a view to changing all facets of higher education in keeping with the needs of a newly democratic South Africa. The NCHE submitted a report: *A Framework for Transformation of Higher Education* on the basis of which the *Green Paper on Higher Education Transformation* was released in December 1996. This was followed by the *White Paper on Higher Education Transformation* (DE 1997) culminating in the Higher Education Act (DE 1997). In keeping with the notion of a restructured and integrated system of education and training in South Africa, higher education and training was defined as education and training that follows matriculation at the end of level 4 of the National Qualifications Framework (NQF). Under the new dispensation this is provided by universities, technikons, private or public colleges such as those supplied for the training of teachers, nurses, police, correctional service officials, agriculturalists and so forth as well as professional institutes. Among the public institutes, universities and technikons are regarded as a national function while the colleges should fall under the management of the provincial departments of education.

The restructured system of higher education in South Africa created by the new policy directives and ensuing legislation reflects a number of global trends. International reviews of university reform (Dill & Sporn 1995; Watson 1992) include most issues which South African higher education belatedly confronts as it emerges from the isolation of the apartheid period. These include the massification of higher education; the blurring of the binary divide between the university and the non-university sector; the debate around the location and status of teacher education; the marketisation of universities; and most recently, the shift to a commercial model of management in higher education (Watson 1992:322).

Knowledge of international patterns of higher education policy and practice are useful to the study of higher education reform in South Africa. According to the eminent comparative educationist, Noah (1984:551), an international perspective enables us 'to understand better our educational past, locate ourselves more exactly in the present, and discern more clearly what our future may be'.

Not only is South African higher education a latecomer to international developments, but the ideological discourses which now frame policy at the national level have already been globalised and these global discourses inform national policy options (Taylor, Rizvi, Lingard & Henry 1997:71). While the historical context of higher education transformation in South Africa (i.e.

apartheid ideology and its creation of an unequal system of education) should not be underplayed, policy and legislation on higher education transformation, in several respects, follows closely the contours of policy already implemented elsewhere. This convergence is, however, not uncommon (Cowen 1996a; Taylor et al. 1997). As governments worldwide grapple with similar societal changes, educational policies, despite their quite different points of origin become, not identical, but somewhat more alike. Globalisation brings a new slant to the research agenda of the comparative educationist. According to Cowen (1996a:151), instead of selecting problems at home and then looking for lessons from abroad, we would do well by beginning our studies outside the 'nation-state' – commencing in a reading of a global problematique associated with the late modern era. Thus, higher education policy is a kind of second-order consequence of change elsewhere in the political and social fabric. Homogenisation, however, does not rule out cultural particularity. Naturally educational policies converging in the global must still be worked out in local settings (Usher, Byrant & Johnston 1997:4).

Furthermore knowledge of global patterns enhances the critical scrutiny of national policies in another way. At present the current policy environment in South Africa is so dynamic that educators are tempted to accept its direction as inevitable and normal. To problematise current changes more rigorously, fresh and alternative discourses are required. In this regard, the post-modern debate may contribute to this end (Rust 1991:625) in spite of the reluctance of educational practitioners (Edwards & Usher 1994:1) and, specifically, comparative educationists to incorporate post-modern discourse into their field of inquiry (Cowen 1996a:151). It is possible that educationists in developing countries may feel that the complex post-modern discourse is best read from the contemporary anxieties of Europe and North America and suffers in its application elsewhere. However, as the social conditions emerging in post-industrial societies become more widespread, the literature of post-modernism offers the comparativist valuable 'new ways of interpreting' in a wide range of contexts. Thus, this chapter will draw, albeit selectively, on the post-modern critique of the contemporary university which has salient application in the study of the system of higher education in general.

8.2 The university, modernism and post-modernism

A brief explanation of the use in this chapter of *modernism* and *post-modernism* is necessary, however highly contested the terms are. Modernism is understood as a faith in universals discovered through reason; in science and the scientific method as superior means for arriving at truth and reality; and in language as a credible and reliable access to that reality (Bloland 1995:523). Modernism has long been considered the project for humankind's emancipation, progress and benevolent change. Education has been the vehicle to substantiate and realise modernism's overarching explanatory theories and to carry the modernist project forward (Edwards & Usher 1994:8). Hence, educational theory and practice are deeply embedded in modernism's ideals, vocabulary and institutions.

Cowen (1996a:158) elaborates on the characteristics of being modern by identifying dimensions of the modern education system. Herein the nation-state is the provider of mass education and the system is state-created and state-driven. Education's moral message relates to the formation of a common political identity (Cowen 1996a:158) and this message is balanced by the *general* contribution that education systems can make to economic growth. The structural and cultural linchpin of a modern system is the university. As a quintessentially modern institution, the university is distinguished by fundamental features: its grand purpose or metanarrative which is the search for disinterested Truth, and the belief in Truth's emancipatory power (Bloland 1995:523). Its fundamental function is the production of scientific knowledge. In this context, the *academic professional expert, the professor/scholar* enjoys special status and autonomy, making key decisions concerning what and how to research and to teach (Van Vught 1995:202). However, over time, modernism has displayed a less inviting face – its spectacular successes marred by totalitarianism, uncontrollable technology and the instrumental rationality which has created a consumer society (Lyotard 1993:29). Thus modernist values and institutions, including the university, are increasingly viewed as inadequate, irrelevant and expensive (Bloland 1995:521). This scepticism towards the contemporary university resonates in both intellectual and public critiques of its essential purpose; the questioning of the kind of knowledge it transmits; the tenuousness of the status of the scholar and the rapid alteration of the university's historical principles of self-organisation – community, collegiality and autonomy.

Foremost among the challenges to the certainties of modernism is the *post-modern discourse*. A definition of the latter is neither possible nor entirely desirable since definitions vary with every citation. Moreover, a definitive perspective is inconsistent with the post-modern stance – knowledge cannot be systematised into a singular, all-encompassing framework. However, Edwards and Usher (1994:7) suggest that post-modernism is '... an umbrella term for a historical period, a condition, a set of practices, a cultural discourse, an attitude and a model of analysis'. Underlying these dimensions is an incredulity toward the modernist project – a scepticism, a doubt, even disbelief, expressed towards modernist ideals in the light of a rapidly post-industrialising society. While the modern and post-modern are clearly distinguishable, both as historical periods and as cultural movements (Lyotard 1984), they can, and indeed do, exist recursively in any period in an oppositional tension (Lyotard 1984:15). Thus, universities, and by extension higher education policies, are the sites of competing discourses. For example, the guiding principles of the *White Paper on Higher Education Transformation* (DE 1997:12-13) embody the rhetoric of several alternative discourses – equity, redress, democracy, efficiency, effectiveness, affordability and economic competitiveness. These incorporate rival conceptions of being human and concomitantly serve different political, social and philosophical agendas (Barnett 1992:3).

8.3 The post-modern condition

For further elucidation of the post-modern stance, reference is made to the work of JF Lyotard (1984) who is one of the few post-modern writers who specifically comments on the university in the aftermath of the industrial age. The work on which this chapter primarily but not exclusive draws, *The postmodern condition: A report on knowledge*, although written in 1979 (in French; translated in 1984) anticipated current conditions in higher education with such uncanny accuracy that its relevance remains remarkably valid today. Admittedly, other difficulties are created which should be addressed: as with any other writer, Lyotard may be co-opted to serve a particular bias; the intricate complexity of his argument can be trivialised or his stance exaggerated by selective quotation (Cowen 1996b:247). Notwithstanding, Lyotard's provocative analysis remains most useful.

According to Lyotard (1984:xxiii) the post-modern movement emanates from and results in a scepticism towards the metanarratives or foundational theories developed during the Enlightenment. As we move from being a reproduction to a consumption society, the grand functions of the university – the metanarratives of *speculative unity* and of *emancipatory humanism* – lose ground (Lyotard 1984:33). The metanarrative of speculative unity which sought to unify scientific knowledge by the master discourse of metaphysical philosophy affords knowledge a legitimacy found in itself, not in a principle of usefulness, either to the state or civil society (Lyotard 1984:34). The metanarrative of emancipatory humanism points to individual freedom through knowledge, which in turn leads to progress (Lyotard 1979:32). But in the post-modern world, Lyotard proposes, these metanarratives have become redundant and thus can no longer legitimise science or the university. The status of these metanarratives is therefore reduced to a language game in a world characterised by a multiplicity of language games.

This displacement of metanarratives permits a redefinition of knowledge: knowledge becomes 'technically useful knowledge'. Knowledge is exteriorised with respect to the knower while the educational processes between learner and teacher are reconstituted as a *market relationship* between producer and consumer. Knowledge is exchanged on the basis of the value it has for the consumer – it becomes 'value-added' (Lyotard 1984:4-5). Hence, the world of international relations is read as a place where competitive advantage is based on knowledge and its applications in the economy (Lyotard 1984:48). Consequently certain knowledge is more important than other knowledge. The leading sciences and technologies are considered leading because of economic usefulness, their creation of competitive advantage and their translatability into information (computer) knowledge (Lyotard 1984:48).

Yet Lyotard's observations are even more incisive than a mere concern about the advantages of access to certain disciplines over others. By removing the traditional basis for legitimising knowledge, the subjugation of science and the university to a *new ideological legitimation* is possible. In this climate, the primary goal of universities (and of knowledge) becomes their optimal contribution to the best, the most efficient performance of the social system. Lyotard calls this criterion for legitimation, *performativity* aptly described by Bloland (1995:536) as '... the capacity to deliver outputs at the lowest cost, [a principle] which replaces truth as the yardstick of knowledge'. Subsequently, performativity supplants the agreed-upon, rational criteria for merit and instead efficiency and effectiveness become the exclusive criteria for judging knowledge, behaviour and social systems. In particular, the university becomes subject to a *post-modern condition* in which its historic claim to have special knowledge, to be creating special knowledge and to be testing truth, is undermined as the following quotation demonstrates:

> The question now asked by the professionalist student, the State or institutions of higher education is no longer 'Is it true?' but 'What use is it?' In the context of the mercantilisation of knowledge, more often than not this question is equivalent to: 'Is it saleable?'... 'Is it efficient?'. (Lyotard 1984:51)

In effect, this argument removes from the university its traditional defence against co-option by the state with regard to its key practices. For example, the decisions affecting the exclusion or inclusion of certain knowledge in the curriculum; the privileging of certain fields of study; the introduction of new management practices or new and external definitions of excellence. Instead of competence measured by the criteria of true/false, just/unjust, a technical game of efficiency and inefficiency is played in which the key questions during university decision-making are: 'Is it sellable? Is it translatable into information?'

Against this background, Lyotard (1984:xxv) predicts a bleak future for the university which now should '... create skills, and no longer ideals'. Under conditions of post-modernity, the university loses its monopoly in the production of knowledge. Instead of the acme of a higher education system, it becomes a mere component of the market made up of innumerable competitors – the polytechnic (technikon) which looms supreme, private research institutes, think tanks, industrial and government laboratories and corporate classrooms, to mention only a few. Hence universities are forced increasingly to reconstruct themselves as commercial enterprises competing in the knowledge business (Edwards & Usher 1994:175). In this context the student's role shifts from a calling requiring a cultural outlook to one which requires mere technical expertise (Lyotard 1984:53), a consequence which Lyotard describes as the death of the professorship.

8.4 Emerging patterns of higher education policy

In the light of Lyotard's analysis interrelated policy issues are focused upon: the university as instrument for economic development, the shift to supervisory state and a market-driven university, the new ideology of quality and its relation to the massification of higher education, and finally, corporate managerialism.

8.4.1   The university as instrument for economic development

The collapse of the university's metanarratives and the concomitant shift towards performative knowledge foreseen by Lyotard reverberate in several government reports appearing in the last decade. Although certainly not consciously informed by post-modern writing, the reports overlap strikingly with the post-modern critique in their definition of the so-called crisis of higher education. Commencing with the influential Organisation for Economic Co-operation and Development's report entitled *Universities under scrutiny* (OCED 1983; 1987), universities worldwide were accused of having fallen gravely short of meeting the economic challenges of the late twentieth century. This created 'a crisis of performance' which, in turn, created an 'internal crisis of purpose'. Similar anxieties are expressed in several subsequent government reports on the state of higher education – Australia, Canada, Britain, USA, Singapore and South Africa to name a few (Cowen 1996b:247). Keenly aware of international competition, governments called on universities to promote regional and national development and ensure economic efficiency. The *White Paper on Higher Education Transformation* (DE 1997:1.10) captures the aspirations of many governments when stating that higher education must be restructured to meet the '... needs of an increasingly technological economy with the capacity to participate in a rapidly changing global context' and '... to prepare for integration into the competitive arena of international production and finance'.

To address this crisis, policy-makers suggest an apparently simple solution: higher education should produce an indigenous supply of able and highly qualified personpower, particularly in areas of science, technology and management which are considered the engines of progress (Cowen 1996b:250). A strategy for partially addressing the skills shortage has been to create, virtually overnight, new universities by dint of giving university status to the relatively cheaper, more vocational polytechnic and vocational schools (Neave 1995:51). Britain is an obvious illustration of this move when it changed the status of polytechnics creating the 'new' universities. Furthermore, higher education policies from a wide range of countries converge in their steering of university education and research, often via preferential funding, towards the physical sciences and technology, complemented by professional subjects. In line with this growing *instrumentalism*, the White Paper, similarly, singles out the '... need for graduates particularly in career-oriented courses, science, engineering and technology' (DE 1997:1.8) so that higher education can 'yield a good return to the nation' (DE 1997:1). The privileging of functional, utilitarian, technical knowledge, an endeavour Smythe (1997:58) calls 'pedagogy for profit', inevitably renders vulnerable the traditional academic core – the arts and humanities – disciplines which do not have a measurable output in the new budgeting lexicon (Nowotny 1995:87).

But is this not merely a revisiting of the inevitable tension between what Snow (1959) dubbed the two cultures: the natural sciences versus the human sciences. Geiger (1995:45), commenting on shrinking enrolments in the humanities in American universities during the 1970s through the 1990s, disagrees. The future of the natural sciences and technology is assured, but, he states '... the future of the humanities, vital to a free society, remains contested'. This is not due to the inherent tension between the two academic cultures, but because of overriding mercantile determinants. This does not mean that the humanities would disappear, but they will increasingly be reconfigured as saleable, marketable commodities. For example, the literary disciplines may continue but in a new role, as generic language skills aimed at improving cognitive, social and personal proficiencies, not as the entrée to culture and civilisation (Rothblatt 1995:45). In this context, Watson (1992:319) suggests that what he terms 'the irrelevant, liberalising subjects' will be consigned increasingly to continuing education programmes and no longer form the core of a liberal university education.

It can be asked whether the redefinition of the university's role according to economic imperatives and the instrumentalism of knowledge is necessarily flawed. After all, the university's responsibility towards the labour market is neither new nor unjustified. Most countries expect the higher education sector to produce economic invigoration, increased international competitiveness, and a better educated and skilled workforce. Yet policy analysts appear concerned. Brady (1988:29), critiquing the 1987/88 Dawkinsian reforms of higher education in Australia, warns against allowing sheer commonsense to seduce us into accepting instrumentalist policy: '... the discourse of common sense has little awareness of its own, taking for granted ideas, practices and values which may be open to question'.

The view that the sole purpose of the university is to ensure economic vitality requires interrogation through a process of sifting and sorting, selecting and rejecting policy options (Brady 1988:31). When the economic role is thus problematised, it implies the university's co-option to become predominantly a locomotive of economic development. Moreover, this constitutes a clearly discernible element of an even broader global trend in educational policy-making. As Lyotard predicted, education, at all levels, is being rapidly *commodified* amidst a kind of cultural cynicism towards larger philosophical issues. Education systems are being made objects of macro-economic reform, with educational activities turned into saleable or corporatised market products as part of a national efficiency drive (Taylor et al. 1997:77). Nor is this pattern limited to developments in the university in influential Western democracies. Castells (1994:15) points out that a shift to an economic role is also occurring in less developed countries where universities are becoming fundamental tools of progress in a very different way to what used to be proposed by the humanistic approach to development. Previous educational objectives, such as improving literacy and fulfilling cultural needs, are now subsumed and made the condition for the larger aim of competition in a new informational-international economy. Neave (1995:56) of the International Association of Universities, corroborates this pattern. He observes that in the last five years the discourse in higher education policy has changed so drastically that it '... is less part of social policy [rather] it is increasingly viewed as a sub-sector of economic policy'. The *White Paper on Higher Education Transformation* is unabashedly explicit in this regard: higher education (also schooling) is a sub-element of various overarching economic policies, the Reconstruction and Development Plan, GDS and GEAR (DE 1997:12).

8.4.2 Towards a supervisory model by the state

But even if the metanarratives of the university have collapsed in a post-industrialist era, universities must be persuaded to comply with the performative purpose which policy-makers now envisage as their replacement. The means to do this lie partially in a shift from *state regulation* of education to *state supervision*. This is indicative of another feature of post-modernity – the weakening of the modern nation-state and the slackening of its characteristic function as the chief financial supplier of education. The supervisory model falls squarely in the current policy developments in the US, UK, Europe and Australia and the White Paper is a harbinger of its introduction in South Africa (DE 1997). By *downsizing* or *customerising* government's basic operations including educational provision and funding, the state seeks to offload financial responsibilities to either regional governments (e.g. the predominant pattern in Western Europe), to students in the form of fees and loans (e.g. the convention in the US and most recently introduced in the UK) or to business and industry. The White Paper (DE 1997:30) suggests a range of sources of external funding to which universities may appeal in lieu of state involvement: 'employer contributions, bequests and donations, ... institutional investments, contracts and consultancies and the expansion of private programmes and institutions'.

In the face of the reduction of state funding, universities must rely on their success in the marketplace to raise funds from external sources in a climate of new inter-institutional competition (Neave 1995:60). But a consequence of a market-driven university system is that research and teaching are judged by their ability to promote the university's financial cutting edge rather than advance a particular academic discipline. A strictly performative view of educational activities is a logical outcome. As Gibbons (1995:97) notes in words, strongly reminiscent of Lyotard:

> In a market-driven university system, further questions are posed to the criterion of intellectual interest: Will the solution [to a research problem], if found, be competitive in the market? Will it be cost effective? Will it be socially acceptable?

Moreover, this delegation of funding is hazardous: multiplying the pipers raises a cacophonous policy environment for the university which is exposed to a new variety of stakeholders all wielding the power of the purse (Neave 1995:63). In a most sober comparative report on European university systems, Veld, Fussel and Neave (1996:31) warn of the dangers of wooing the market. For example, powerful high-tech communication conglomerates, hungry for new merchandise, are becoming interested not only in funding universities, but also in buying them. Probably, they argue, one global conglomerate could afford to buy several European universities. 'How could the necessary independence and integrity of science be maintained in such situations?' asks Veld et al. (1996:31).

Ironically state offloading is usually accompanied by granting greater self-regulation to a university which should devise strategic plans in line with national goals. But such institutional self-regulation should not be misconstrued as greater autonomy. It is rather a mutation of autonomy, an autonomy conditional on institutional performance contained in performance indicators. The latter may relate to cost, student throughput, exit trajectories, research contracts, ratings compared with other institutions and, in a South African context, evidence of redress (Watson 1992:321). Self-regulation is then a reward for performativity in which various devices, such as discretionary funding and budget cuts, are at hand to punish the laggard or reward the virtuous (Veld et al. 1996:26).

Again the White Paper with international patterns of higher education policy states in this regard: 'the suggested adoption of performance based allocations of public funds could be used to steer the development of the system in South

Africa in accordance with national goals' (DE 1997:22). Suggested performance indicators are: broad fields and levels of study (which will doubtlessly privilege the natural sciences and technology), student completions and research publications (DE 1997:33). Drawing on the painful experience of British universities, Peters (1992:127) cautions that performance indicators are never value-free, but embody judgements about what the state considers useful knowledge and the correct measurement of efficiency. Performance indicators determine earmarked funding and the rationale for government budget cuts which, in turn, force university administrators to prune certain programmes, rationalise posts and direct research. If the government rewards the completion of a certain learning programme but not any other successful programme, it provides a strong bias in the direction of a single type of education (Veld et al. 1996:79). Moreover, universities in the UK and Netherlands have encountered an unanticipated and negative side-effect of performance funding. As the number of graduates in earmarked programmes rose dramatically, successful institutions began to face diminishing not increasing resources. The reason: the national education budget did not increase in relation to the increased production. Instead the 'price' for performance units, that is graduates in fields deemed appropriate, fell sharply.

8.4.3 Higher education and a new context for academic quality

Performance budgeting as an instrument for state steering is accompanied by the establishment of a new quality assurance system in higher education. Historically mechanisms to ensure quality have been part of the university since medieval times (Van Vught 1995:195-6). An appreciation of quality has been embedded in the university's grand purpose, the quest for disinterested Truth, and in this context faculties and their appointed scholars were the primary guardians of excellence and veracity. Moreover, as public good, universities could not shirk accountability to external constituencies and various mechanisms have existed for the purpose. Yet, since the late 1980s the conviction that determining quality is no longer a liberty of students to be based on internal regulation and peer judgement has emerged. The new understanding of quality rests heavily on an extrinsic definition of higher education. A crude yet watershed illustration of the new thinking is the former British Minister of Education's definition of quality in higher education as 'value for money', thus echoing by default Lyotard's anticipation of value-added knowledge. This definition of quality skirts the more elusive, intrinsic features of excellence associated with the metanarrative, which Van Vught (1995:201) calls 'a deep caring for the fundamental values of the search for truth and the pursuit of knowledge'. The White Paper also espouses a performative view of quality (DE 1997:13) undergirded by crucial notions of efficiency, effectiveness and relevance (Van Vught 1995:199) defined narrowly in cost terms or 'functioning without waste' (DE 1997:21). This is illustrated by some of the definitions of quality contained in a recent document produced by the South African University Vice Chancellors Association (cf SAUVCA 1997:5-6) which include:

- *The IS (9000) concept approach to quality in terms of a product which is being delivered to customers and quality is evaluated against customer satisfaction.* This concept is not without grave difficulties, however, since the concepts of a product and the customer cannot be extrapolated from the world of commerce or industry to the school without considerable adaption.

- *The concept of quality in terms of value for money.* This concept is particularly popular among providers of funding such as government and donors to educational institutions. According to this model, quality is measured in terms of performance indicators (or quality indicators) such as student pass rates and teacher-student ratios.

- *The concept of quality as the quest for zero defect.* Here comparison is made to certain pre-ordained standards.

- *The concept of quality according to ratings.* In this approach certain institutions are identified as maintaining high standards such as exceptional pass rates in examinations or research outputs. Institutions are then rated and ratings are often published. Other institutions would compare themselves to these role models.

- *The concept of quality in terms of the idea of fitness for purpose.* This definition is commonly used in education. An institution is asked to formulate its mission and goals within its own particular context and is then evaluated against these. Related to this idea is the concept of fitness of purpose. According to this approach the institution's mission, goals and objectives are evaluated against national policies, regional requirements and societal expectations.

- *The concept of quality in the sense of transformation processes and equity issues.* This concept is particularly popular in South Africa where education is called to transform its structures, content and processes from that of the previous political regime. In terms of equity and issues of redress, quality of educational institutions may be measured by the number of disadvantaged staff and students and the presence and effectiveness of developmental programmes to assist these people.

Similar to overseas models, quality assurance in South African universities is to be driven by external audits which will allow for appraisal in terms of institutional mission and vision and strategic planning done within the unique context of the institution.

This development of a new context for academic quality is quite comprehensible after a reading of Lyotard (1984:46) who anticipated that in a post-industrial society the university's goal fast becomes the best input/output equation. In this respect, the convergence of the White Paper (DE 1997:21) with international policy is striking and introduces South African higher education to a quality performatively defined and operationalised through self-assessment and external audits. In the US, Europe, East Asia and South America, similar systems already in place have rapidly led to a vast corpus of literature and a lucrative quality industry manned by civil servants and consultants who conduct and advise on university audits (Van Vught 1995:204) also making staggering demands on the time and energy of academics. If the enthusiasm for the new context for quality can be judged by the fact that implementation of university audits in South Africa have been one of the first recommendations of the White Paper to be implemented, then South African higher education has embraced quality with vigour. This demonstrates that higher education in South Africa together with many other university systems has entered 'the age of disenchantment ... in which society is no longer prepared to accept that higher education is self-justifying and wishes to expose the activities of the secret garden' (Barnett 1992:216).

8.4.4 Massification

The quest for quality in higher education is partly an outflow of the massification of higher education which took place mainly in the industrialised countries in the 1960s and appeared in most Third World countries in later decades. The American system was one of the world's first systems to make the transition from the élite to the masses successfully. Massification refers to the extraordinary growth in enrolments which marked the transition from élitist education to mass education and eventually, in some countries, to universal higher education. Higher education has traditionally served as an important means whereby young people joining adult society are filtered for different employment positions and, in large measure thereby, for the life opportunities which accompany them. It was hoped that widening access to higher education would create greater social quality and stimulate upward mobility particularly for groups that had been excluded such as manual working class and certain minority communities (Duke 1997:26). Statistics give us an idea of the extent of the result of massification: worldwide the number of students in higher education was 29,2 million in 1970; 58,4 million in 1988; and in 1990 appeared to be about 61 million. In other words enrolments more than doubled within two decades. Massification of higher education in South Africa is also referred to by the White Paper (DE 1997) as a desirable goal for South Africa particularly in relation to the redress of disadvantaged groups who were historically prevented from optimising educational opportunities.

It was rapid growth in higher education and consequent expansion that alerted governments to concerns about preserving high quality on massively and rapidly expanded systems. Massification has diverted university budgets and resources towards teaching at the expense of research and produced an assortment of degrees which, because of the large numbers of graduates, have become devalued in the marketplace. This growth has also contributed to unemployment since many graduates are unable to find employment. In many cases large numbers of undergraduate students find themselves in overcrowded conditions in which they are not given sufficient support in making the transition from secondary to higher education and thus drop out of the system. Since the 1960s many traditional universities have not been able to cope with the extraordinary growth in the demand for higher education and the emergence and implementation of lifelong education and recurrent education. The creation of open universities and distance education emerged to offer people a chance to improve education without following the traditional university path.

8.4.5 Corporate managerialism and its effect on academe

The cumulative effect of economic imperatives, state offloading, marketisation of universities and a new ideology of quality while widening access to larger and larger numbers of students brings irresistible pressure to bear on universities to adopt business-like modes of internal operation. It is not surprising that since the 1980s a 'managerial revolution' has swept higher education throughout the world. The corporate model is a rational, output-orientated, plan-based view of organisational reform which embraces the management values and techniques of business and industry (Taylor et al. 1997:81). Corporate values, procedures and management techniques and a bottom-line budgeting mentality, it is argued, will make universities more cost effective and productive, in other words able to 'do more with less'. Accountancy procedures, planning and control techniques and cost benefit analyses become tools in the hands of institutional administrators (Watson, Mogdil & Mogdil 1997a:xvi). Managerialism pervasively infiltrates the metaphor, symbols and language of both national policy and university discourse. Consider the new policy lexicon which includes such terms: core business, re-engineering, retooling, multi-skilling, products, packages, sponsors, clients and user charges. Academic leaders are replaced by line managers; vice chancellors become chief executive officers; management boards evolve alongside senates and councils (Taylor et al. 1997:91). But borrowed robes fit uneasily and as even the most ardent disciple of can-do managerialism must admit, universities are not entirely similar to business firms. According to Duderstadt (1995:44), professor of nuclear engineering charged with strengthening links between industry and science at the Massachusetts Institute of Technology (MIT), 'the simple and very persuasive injunction [to adopt business modes] translates into something a lot more complicated in the context of universities'.

Finally, this corporatist revision of higher education transforms the way institutions are run and impacts on the personal working lives of individual academics. It is here that what Cowen (1996b:255) terms 'the daily, lived experience of performativity' affects academics most powerfully. The changing academic ethos reported from many parts of the world is most familiar. Universities report a widespread demoralisation of academic staff (Smythe 1995:74). Time for scholarship and research is eroded by the demands made by financial and institutional management, demands for which many academics do not have either the training or the propensity (Adelman 1997:84).

The detailed measurement of performance of individual academics, departments and institutions by means of performance indicators shifts the academic culture of collegiality to a management culture where people and organisations often find themselves trapped by incentive systems (Veld, Fussel & Neave 1996:79). Workload distribution is carefully measured and job evaluation and performance appraisals systems wrested from the business world are applied in academe. Academics are being tempted to withdraw from community service or to diminish teaching responsibilities in order to devote more time to the measurable products of research. Where institutional efficiency is equated with reduced running costs, rationalisation and retrenchment operations have become a litany of academic life worldwide (Peters 1992:124). In many instances this has led to the splitting of the academic profession into a core of full-time workers and a larger group of part-time workers functioning via short-term contracts who pose a much cheaper option (Cheng 1996:213). Bertelsen (1998:135) points out that while South African academics agree on the need for institutional transformation, there is insufficient debate about the manner in which the change is being effected. The virtual revolution in the university culture in this country, as in others around the world, is being superheated by administrators who have adopted the business model to define and drive the process of change.

8.5 Teacher education and training

In many education systems worldwide there is as an ongoing debate about the role of the teacher and the place and content of teacher preparation. The debate, both in developing countries and the industrialised world, has concerned the location of teacher education within the system of higher education as well as the content of teacher education. When it is considered that generally teachers' salaries consume between 75% and 95% of the education budget, it is obvious that governments have a particular interest in the efficacy of teacher education. Moreover, as teachers acquire years of service they become more expensive. This principle operates in all societies. Typical questions raised among policy-makers are whether training should be prior to a teacher commencing practice in a school or whether it should be in-service while teaching occurs; whether it should be based in higher education, either through specialised teacher education institutions such as colleges of education or through university departments of education; and whether the content of teacher education should focus on pedagogical training with the emphasis on classroom and school practice or whether there should be a weighty input of general education and theory (Watson, Mogdil & Mogdil 1997b:ix).

In most countries teacher education is coupled in some way with higher education. In Germany training is in two phases the first of which is university-based and concerned with subject study. This stage takes a minimum of three years and is followed by two years of professional training organised in regional training centres working closely with training schools. The professional phase is controlled by each separate *Land* ministry of education. In the United States a series of reports on teacher education reflect concerns about the preparation of teachers, many of them focusing on the location of teacher education within the university. Departments of education in universities are often criticised as being removed from the concerns of classroom teachers; educational research is either not useful enough to influence practitioners or not of good enough quality to command the respect of academic scholars and there has been little success in developing durable models of teacher training. This has led to a move to reform and develop the role of the university in teacher education rather than supplant its involvement. This view of teacher training as an integral part of the university is based on the view that teaching is a complex activity requiring highly developed approaches to preparation. So it appears that the direction that teacher training takes in most countries is towards the involvement of higher education rather than away from it (Blake 1997:103).

In Europe there has been a tendency to assign a fundamental role to the universities in the education and training of teachers. A general pattern in the development of teacher training can be illustrated by what has happened over decades in the Netherlands. The training of primary teachers moved from an apprenticeship model through to normal schools run by teachers and principals, to the creation of teacher education colleges from 1935 onwards. In 1967 these colleges were renamed 'pedagogical academies' in an endeavour to raise the status of teacher education. In the 1970s there was criticisms that the teacher education programmes were too theoretical and emphasised method and pedagogy at the cost of subject knowledge. By 1984 the number of teacher education centres had been halved and almost all were incorporated into large institutes of higher vocation education. Similarly in France the formation of the *Institute Universitaire de Formation des Mitres* brought together the training of all teachers in institutions of university rank. In Canada the control of teacher education by the universities is a comparatively recent development. It has been argued that the involvement of universities in teacher education has raised the status of teaching in Canada. All teachers have degrees and this raises the esteem in which teachers are held (cf Blake 1997:105).

8.5.1 Change in teacher education in South Africa

South Africa has never had a coherent national policy on teacher development or governance. As a result of its apartheid history there were 17 different employing authorities for teachers and a range of different institutions and procedures to manage them when the first democratic elections were held in 1994. Furthermore the system of teacher education was fragmented and racially and regionally determined. Teacher education in South Africa has primarily been provided by teachers' training colleges or colleges of education which fell under the administration of the former four provinces prior to 1994. In addition to teacher training colleges, faculties or schools of education at universities as well as the technikons under the national department of education have also trained teachers. The number of teacher training colleges proliferated dramatically during the 1980s in an attempt to address the educational crisis of the apartheid era. The vast majority of newly established colleges catered for African students as part of the previous government's attempts to upgrade teacher education in racially segregated institutions. These colleges were often inefficient and cost-ineffective (Claassen 1995). Moreover, in-service teacher education has not been guided by any coherent policy. Education departments, non-governmental organisations (NGOs), distance education institutions and the private sector provide in-service teacher training (INSET) often in association with teacher organisations. As a result of these problems the need to reconstruct policies of teacher development, utilisation and supply became evident.

However, the process of policy development was hampered by a general lack of comprehensive, recent and comparable data on teacher demand and supply and the provision of teacher education in the countries. In the light of this need the first national teacher audit was held in this country. The National Teacher Audit completed in 1995 transcended racial, regional, departmental and institutional divisions (Hofmeyr & Hall 1996). The National Teacher Audit thus provided a much-needed database from which policy planning for teacher development could be launched. Contrary to popular opinion, the Audit disclosed that there was actually an oversupply of teachers in South Africa. In 1994 the total output of newly qualified teachers from all teacher education institutions was approximately 26 000. The oversupply of teachers was observed to be most acute in the Northern Province, Gauteng and the Western Cape. This situation is intensified by the low national attrition rate of teachers which was only 6% per annum at the time of the Audit.

At present the system of teacher education is under review. In this regard the *White Paper on Transformation of Higher Education* (1997) and the discussion document on National Policy on Teacher Supply, Utilisation and Development (DE 1996) recommend that teacher education should be seen as a unified field which should be located in the system of higher education. This new development has already led to the closing of several teacher training colleges and the planned incorporation of these into the system of university governance. Thus, the location of teacher education is envisaged as a single system of higher education, although teacher education is placed somewhat ambiguously between national and provincial administration depending on whether the programmes are offered by college or university.

Furthermore, the content of teacher education programmes required reform. The ideology of apartheid had a major influence on teacher education and was mainly expressed in the philosophy of Christian National Education. This philosophy propagated a segregationist, authoritarian approach to education which dominated the relevant curriculum. According to the discussion document on National Policy on Teacher Supply, Utilisation and Development (DE 1996), in the new educational dispensation teacher education should be based on the five basic principles underlying education according to the 1996 Constitution. These are: global and national relevance, learner centredness, professionalism, co-operation and collegiality, and innovation. Furthermore, an integrated approach to the policies for teacher supply, utilisation and development is recommended. This will require close co-operation between those engaged in teacher education and in conditions of service. The curriculum for both teacher education and in-service education could be congruent with another policy initiative: norms and standards as proposed by the newly established National Qualifications Framework and the Committee on Teacher Education Policy (COTEP) (1998). The curriculum should include training for Early Childhood Education, Adult Basic Education and Training, Workplace Education and Education for Learners with Special Needs. A coherent funding strategy should be devised for teacher education. According to this policy, mechanisms to define quality and quality-assurance procedures for all educators would be put into place. Finally capacity building i.e. the development of the necessary knowledge, attitudes and skills is required by staff in the system of teacher education at provincial and national levels.

In particular, COTEP calls for the adaptation of courses for teacher education over a period of four years to the new norms and standards for teacher education. COTEP also made important recommendations regarding the governance for teacher education to the National Commission on Higher Education and has conducted a situation analysis of all teacher education institutions in order to develop a database for future planning. The norms and standards for a teacher education document constitutes a radical departure from previous policy on teacher education. The norms and standards are based on competences presented in the form of outcomes and will be brought into line with the

National Qualifications Framework which is linked to roles for teachers. All teacher educators are faced with the formidable task of recasting their syllabi and curricula in terms of the outcomes (DE 1996:1). Principles guiding teacher education curricula are: sensitivity to the diverse contexts in which teachers work; lifelong learning which seeks to increase access to education across a lifespan; congruence of teacher education curricula with the principles of the Constitution and greater articulation among teacher education programmes.

8.6 A new context for higher education

This chapter has outlined the new international context in which higher education, in particular the university, functions – a context which is most relevant to the development of higher education in South Africa. The *White Paper on Higher Education Transformation* and the Higher Education Act comprise a rigorous endeavour to construct an own educational policy, but it simultaneously mirrors a globalising post-modern condition and endorses performativity, both in spirit and intent. According to Cowen (1996b:256) international patterns of higher education in the context of a late modern/post-modern world leave a university attenuated in all its functions. As the non-university technical and vocational sectors are retitled and absorbed into the higher education system, the university ceases to be the apex of that system and carries no major cultural messages. Its students are no longer apprentices to be immersed in intellectual fields, but become consumers and demanders of education whose choices of knowledge packages are determined by the whims of the marketplace. The university's pedagogic purposes are dominated by the transmission of occupationally useful knowledge and its mode of existence is entrepreneurial (Cowen 1996a:161).

In the light of this scholars urge university presidents, rectors and vice chancellors to seize the high moral ground and redefine and recapture the university's essential calling (Watson 1992; Kerr 1994). Perhaps, others optimistically suggest, a solution to the university's dilemma will lie in a new synergistic plurality of goals: teaching, research, service and – equal to these – economic development. The latter acquisition, they propose, is non-threatening. It constitutes only another revolutionary extension of the university's functions, just as the Humboltian paradigm of the late nineteenth century added the function of research to the teaching university; and civil rights awareness of the 1960s contributed the function of community service (Van Glinkel 1995:17).

Furthermore, at the heart of the worldwide debate about the relationship between teacher education and higher education lies the status of teaching as a profession. Many criticise the influence of higher education arguing that it has developed as an over-academic, theoretical curriculum that is remote from the actual needs of teachers in the classroom. On the other hand there are defenders

191

of the role higher education plays in teacher education who argue that progress has been made in developing good training programmes characterised by intellectual rigour and practical insights. A key trend today is the growing tendency for governments to seek control over initial teacher training programmes in order to control the intake of new teachers into the state's teaching corps and to align this intake with market needs. This is also true in South Africa. However, what has become clear to policy-makers is that where teacher education is decoupled from the university, it has severe implications for the status of the profession. Over-emphasis on practical teaching skills and the distancing of teacher education from the university does lead to a loss of status in the profession and a failure to attract candidates of an appropriate quality and can thus endanger the quality of teaching itself (Blake 1997:112).

References

Adelman, C (1997) Judging quality in higher education: towards bureaucratic conformity. In K Watson (ed) *Educational dilemmas: debate and diversity Vol 1.* London: Cassell.

Barnett, R (1992) *Improving higher education.* London: SRHE.

Bertelsen, E (1998) The real transformation: the marketisation of higher education. *Social Dynamics,* 24:2:130-158.

Bloland, HG (1995) Postmodernism and higher education. *Journal of Higher Education,* 66(5):521-559.

Brady, V (1988) The long perspective. *Australian society,* 29-30:54-55.

Blake, D (1997) The place of higher education in teacher preparation. In K Watson (ed) *Educational dilemmas: debate and diversity Vol 1.* London: Cassell.

Castells, M (1994) The university system: engine of development in the new world economy. In J Salmi and AM Verspoor (eds) *Revitalising higher education.* Oxford: Pergamon Press.

Cheng, K (1996) The evaluation of the higher education system of Hong Kong. In R Cowen (ed) *The yearbook of education: the evaluation of higher education systems.* London: Kegan Paul.

Claassen, C (1995) The education system of South Africa. In EI Dekker and OJ van Schalkwyk (eds) *Modern education systems.* Second edition. Durban: Butterworths.

Committee on Teacher Education Policy (COTEP) (1998) *Norms and standards for teacher education.* Pretoria: Department of Education.

Cowen, R (1996a) Last past the post: comparative education, modernity and perhaps post-modernity. *Comparative Education Review,* 32(2):151-170.

Cowen, C (1996b) Performativity, post-modernity and the university. *Comparative Education Review*, 32(2):245-258.

Department of Education (1996) An agenda of possibilities: national policy on teacher supply, utilisation and development. Discussion document.

Department of Education (1997) Draft White Paper on Higher Education. *Government Gazette*, 382 (17944).

Dill, DD and Sporn, B (eds) (1995) *Emerging patterns of social demand and university reform: through a glass darkly*. Oxford: Pergamon Press.

Duderstadt, J (1995) Academic renewal at Michigan. In JW Meyerson and WF Massy (eds) *Revitalising higher education*. Princeton: Petersons.

Duke, C (1997) Diversification and élitism in higher education. In K Watson (ed) *Educational dilemmas: debate and diversity Vol 2*. London: Cassell.

Edwards and Usher, R (1994) *Postmodernism and education*. New York: Routledge.

Geiger, R (1995) The future of the humanities. In DD Dill and B Sporn (eds) *Emerging patterns of social demand and university reform: through a glass darkly*. Oxford: Pergamon Press.

Gibbons, M (1995) The university as an instrument for the development of science and basic research. In DD Dill and B Sporn (eds) *Emerging patterns of social demand and university reform: through a glass darkly*. Oxford: Pergamon Press.

Hofmeyr, J and Hall, G (1996) *The national teacher education audit*. Pretoria: Department of Education.

Kerr, C (1994) *Higher education cannot escape history*. New York: Suny.

Lyotard, JF (1984) *The postmodern condition: A report on knowledge*. Manchester: University Press.

Neave, G (1995) The stirring of the prince and the silence of the lambs. The changing assumptions beneath higher education policy, reform and society. In DD Dill and B Sporn (eds) *Emerging patterns of social demand and university reform: through a glass darkly*. Oxford: Pergamon Press.

Noah, H (1984) The use and abuse of comparative education. *Comparative Education Review*, 28(4):550-562.

Nowotny, H (1995) Mass higher education and social mobility. In DD Dill and B Sporn (eds) *Emerging patterns of social demand and university reform: through a glass darkly*. Oxford: Pergamon Press.

OECD (1983) *Universities under scrutiny*. Paris: OECD.

OECD (1987) *Structural adjustment and economic performance*. Paris: OECD.

193

Peters, M (1992) Performance and accountability in post industrial society: the crisis of British universities. *Studies in Higher Education*, 17(2):123-139.

Rothblatt, S (1995) An historical perspective on the university role in social development. In DD Dill and B Sporn (eds) *Emerging patterns of social demand and university reform: through a glass darkly*. Oxford: Pergamon Press.

Rust, VD (1991) Postmodernism and its comparative education implications. *Comparative Education Review*, 35(4):610-626.

Smythe, J (1995) Higher education policy reform in Australia: an expansive analysis. In JE Mauch and PLW Sabloff (eds) *Reform and change in higher education: international perspectives*. London: Garland.

Snow, CP (1959) *The two cultures and the scientific revolution*. Cambridge: Cambridge University Press.

South African University Vice-Chancellors' Association (SAUVCA) (1997) Quality manual. Pretoria: Department of Education.

Taylor, S; Rizvi, F; Lingard, B and Henry, M (1997) *Educational policy and the politics of change*. London: Routledge.

Usher, R; Byrant, I and Johnston, R (1997) *Adult education and the postmodern challenge*. New York: Routledge.

Van Glinkel, H (1995) University 2050: The organisation of creativity and innovation. *Higher Education Policy*, (94):14-18.

Van Vught, F (1995) The new context for academic quality. In DD Dill and B Sporn (eds) *Emerging patterns of social demand and university reform: through a glass darkly*. Oxford: Pergamon Press.

Veld, R; Fussel, HP and Neave, G (1996). *Relations between state and higher education*. The Hague: Kluwer.

Watson, K (1992) Towards a reassessment of higher education. *Comparative Education*, 28(3):316-317.

Watson, K; Mogdil, C and Mogdil, S (1997a) Tradition and change in higher education: Have the managers triumphed over the academics? In K Watson (ed) *Educational dilemmas: debate and diversity Vol 2*. London: Cassell.

Watson, K; Mogdil, C and Mogdil, S (1997b) Should teachers be educated or trained? The ongoing debate. In K Watson (ed) *Educational dilemmas: debate and diversity Vol 1*. London: Cassell.

CHAPTER 9

ASPECTS OF LIFELONG LEARNING

Prof Louis J. van Niekerk
University of South Africa

Table of contents

9.1 Introduction

It can be asked whether lifelong learning is really a new phenomenon. One could argue that lifelong learning is a new 'myth' created to provide hope to a generation which has become increasingly cynical about the so-called Utopia which technology was to have established. However, the notion of lifelong education was first used as early as the 1920s in the educational literature of the English-speaking world. The tradition of adult education, a related concept, appeared as far back as the 1800s in Northern Europe. Impetus was given to the trend of providing lifelong learning by the international conference on Adult Education held by UNESCO in 1960 which sought to promote adult education in a global context. The growing commitment to adult education gave rise to the concept of lifelong education which began increasingly to be used internationally in the 1970s (Sutton 1994:3417). During the 1970s and 1980s major international organisations gave attention to the promotion of lifelong learning. During the early 1990s, greater emphasis was given to the provision of universal basic education. However, the need for a learning society which can cope with changing workplace patterns and rapid technological change has shifted the focus again to lifelong learning (Sutton 1994:3419).

9.1.1 The terminology of lifelong learning

A survey of literature over the past 30 years or so would indicate that what has become known as 'lifelong learning' can be discussed under different headings. In this regard the following terms have been used to describe aspects of lifelong learning:

- vocational training
- adult education and training
- continuing education
- learning across the lifespan
- community education
- lifelong education
- permanent education.

This variety of terminology used to describe the field, however, should not be seen purely as a matter of semantics. Shifts in emphasis and differing theoretical frameworks require a different vocabulary in order to focus the attention of students on particular aspects. Most of these terms are still used within specific contexts depending on which aspect of lifelong learning is emphasised. According to Sutton (1994:3420), different terms form a spectrum. This commences with the concept of lifelong education which embodies the vision of a learning society in which education is accessible to all and is provided in a variety of formal, nonformal and informal settings. Lifelong learning includes the idea of the development of the capacity for self-learning. Recurrent education focuses on creating the opportunities for lifelong learning and seeks to remove the obstacles of formal institutions, structures and funding. Continuing education refers more narrowly to post-initial courses paid for by government, employers and learners. Adult education has been revitalised by the perceptions of these concepts and frequently subsumes them. More recently the Report to UNESCO of the International Commission on Education for the Twenty-first Century, also entitled *Learning: the treasure within* (1996), introduced the descriptor 'learning throughout life' rather than 'lifelong learning'.

Different viewpoints concerning education lead to different interpretations of these concepts. A capitalist approach would propose that lifelong learning allows the individual to remain competitive throughout his or her lifespan. Critical theorists would probably argue that lifelong learning is a form of exploitation of the labour force, especially when the learning emphasis is predominantly on skills training aimed at increasing economic productivity. A liberal viewpoint would describe lifelong learning in terms of the continued emancipation of humankind whereas a hermeneutic (one who seeks to gain a better understanding of human existence) might interpret lifelong learning as a means to continue the lasting search for meaning.

9.2 Teaching for lifelong learning

Lifelong learning is based on the view that education does not cease once an individual has finished school or has obtained a diploma or degree. In this respect it is interesting to investigate the origin of the term 'degree'. In ancient times a circle – consisting of 360 degrees – symbolised completeness and fullness. A degree or number of degrees would therefore indicate that the student has not yet attained 'fullness' or absolute knowledge. It was accepted that there would always be unanswered questions. It should also be characteristic of learned people to show humility in their awareness of how little they actually know.

The assumption that learning takes place throughout life and is not confined to childhood and adolescence nor to educational institutions (Sutton 1994:3416) contrasts sharply with the epistemology that emerged during the Enlightenment (the age of reason) which viewed knowledge as static. This assumed that there was a body of knowledge that one could access through study and that the more one studied, the more one would know. It was also assumed that, if not the individual, then at least humankind in general would one day know everything there is to know.

The realisation that learning and education are lifelong endeavours has become more acute as a result of the increasing complexity of modern and post-modern society together with the so-called 'information age' and the concomitant information technologies which have been developed. Change is thrust upon society and the ever-increasing demands of life lead to fragmentation of experiences and interpretation of realities. The challenge to the individual is not only to survive but to live life meaningfully in terms of a set of values to which he or she subscribes as a member of a community. The function of lifelong learning is to enable a person, an organisation, a community or even a nation to adapt to a changing environment and to different needs and demands which are the result of a worldwide paradigm shift about the nature of knowledge. This shift in the way we perceive, think and talk about reality even affects our ideas about knowledge. In the UNESCO Report (1996:85) it is stated:

> It is not enough to supply each child early in life with a store of knowledge to be drawn on from then on. Each individual must be equipped to seize learning opportunities throughout life, both to broaden her or his knowledge, skills and attitudes, and to adapt to a changing, complex and interdependent world.

That there is a close relationship between knowledge and power to the point of stating that knowledge *is* power has long been known. If this is so, then those who control access to knowledge are powerful and have an advantage over those who do not. Education must therefore prepare learners to acquire the knowledge needed not only to survive, but also to live a meaningful life. Meaning is therefore closely associated with one's ability to exercise a degree of control over one's own life. One might assume that the acquisition of knowledge in the information age is a simple process as technology in its varied forms makes information readily available. Yet there is a distinction between information and knowledge. The ability to access information does not necessarily lead to the acquisition of knowledge. In much the same way, one could argue that being able to read does not necessarily mean that all texts will be meaningful to the reader. Lifelong learning is closely associated with the learner's ability to interpret textual information and to relate it to a particular situation or context. The different spheres of life which represent different contexts will require of a person to be able to continually readjust or adapt to new situations. Learning can never stop because it is about discovering new ways of living, reinventing roles, demythologising grand narratives (assumptions and beliefs) and liberating one's mind from oppressive ideas.

In this vein, Paulo Freire (1972) indicated in his work *Pedagogy of the Oppressed* that the notion of 'banking' knowledge for future use is no longer applicable. 'Banking' in this sense refers to accumulating knowledge to be used later in life. If one allows long-held assumptions or beliefs to dictate the way one thinks, one becomes one's own worst oppressor. Lifelong learning concerns democratising knowledge and thus avoiding being at the mercy of 'experts' who propose solutions. It leads to understanding one's own context and discovering solutions to problems that affect oneself. It opposes rigidity and proposes fluidity in our thinking. Realising that there is more than one solution to any given problem is essential.

9.2.1 A curriculum for lifelong learning

The notion of lifelong learning should be seen as a principle underlying curriculum development in any field and the challenge is to find ways to incorporate it into the curriculum. According to the UNESCO Report (1996) all education is built on the following four pillars:

- learning *to know*
- learning *to do*
- learning *to live together* and learning *to live with others*
- learning *to be*.

These four broad themes should also provide the cross-curricular content for lifelong learning.

Learning to know would enable the learner to combine 'a sufficiently broad general knowledge with the opportunity to work in depth on a small number of subjects. This also means learning to learn, so as to benefit from the opportunities education provides throughout life' (UNESCO Report 1996:97). A broad general knowledge allows the learner to interpret information intelligently. The report does not denigrate the role of the specialist but warns against the kind of specialist who is unable to relate activities in one field to those in another. Consider, for example, the roles technologists and environmentalists play in society. It is important for technologists to be aware of the impact of technology on the environment. In the same way, environmentalists need to understand the constructive use of technology to rectify the negative effects of human behaviour on the environment. Learning to know is also about realising and having the courage to acknowledge that one does not know and questioning previously attained knowledge.

Learning to do relates specifically to the world of work and emphasises learning as an economic activity. In this respect, lifelong leaning is described in terms of vocational training and career development. Workers need to acquire the necessary skills and terms such as 'multi-skilling' and 're-skilling' should become part of the vocabulary of the workplace. However, learning to do should not be narrowly and simply viewed only in terms of vocational training and the acquisition of occupational skills. It refers more broadly to 'the competence to deal with many situations and work in teams. It also means learning to do in the context of young people's various social and work experiences which may be informal, as a result of the local or national context, or formal, involving courses, alternating study and work' (UNESCO Report 1996:97).

In a learning programme where commercial preferences supersede other values the focus in providing learning experiences would be on cost-efficiency, functional skills and performance. In this context Lyotard (1984) coined the term *performativity* to describe the human behaviour that is most valued. Governments who seek to develop the economies of their countries could apply the curriculum as an instrument in the achievement of performativity. The curriculum is then accorded an instrumental role. Learning activities would be designed to promote learning performance in a particular area. Learning 'by doing' in this context means that learners should be able to demonstrate their competence in doing a task.

Learning to live together would naturally focus on the values that govern interpersonal behaviour. The UNESCO Report states this ability is 'developed by an understanding of other people and an appreciation of interdependence – carrying out joint projects and learning to manage conflicts – in the respect for the values of pluralism, mutual understanding and peace' (1996:97). However, an over-idealistic view of this principle should be avoided. By learning to live together one should also be aware of the power relations that underlie and affect the way humans behave towards each other. Although pluralism allocates equal status to differing viewpoints and advocates tolerance for views that are different from one's own, tolerance tends to wear thin where conflicting interests are at stake. Once a group or person is marginalised and starts to feel threatened by a dominant group, conflict could arise. Mere 'conflict resolution' is often inadequate in addressing the issue of disturbed power relations where a person or group feels that they are being discriminated against. There are many examples of minorities being treated unequally in spite of so-called minority rights. An example of this is women's struggle for equal rights. Cultural influences on the role of women in society is so strong that many have come to adopt and accept roles in which they are exploited. Lifelong learning would require of them and all other minorities to critically reflect on their position and to 'unlearn' behaviour associated with subordination.

Learning to be is closely related to learning to live together. While interdependence is the core value in learning to live together, learners have to take responsibility for their own learning and become independent learners. Learning to be is seen by the UNESCO Report as the ability to 'develop one's personality and be able to act with ever greater autonomy, judgement and personal responsibility' (1996:97). It proposes a holistic approach in that '... education must not disregard any aspect of a person's potential: memory, reasoning, aesthetic sense, physical capacities and communication skills' (UNESCO Report 1996:97). Although freedom of individual expression is highly valued in Western civilisation, individuals do not have absolute freedom. They continually relate to someone else which is called the relationship of the self to the other. This can be illustrated by people's use of public roads. Both pedestrians and drivers form part of the traffic and must accommodate other road users. The relationship with other users is determined by the right of others to be road users too. It is based on mutual understanding and respect for the other which forms the rationale for a complex set of rules which governs the behaviour of road users. Similarly, every individual plays many different roles. For example, a man can simultaneously be a father, a son, a brother, an employer or employee. Each role is regulated by different rules or expected behaviour patterns.

9.2.2 Curriculum change and lifelong learning

A curriculum that encourages learners to participate in the process of knowledge production will empower them to become lifelong learners with the emphasis on 'learning to learn'. This approach represents a shift from a so-called product-orientated curriculum to a process-orientated curriculum.

In the *product-orientated curriculum* the learning content was presented to the learners as the result of research carried out by specialists elsewhere. The learners had to study the content and make it their own regardless of their context or situation. Very often, learners had great difficulty in understanding the content simply because it did not make sense to them. They consequently resorted to merely memorising the 'facts' which would then be reproduced in an examination. Cognitive activities such as understanding, application and critical evaluation in most instances merely reflected the teacher's conceptualisation.

In the *process-orientated curriculum* the learning activities constitute the learning content. The emphasis is on the skills required to produce knowledge. Although there is no clear definition of a skill one can accept that this refers to the ability to do something and includes concepts such as method and methodology, technique and technology (cf Spector 1993). For example, in a subject like biology, the ability to observe would be described as a skill. In the study of the grasshopper as an insect, the grasshopper would represent a specimen or example of an insect. The teacher would demonstrate certain features that all insects have in common and indicate what to look for when the learners come across insects. Acquiring the skill to observe could eventually lead to a heightened awareness of the role of insect life in our environment. Without this skill, learners could easily acquire the view that all insects are 'bugs' that harm humans and should be exterminated. This presupposition, based on previous experience and other people's interpretation of reality, clearly represents a false notion. Acquiring the skill of observation could be the first step in freeing learners from ignorance and setting them on the path towards ecological enlightenment.

It is also clear that in order to develop the skill of observation one has to look at something in a certain way. A skill cannot be practised on its own since it is always related to a particular context. If thinking is regarded as a skill, one has to think about something. Thinking can therefore never be 'content-free'. Applying a skill without proper understanding of its context will result in meaningless activities. In order to be effective, teachers require knowledge of the learner, educational theories, appropriate methodologies, the education system and so on.

Baine and Mwamwenda (1994:116), in their criticism of secondary school curricula, demonstrate quite succinctly that skills form part of a holistic approach to curriculum construction when they state:

> The most common criticism of secondary schools is that they fail to prepare young people for the world of work, and that the students fail to develop essential values, attitudes, respect for self and others, social skills and life skills.

Addressing these needs requires intellectual activity that enables the learner to understand past causes, to evaluate the present situation and to plan how to act in future. It requires of the teacher not merely the presentation of content as facts or values that learners have to acquire and repeat at some future stage, but also the planning and preparation for intellectual activity. By working inductively, that is applying the problem-solving approach, the teacher formulates problems that relate to the learners' field of experience and cognitive development. In this context teaching should become the science of discovery and invention. De Beer (1994:2) suggests that a better understanding of education can be acquired by clarifying one's views regarding culture, knowledge and thought. He analyses the dimensional character of culture and identifies one outstanding aspect of it which he calls 'the convivial' – being together. In science which produces knowledge the emphasis should be on conscience. Real knowledge is shared knowledge. Thought should be contemplative rather than calculating. Education should create an awareness in learners of the relationship between language and meaning. We should have learners who are conversant – not education as/for reproduction, but as/for inventiveness. To echo De Beer (1994:9), a post-modern approach to learning should foster learners who are convivial, conscientious, contemplative, conversant, and willing to confront problems and to improvise.

In recent years there have been moves to democratise curriculum construction by involving all those who have an interest in the curriculum. This means teachers, parents and learners alike. Adult learners who are involved in lifelong learning are no longer willing to enrol for courses that do not cater for individual needs and preferences and nor do they appreciate an authoritarian approach by teachers or lecturers. Participation in curriculum construction is titled the 'socio-constructivist perspective' where a curriculum is the result of negotiation by stakeholders. It is hoped that curricula that are developed in this way will serve the needs and aspirations of particular communities. Curricula will have to be contextualised in order to address the problems, topics and issues that face a society. According to Spector (1993:9-19) a curriculum that is built on a socio-constructivist approach to learning reveals the following characteristics:

- It reduces the amount of content information and does not merely add more facts annually as research produces new information.

- The focus is on processes to develop connections forming conceptual frameworks into which new information may be integrated, rather than to teach content loaded with detail. The emphasis is on holistic concepts.

- Disciplinary boundaries become blurred as content and methods become more trans-disciplinary.

- Instead of the content being selected and organised around the structure of the discipline, it is organised around themes, current issues and real-life problems. The curriculum thus becomes problem-based rather than discipline-based.

- Science is portrayed as a dynamic discipline challenging established truths – science as doing rather than as a set of abstract rules defining reality.

- Learning is seen as scientific enquiry where new meanings are constructed. Scientific activity is regarded as a human endeavour and responsive to human perceptions and interpretation, contrary to the established view of science as impersonal, objective and mechanistic. The scientist is regarded as someone who is empowered to look for answers and solutions to societal problems.

According to Spector (1993:9-19) in teaching a socio-constructivist curriculum, the teacher will:

- be guided by learners' questions and their need to know

- assume that students have pre-knowledge and a frame of reference based on experience

- be sensitive to the values of multiple cultures, races, females and males

- incorporate different ways of knowing and allow for different learning styles and expression

- focus on inquiry and communication rather than drill and practice

- exemplify lines of reason to build theories, rather than focus on the rhetoric of conclusions

- respond to questions, not with closed-ended answers but with questions developing lines of questioning (patterns of reasoning)

- support open-ended activities, active learning and inductive reasoning

- break free from a textbook and worksheet approach to a hands-on/minds-on experience

- create learning experiences rather than present learning content
- devise co-operative learning strategies that foster a collaborative environment and discourage a teacher-dependent attitude.

9.2.3 The role of the teacher in lifelong learning

Dramatic social change requires all people to become lifelong learners. This, together with change in the way knowledge is viewed, has created a new role for the teacher. De Beer (1994:3) elaborates on the dramatic epistemological transformation of the past decades: 'This transformation meant a break with opposites that always consisted of two poles such as good and evil, knowledge and ignorance and accepting that although they are dialectically connected, they are not always positive and negative'. These poles are complementary – not opposing, but different. In the same way teaching is viewed as being either teacher-centred or learner-centred, based either on prescription or self-discovery, content-based or outcomes-based. In the light of a changed view of knowledge, teachers are becoming aware though that there are alternatives to prescriptive teaching. One suggestion is that we speak of an heuristic approach to teaching – the science of discovery and invention. To echo De Beer (1994:9), teachers today should create a learning culture that will foster learners who are convivial, conscientious, contemplative, conversant and willing to confront problems.

The current paradigm shift requires a learner-centred approach and a 'deconstruction' of the teacher's role. Traditionally those involved in education had their task clearly defined: teachers were the experts who made their knowledge available to learners mostly through lecturing. The teacher was seen to be the source of knowledge and the learner the recipient. Teaching practices could therefore be organised around the relationship between the teacher and the learner. This relationship, however, was based on the idea that knowledge could be packaged and presented to learners. It was also governed by a specific power relationship: the teacher as information-giver, the learner as information-receiver. The teacher had the task of transmitting the accrued body of knowledge didactically and learning was equated with reproducing what the teacher wanted. Teaching was also teacher- and content-centred. Learners were not encouraged to question the subject which they were expected to 'make their own'. According to the new paradigm, the teacher must create the conditions for learning and to be instrumental in establishing a learning culture.

This shift in the role of the teacher introduces salient aspects that open up new ways for lifelong learning to take place. Spector (1993:12) summarises this paradigmatic shift in Table 9.1, possibly presenting extreme views in a binary relationship that is not necessarily mutually exclusive. While it may also be argued that this view is reductionist, it focuses on important aspects of the new role of teacher, lecturer or tutor.

Teachers in the still dominant paradigm	Teachers in the new paradigm
• view students as uninformed and naïve.	• view students as equal partners.
• know and transmit best practice.	• collaborate with other teachers as equals to determine options for practice.
• are isolated from other teachers and school personnel.	• are integrally involved with practitioners in schools.
• are housed exclusively in schools or on campuses.	• are housed full- or part-time in schools.
• conduct research individually, frequently isolated from learners.	• conduct collaborative research in schools with teams of teachers.
• work in schools/colleges (faculties), frequently separate from members of staff of other schools/colleges.	• serve as change facilitators, designing and implementing strategies for improvement in university and teacher education. • serve as linking agents and interpreters among national and other professional associations. • establish networks of teacher education centres. • advocate the professionalisation of teaching.
• teach discipline-specific methods separately from discipline content.	• integrate the teaching of discipline-specific methods into discipline content by modelling, reflection and analysis.
• tend to adopt the common teaching strategy: 'Do as I say, not as I do'.	• adopt teaching methods that are congruent with the way learners learn the subject.
• add to learners' collection of segregated facts.	• reflect on an acquired collection of facts to create multiple linkages among concepts and develop and select umbrella concepts.

Table 9.1: The paradigmatic shift in education

9.3 Provision of lifelong learning through open and distance learning

Lifelong learning emphasises the autonomy and independence of the learner. In this context, learners are less teacher-dependent but rely on well-structured learning opportunities that are designed to lend them maximum support. Open and distance learning (also referred to as distance education) is therefore an excellent means to provide the learning needs of lifelong learners. It is often impossible for adult learners to return to school, college or university to resume their studies. These learners cannot be bound by time and place, and should be free to study at their own pace and in their own time.

However, it is not surprising that the organisation of distance education (which evolved from correspondence teaching) as a main provider of lifelong learning also reflected the traditional relationship between teacher and learner. In distance education this meant that the learner was presented with knowledge as text. In large distance education institutions the production of texts evolved into an industry. The need for mass education as well as the lack of personal contact with teachers and lecturers allowed for the use of the media other than print. It is fair to say that in large-scale distance education institutions teaching became 'industrialised' in the sense that the emphasis was on the efficient delivery of study materials to students. A system was set up to process teaching with scant regard for the needs of learners. Everyone involved in the system had a specific task to do. This linear, assembly-line type process started with the teacher as the authority and the author of texts. Teachers therefore occupied positions of power which influenced all power relations in the organisation.

9.3.1 Developments in distance education and the impact on lifelong learning

In more recent years a different model of distance education has developed in which the focus was on the production of high-quality learning materials. The emphasis shifted from the teacher to the content. These institutions are much like publishing houses: a core group of curriculum specialists appoints authors on a contract basis to write materials for the institution. The author forms part of a team that could include a media specialist, language editor, academic editor, graphic artist, instructional designer and so on. The team meets regularly under the guidance of a project manager. The materials developed are usually sent to critical readers for evaluation. This implies that the role of the teacher as author is decentralised: producing learning materials has become a team effort. The teacher is now subsumed in the materials with the aim of providing integrated learner support. Advancements in technology also make it possible to provide multi-media learning packages. Learner support and the marking of assignments are contracted out to a network of tutors. Although these tutors might not necessarily have been members of the course development team, they could be involved in the evaluation of course materials.

In South Africa attention was focused by the National Commission for Higher Education on the growing importance of distance education in the provision of lifelong learning. It seems clear from the NCHE report that resource-based learning will eventually signal the collapse of the traditional sharp distinction between contact and distance education (NCHE 1996:273). In the past distance education was largely based on the transmission of knowledge through correspondence. One could easily be misled into thinking that it is simply a matter of bridging the distance in time and space between learner and lecturer whereas the real distance is between teaching and learning where the learner becomes her or his own teacher. In a new model of distance education a curriculum must be presented that does not, through the practice of textual interpretation, inculcate obedience in the learner. Distance education should be underscored by the principles of open, independent and flexible learning.

9.3.2 Transforming distance education institutions

It has already been mentioned that paradigm shifts in the theory of knowledge require a different approach to teaching and learning. This also applies to distance education curricula. Transformation of the curriculum should form part of institutional transformation in order to qualify as a provider of lifelong learning. The question that follows is how a transformed curriculum would affect the way in which a distance education institution is managed and the impact it would have on organisational structures.

9.3.3 Organisational structure

According to Mackintosh (1997) '... a critical analysis of organisational structures and policy, [necessitates] an analysis of the authority, roles and functions of academic, professional and support departments'. Mackintosh (1997) conducted an investigation into re-engineering the open and distance learning (ODL) materials process at the University of South Africa. He views the paradigm shift characterising education in terms of a shift from an industrial to a post-industrial approach to teaching and learning, especially in ODL. Transformation would therefore imply a move from industrialism to post-industrialism. The practical implications of such a transformation for division of labour and managerial control are shown in Table 9.2.

Industrial	Post-industrial
The teaching-learning process is split into many specialised, centralised, departmental subfunctions, for example writing instructional design, graphic design, scheduling, editing, assessment design, administration, teaching and so on.	Smaller professional working groups, comprising individuals who are multi-skilled in the areas of expertise required in open and distance learning development and provision, work together in project teams.
Centralised administration and managerial control over processes and the characteristic division of labour.	Decentralised administration and managerial control where the professional working groups hold decision-making authority and accountability.

Table 9.2: The implications of transformation

This requires a reconfiguration of the organisational structure to meet the demands of the ODL learning materials process which, in turn, implies the multi-skilling of staff in the ODL materials process. The organisational structure thus becomes more organic and participative. This could be achieved through a matrix-based, decentralised decision-making model. According to Mackintosh (1997) the institution would be 'characterised by task-based project operations, designed to be flexible, dynamic and not permanent'. Although Mackintosh's approach suggests an integration of responsibilities and an overlap of roles, one can still distinguish separate functions.

Rumble (1992) identifies a number of functions of distance education which he describes in terms of organisational structure. In large distance education institutions education becomes industrialised and therefore it becomes important:

> to establish specialist production departments – specialising in print, video, audio, computer-based systems, etc. Warehouses and materials

distribution and mailing facilities need to be set up. Assignment-handling offices are needed. The growth in tutorial staff engenders its own demands for structures to manage recruitment, selection, induction, performance appraisal, career development and discipline. If face-to-face tuition is used, then local facilities have to be identified and tutorials timetabled and put into effect. A local presence is desirable. Production, distribution and presentation need to be scheduled and co-ordinated. And, alongside of all these developments, are the normal functions of financial management and accounting, purchasing, data processing, buildings and estate management, human resource management, personnel, etc. In broad terms, there is a remarkable similarity in the structure adopted by different kinds of distance education institutions. This convergence derives from the common technologies used in distance education systems and the high level of invitation that has taken place as particular distance learning systems have 'exported' their structures to newer institutions. Structural differences can, however, be seen between institution-centred, individual-centred, and community-centred systems. (Rumble 1992:48-49)

Small-scale institutions are more flexible and they are able to outsource many of the functions listed by Rumble. According to Rumble (1992:55) small-scale institutions can, on the whole, focus much more on individual learners – even if they do not subscribe to a learner-centred approach. Such institutions tend to emphasise the interaction between the lecturer and the learner. In some systems, the tutor's role is central as the negotiator and arbitrator of a learning contract with the learner. One of the tutor's main jobs is to direct learners towards appropriate learning materials and experiences and to motivate them once they embark on the programme. In others, the learner has the freedom to 'contract' a tutor's services as and when he or she feels the need. Within a community, a group of people representing a particular interest (non-governmental organisation or foundation) may decide to develop a training programme to meet a specific need. In this regard one may refer to environmental education programmes targeted at specific communities.

In community-centred projects, the facilitator plays a major role in identifying community-based problems and encouraging the formation of study groups. The facilitator may be supported by a co-ordinating body which can arrange for suitable materials to be designed and delivered to support group learning. Alternatively, the facilitator may encourage group members to design their own materials. Very often this results in collaboration with an academic institution which makes its expertise available. The end-result of the process may be an action plan which works at individual, group and community level.

Rumble (1992) makes it clear that there is no single way of organising a distance learning system. The organisational structure appropriate for a small-scale, person-centred distance learning system will be very different from that aimed at a large institution-centred system. An institution-centred system embedded in a dual-mode institution (distance education and face-to-face instruction) is likely to be organised very differently from a single-mode institution. Nevertheless, similar functions will need to be performed and there are, for example, surprising similarities between the structures in the various distance-teaching universities. Generally speaking, the following areas exist:

- Academic faculties, schools and departments responsible for curriculum development and the development of materials. They may be assisted by specialist departments of educational technologists.

- A department which organises the tutorial and other local services provided to learners and enquirers. This usually consists of a small central co-ordinating section and decentralised offices at local level.

- A department dealing with the production of materials in various media, e.g. print, audio and video including editing, design and production of materials.

- A distribution department (warehouses, mailing facilities and so on).

- An administration unit dealing with finance, personnel, data processing, estates and buildings, secretariat and student administration.

Course development, production and distribution can be organised in different ways depending on the needs of the institution. This is a specialised field of study and requires a greater investment of academic time than does, for example, the preparation of a lecture. Sparkes (in Rumble 1992:55) suggests that developing a lecture which requires one hour of student work takes an academic from two to ten hours. Developing a teaching text which takes students the equivalent of one hour's work requires 50 to 100 hours of academic time. Not surprisingly, therefore, developing anything other than a simple course requires an input from a team of people.

Stone (in Rumble 1992:55) suggests that there are four different approaches to the organisation and management of the development phase:

- In the *specialised* approach, the various tasks like curriculum planning, writing, editing, design and so on are allocated to professional staff. Each specialist works on his or her own tasks, the analogy being an assembly line.

- The *chain* approach modifies the specialised approach in as much as each specialist works with the assembly-line specialist immediately preceding or succeeding him or her.

- In the *interdisciplinary team* approach, people from different specialities are brought together and given joint responsibility for the overall development and production of the project or course.

- In the *matrix* approach, projects are staffed by appropriate specialists who are borrowed from functional departments (academic faculty or department, editing, design and so on) to perform specific tasks for the group. Such specialists continue to have a functional responsibility to their parent department, but are responsible on a day-to-day basis to the project head.

The main problems with the specialist approach are those of discontinuities of work, poor communication between specialists and the fact that there may be no integrated overview of the project. These are very likely because the specialists come from widely differing functional groups. The chain approach tries to ameliorate the situation, but only the team and matrix approaches can provide a really satisfactory basis for co-operation and interaction.

Finally, there is the question of checking on the quality of the developers' work. One of the issues faced by distance learning systems is the need to ensure that the course materials are:

- of an academic quality appropriate to the level of the course
- of a pedagogic quality appropriate to the level of the learners
- integrated with any other materials being developed for the course
- acceptable in political, religious or other terms.

9.3.4 Management of tutors and learner support services

Although lifelong learning requires independence and flexibility on the part of learners, adult learners still require support. In the past distance education institutions adopted a 'sink or swim' approach to learners. This attitude is no longer tolerated as learners demand value for money. Institutions have had to provide infrastructure to lend support to learners and these services need to be managed. Thus student services and administration exist to ensure that students are:

- admitted to the institution and enrolled in courses
- allocated to tutors and, where appropriate, counsellors
- told what is expected of them in terms of their formal commitment to the institution (e.g. payment of fees, withdrawal from courses, change of address) and appeals against administrative decisions.

Given the increasing diversity of the learner population in many distance-teaching systems, the kind of advice and help needed by individual learners and enquirers and the level of support required by different individuals will vary enormously. A proportion of learners will have problems which need to be handled individually, and the support system needs to be able to deal with such problems efficiently, effectively and humanely. This has given rise to a new need for tutors who are able to interact with and support learners. All distance learning systems need to provide opportunities for learners to interact with tutors and possibly counsellors (where a separate counselling role is identified). How tutor systems are managed will depend on whether or not the tutors:

- are full-time or part-time employees
- are based on campus or are, like the students, at a distance
- have been involved in the development of the course
- also play a counselling role or whether the two roles are separated.

Rumble (1992:70) indicates that full-time tutors are more easily managed than part-time staff. One crucial aspect is lack of communication and availability of information to part-time tutors. Management will have to set up a system to communicate with tutors regularly and provide capacity building for tutors. Although tutors usually have a thorough knowledge of their subject and some might even have experience of face-to-face teaching, a number of tutors have been or still are school teachers who may adopt a somewhat teacher-centred approach to tutoring. Few of them have had much experience in tutoring learners in ODL.

Freeman (1997:75) highlights the problems surrounding capacity building for tutors when he states: 'Developing these skills in open learning tutors is problematic because tutors tend to be part-time and are usually widely scattered.' Although Freeman (1997:74) indicates that capacity building for tutors should concentrate on what is new in open learning, one should not assume that tutors are able to transfer skills gained from face-to-face teaching experience to open learning. Freeman (1997:75) lists a number of generic skills which a prospective tutor should possess as well as the new skills that need to be developed. One would assume that the best way to build capacity in a tutor for ODL would be to model the process by developing a course that could set an example.

Apart from managing capacity building for tutors, there are also the 'other supporters' who support learners such as administrators, technicians, librarians and so on (Freeman 1997:81). These practitioners play an important role in providing support to the learners. Capacity building for these supporters should follow on a thorough task analysis and job evaluation of their tasks. Freeman (1997:85) compiles a table of staff development methods in terms their strengths, weaknesses and possible purpose. Managing capacity building of distance education practitioners requires a paradigm shift that reflects the shifts in knowledge production from an industrial to a post-industrial paradigm. If there has been a move away from a teacher-centred approach to a more learner-orientated approach, this should also be reflected in the management of ODL institutions. Staff members are also lifelong learners. Accountability to the learners requires them to build the capacity to provide learners with quality learning experiences.

9.4 Lifelong learning in the South African context

The first democratically elected government of South Africa which came into office in 1994 has set about a major reconstruction of education which, among others, focuses pertinently on lifelong learning and the creation of a learning nation. The Constitution of South Africa (1996) states that every citizen has the right to education. As the constitution is underscored by the values of equity, non-racialism, non-sexism and democracy these values must be reflected in the national education programme. The South African Qualifications Authority Act, 1995 (Act 58 of 1995) stipulated that education in South Africa would in future be governed by the National Qualifications Framework (NQF) which will play a vital role in the provision of access to lifelong learning by means of nationally recognised levels on which all learning standards and qualifications will be registered. The NQF is based on a system of credits for learning outcomes achieved. Qualifications may be achieved full-time, part-time, by distance learning, by work-based learning or by a combination of these together with an assessment of prior learning and experience. Tobias (1999:10) claims that the NQF 'will promote and encourage many more people to continue their learning', that 'individuals will have greater control over their learning' and that 'individual learning needs will be met more effectively'.

9.4.1 The National Qualifications Framework and lifelong learning

The NQF translates the ideals of lifelong learning into practice by providing a framework for lifelong learning based on the following principles·

- access
- redress
- integration
- transparency
- quality assurance
- flexibility
- portability
- articulation.

Incorporating these principles into educational programmes should enable South Africans to become a learning nation. The NQF therefore attempts to remove some of the barriers to learning that existed in the past and its existence should be interpreted in terms of the history of South Africa. As such it clearly has a socio-political agenda. The NQF is a social construct and it should be noted that it is not so much the result of a power shift but of a paradigm shift taking place in education all over the world. The four main themes for education identified by UNESCO correspond with the critical outcomes formulated by the South African Qualifications Authority (SAQA). The critical cross-field outcomes, as they are called, are generic, can be contextualised to fit any learning programme and must be included in all qualifications. These outcomes will form an integral part of the NQF which has as its focus the

213

promotion of lifelong learning. The focus is on learner outcomes – knowledge, skills and values – and emphasises what the learner is enabled to do, as opposed to teacher input and content.

In terms of the seven critical cross-field outcomes learners should be enabled to:

- identify and solve problems, and make decisions using critical and creative thinking
- deal effectively with others as members of a team, group, organisation and community
- organise and manage themselves and their activities responsibly and effectively
- collect, analyse, organise and critically evaluate information
- communicate effectively using visual, symbolic, and/or language skills in various modes
- use science and technology effectively and critically, showing responsibility towards environments and the health of others
- demonstrate an understanding of the world as a set of related systems by recognising that problem-solving contexts do not exist in isolation.

In terms of developmental outcomes learners should be enabled to:

- reflect and explore a variety of strategies to learn more effectively
- participate as responsible citizens in the life of local, national and global communities
- be culturally and aesthetically sensitive across a range of social contexts
- explore career opportunities
- explore entrepreneurial opportunities.

Apart from these critical cross-field outcomes, the NQF also distinguishes the following 12 learning areas:

- Agriculture and nature conservation
- Culture and arts
- Business, commerce and management studies
- Communication studies and language
- Education, training and development
- Manufacturing, engineering and technology
- Human and social sciences
- Law, military science and security
- Health sciences and social services
- Physical, mathematical, computer and life sciences

- Services
- Physical planning and construction.

Through the NQF people should be able to embark on lifelong learning. The NQF's intention is to organise education in South Africa in order to provide learning opportunities for everyone. It will structure learning experiences so that learning becomes value-added and does not simply result in a 'paper chase'. Before a qualification can be obtained, learners will have to demonstrate their ability in a particular learning area or field. Assessment of an individual's competence, knowledge or skill will be based on his or her achievement of the specific learning outcomes for that particular learning area or field.

In the past learners had to have a fairly clear idea of what they 'wanted to do one day' because once they had embarked on one course of study it was very difficult to switch to another. Students who wanted to change course and pursue their studies in another field could hardly expect any recognition for qualifications already obtained, let alone courses passed in a certain field. Frequently, institutions would not even recognise a qualification in the same field received from another institution. The autonomy of institutions and faculties limited the options open to students. Similarly, adults who changed jobs or switched careers could hardly expect any recognition for workplace or professional experience attained over a period of time.

Through the NQF individuals will receive recognition for any previous effort, experience or qualifications. Achieving equity will, as a matter of necessity, require a systems approach to track different learning paths. In this regard the NQF structures education into eight levels which are subdivided into the following three bands:

- General Education and Training (GET)
- Further Education and Training (FET)
- Higher Education and Training (HET).

Each of the levels and bands are structured to suit their own unique requirements and to allow passage to a next level/band or from one institution to another. Whereas government policy provides clear guidelines for programme development in the GET and FET bands, higher education and training providers in each field will:

> together with other stakeholders have to devise and organise their own programmes and assessment in their fields in accordance with standards and/or qualifications that have been registered on the NQF through the National Standards Bodies (NSBs). (NADEOSA 1999)

By registering qualifications, it will be possible for a learner to compare different qualifications and to plan a learning path. The specification of exit levels, prior learning requirements and minimum credits needed as well as articulation possibilities should provide a mechanism to prevent lifelong learning from becoming fragmented, for example where a learner completes a large number of unrelated and often irrelevant short courses. Lifelong learning should not be seen as the collection of certificates where course attendance is the only requirement.

Even though institutions will have the freedom to devise and compile their own programmes, the establishment of ETQAs (Education and Training Quality Assurance Bodies) will regulate the quality of these programmes. The fact that programmes will have to be registered and approved will mean that the distinction between formal and so-called non-formal education will become less pronounced. It will lead to the de-institutionalisation of education as any individual or organisation with an interest in education (such as NGOs, professional bodies and associations) could develop programmes that they register with SAQA. Should these programmes be approved by quality assessors, they are then certified to become education providers.

By adopting a systems approach, the NQF enables one to obtain a holistic view of education that will require not only learners but also practitioners and providers to 'think more interconnectedly, both in terms of knowledge and of people' (Teasdale & Teasdale 1998). Learners who are able to take control of their own learning will continue their exploration of issues and themes long after a particular course has finished. Achievement of every learning outcome should set the learner on the path to the next outcome. Teasdale and Teasdale (1998) believe that:

> by role modelling these processes of thinking and learning we are contributing ... to developing the spirit of global interdependence, cultural pluralism and peaceful interchange that the Delors Report (UNESCO Report 1996) believes is essential for the survival of humankind.

9.5 Conclusion

Lifelong learning expresses the idea that learning is a continuous process which takes place throughout life and which is necessitated by the fact that information is growing rapidly and changing throughout one's lifetime. Learning does not stop once an individual leaves school or an institution that provides formal education. The world of learning has become part of everyday life and also of the world of work. A lifelong learner is someone who understands different learning strategies and who is able to apply strategies appropriate to the learning task at hand. Those who have embraced lifelong learning should be able to explore many educational and occupational possibilities.

References

Baine, D and Mwamwenda, T (1994). Education in Southern Africa: Current conditions and future directions. *International Review of Education*, 40(2):113-134.

De Beer, CS (1994) *Epistemology of knowledge utilisation*. Paper delivered at the conference: Research at Unisa: an interfaculty deliberation, 16 March.

Freeman, R (1997) *Managing open systems*. London: Kogan Page.

Freire, P (1972) *Pedagogy of the oppressed*. Harmondsworth: Penguin.

Lyotard, JF (1984) *The postmodern condition: a report on knowledge*. Manchester: Manchester University Press.

Mackintosh, WG (1997) Report on re-engineering Unisa's learning materials process. Unpublished research report. Pretoria: Unisa.

NADEOSA (1999) Education and training in our new South Africa. A wall chart. Johannesburg: Shuter & Shooter.

National Commission on Higher Education (NCHE) Report (1996) *Report by the National Commission on Higher Education: a framework for transformation*. Pretoria: Government Printers.

Rumble, G (1992) *The management of distance learning systems*. Paris: UNESCO.

Spector, BS (1993) Order out of chaos: restructuring schooling to reflect society's paradigm shift. *School Science and Mathematics*, 93(1):9-19.

Sutton, PJ (1994) Lifelong and continuous education. In T Husen and N Postlethwaite (eds) *The International Encyclopedia of Education*. Second edition. Pergamon Oxford: Elsevier Science.

Teasdale, B and Teasdale, J (1998) *Teaching for peace and international understanding: a process approach*. Paper prepared for the 'Educating All for Peace and Justice' Commission, Tenth World Congress of Comparative Education, Cape Town, 12-17 July.

Tobias, R (1999) Lifelong learning under a comprehensive national qualifications framework – rhetoric and reality. *International Journal of Lifelong Education*, 18(2):110-118.

UNESCO (1996) Report to UNESCO of the International Commission on Education for the Twenty-first Century. *Learning: the treasure within*. Paris: UNESCO.

CHAPTER 10

EDUCATION FOR DIVERSITY

Prof Thobeka Mda
University of South Africa

Table of contents

10.1 Introduction

Effective schools, effective teaching and relevant education have always preoccupied educators', academics' and communities' minds and thus directed their activities. Continually seeking an answer to what makes a school effective or what counts as relevant education is an indication of society's expectations from education. Educating children has been seen as an investment with, hopefully, high social, financial and economic returns.

Over the years, the focus of effective education has gone through reasons for and against the canon (in education) of common education for all, comprehensive education, specialised education, and co-education teaching, the necessity for everyone to have access to basic, free education and equal educational opportunities. It is the latter that led to the focus on needs of learners from diverse communities.

10.2 Diversity and diversity groups

Diversity, which is also referred to as *cultural pluralism* or *multiculturalism*, is based on differences. The bases for differences are race, culture, ethnicity, language, social class, religion, gender, disability and exceptionality. The cultural groups making up a diverse society may include immigrants, indigenous groups, nomads, gypsies, or ex-slavery, ex-apartheid and ex-colonised communities. The groups are also broadly referred to as 'different' cultures. For the purposes of this chapter culture encompasses all aspects of a community's life that are transmitted socially: the value system, ideology, lifestyle, world-view, norms, traditions, political and economic systems, religion, myths and social structures shared by a group of people who are bound by common history, geographic location, language, social class and/or religion.

A description of the diversity in classrooms refers to racially, ethnically, linguistically and economically diverse learners in public school classrooms and learners who have striking differences in family structure, lifestyle, health, and physical and mental ability. Of course, 'diversity' also includes the gender issue. Cushner et al. (1992:24) define diversity in the classroom and in schools as:

> encompass[ing] not only those individuals whose ethnic heritage originates in another country, but also those among us who may have special educational and other needs (the hearing impaired, the visually impaired), those who may share significantly different lifestyles (rural and urban children, children who live in extreme poverty, drug dependants), those whose identity is critically influenced by their gender and those who are significantly influenced by variations in class and religion.

McNergney and Herbert (1995:250) warn against relying on racial, ethnic and cultural classifications because:

> [t]he classification systems such as race, ethnicity, and culture are arbitrary – established capriciously or by convention, or left generally ill-defined. Moreover, people might, and indeed do, think of many other ways to classify people – by interests, by height, by weight, by religion, by knowledge, by income and so on. Such classification may or not coincide with classifications of race, ethnicity, and culture.

In labelling and classification there are also dangers in lumping groups together that do not exactly form a homogenous group (Nieto 1992:18-19). In the context of education, where diversity in the school or classroom implies different educational needs, an inaccurate classification or a classification based on stereotyping and generalisation might, like medical misdiagnosis, be more detrimental than no treatment at all, and in this case, more detrimental than mainstream regular schooling without interventionist or support strategies. Colleen Howell (in print) argues against, for example, the use of the term 'special-needs learners' when applied to all the learners 'perceived to not "fit in" to the mainstream system' (p. 6), because these may be learners with different disabilities such as being slow in learning, at risk of dropping out, or linguistically incompetent in the dominant language, or learners who are exceptional (gifted and talented). The 'concept of "special needs" does not therefore provide insight into the nature of the particular learning needs of those learners categorised in this way' (Howell in print p. 6).

Because of the unreliability of the classification and grouping criteria mentioned above, it is advisable that the differences be acknowledged only when necessary. Sensitivity also becomes necessary. It is important to identify people as they prefer to be identified. The problem with classifying or identifying others is that the term or the classification criteria used may not be acceptable to them even when it is precise and correct. Sometimes the term or criterion may even be regarded as derogatory by those described or classified as such. McNergney and Herbert (1995:250-1) state that 'different perspectives, not surprisingly, often yield dissimilar concepts'. Illustrating this point, Kendall (1996:12) states that people who use wheelchairs do not refer to themselves as 'wheelchair bound' and children do not describe themselves as coming from 'broken homes' but as coming from 'home'.

Associated with the term 'diversity' or 'cultural pluralism' are the notions of minority and outsider status. The term 'minority' has a quantitative or statistical meaning as well as a political one (McNergney & Herbert 1995). Quantitatively, the term may be used to refer to groups or sub-groups whose numbers are smaller than another group's. Politically, 'minority' refers to the status, position, power or influence the group has in society. In most instances, groups whose members are fewer than those of other group(s) tend to occupy the lowest position politically. In other words, minority in numbers becomes minority in status. It is also common, however, to find a minority group (in numbers) being the one exerting influence in society. Such a group usually has political and economic power.

Nieto (1992:17) points out the questionable use of the term 'minority', even quantitatively, in that some groups who are numerical minorities, for example the Swedish-Americans, Albanian-Americans or Dutch-Americans in the US are never referred to as such. It is obvious, therefore, that even the classification that is supposed to be factual and neutral is also relative and judgemental. Using the US as an example, Nieto (1992:17) explains that 'the term has historically been used only to refer to racial minorities, thus implying a status less than that accorded to the other group'.

Thus, even when the said groups are no longer in the minority, numerically, the 'pejorative classification' persists, such that when African-American students are in the majority in their schools they are called the 'majority-minority' (Nieto 1992:17). Similarly, McNergney and Herbert (1995:249) use the example of women, who do not necessarily constitute a numerical minority but are referred to as a minority because they 'are perceived to exert less formal influence on the operation of government'.

A definition of the term 'minority' is that supplied on 31 July 1930 by the Permanent Court of Justice on the Greco-Bulgarian Convention on Emigration. According to the advisory opinion of the above Court, a minority (group) is defined as:

> ... a group of persons living in a given country, having a race, religion, language and traditions in a sentiment of solidarity, with a view of preserving their traditions, maintaining their form of worship, securing the instruction and upbringing of the children in accordance with the spirit and traditions of their race and mutually assisting one another. (Capotorti 1991:5)

There is no mention of numbers in the above definition. Later in this chapter the centrality of the experience of immigration to learners of minority standing will be discussed.

Other interpretations and classifications of minority groups include the following:

Ogbu (1990:46) identifies the following three minority groups:

- *Autonomous minorities*. These are numerical or quantitative minorities. They are covered by the Greco-Bulgarian Convention definition above in that they preserve their ways and bring up and educate their children according to their traditions and culture. According to Ogbu they have a cultural frame of reference which demonstrates and encourages academic success, and while they may be victims of prejudice and pillory, they are not victims of stratification.

- *Immigrant minorities*. These minorities move to another society with the hope of improving their lot economically and politically. This group has 'primary cultural differences' that existed before emigration and immigration but believe as individuals that it is possible to make it in the new society if only they master the host's way, for example the dominant language in the adopted society. They see the barriers as temporary and to be expected since they are foreigners after all.

- *Involuntary* or *caste-like minorities*. These minorities did not choose to move but were brought to the host society through slavery, conquest or colonisation. They have secondary cultural differences that arose after contact with the dominant group, which resulted in subordination of the minority group by the dominant one, and the need of the minority group to cope with the domination and the minority status. One of their strategies for coping with the new system may be resistance.

Grant (1988:162-163) differentiates between three types of minorities:

- *Minorities forming local majorities*. This group may be strong or weak depending, *inter alia*, on size, autonomy, and educational provision.

- *Dispersed minorities*. This group experiences great pressure to assimilate into the mainstream society even though discrimination and other exclusionary measures may make assimilation difficult, even when it is desirable.

- *Suffused* or *penetrated minorities*. These are numerical minorities who are different from dispersed minorities in that 'they are on their home ground' and have 'no other cultural reference point'.

For the purposes of this chapter, the learners of concern are those who are quantitatively, or politically, minorities (McNergney & Herbert 1995) – the immigrant, the involuntary or caste-like minorities (Ogbu 1990), minorities who are weak though they form local majorities, the dispersed and the suffused or penetrated minorities (Grant 1988), in the school and in their society. In addition to these there are also other learners who are in the minority because their educational or other needs (not based on culture) are different from those of mainstream learners, for example learners with disabilities. Yates et al. (1998:27) refer to minority groups as the 'out group', and that is applicable to all the minority groups above.

As illustrated above, the existence of a minority implies the existence of a majority, and it is in comparison to the latter that the minority occupies the position it does. The majority becomes the yardstick by which to judge membership or acceptance of the other. For example, when the group with the majority status (and therefore with power) belong to the white race, all those who are not white are assigned minority status. Similarly, if it is English-speaking males who have the power, those with limited competence in the English language and females are the minority groups.

In view of the concerns about classification expressed above and to try to accommodate all the groups who are targeted by education for diversity, they will all be referred to as 'learners of minority standing'.

10.2.1 Parallels among diverse, minority populations in the context of education

Parallels among diverse, minority populations may include the following:

- *Racism* and *discrimination* in desegregated and 'integrated' schooling which include the actual withholding of education. Discrimination is often manifested through tracking and testing in desegregated schools. A poor quality of education is often provided for these groups, sometimes including remedial instructional programmes which exhibit low expectations of the group(s). Discrimination is often against the whole social class and manifested in the kinds of schools available and the curricula to which learners from these groups are exposed.
- *Sexism* manifested in sexist school structures in terms of organisation, orientation and goals.
- *Segregation* on the basis of race, ethnicity and disability which may be manifested in separate and unequal curricula and faculties.
- *Persecution* experienced by minorities.
- *Political action* manifested in the ever-present need to combat discrimination, often through collective struggles.
- *Discomfort* and *fear* that the minorities evoke in the members of the dominant culture.
- *Coping* with and *adapting* to the dominant culture which takes up most of the minorities' time.
- *Conformity*, meaning the pressure exerted by the dominant culture on people from different cultures to conform with its practices.

10.3 Education for diversity

Education for diversity came about because standard or mainstream education is accused of alienating some learners (Banks 1993; Cushner et al. 1992; Delpit 1988; Nieto 1992). Proponents of education for diversity or multicultural education assert that there is no single education system that is suitable for everyone regardless of race, language group, ethnicity, social class or gender.

According to Nieto (1992:20) the underlying principle in education for diverse groups or multicultural education is that 'children are educated differently by our schools; in addition, the differences that children bring to school have a profound effect on what they gain [or not] from their educational experiences'.

Another rationale is that education is driven by the philosophies of those in power. As a result, education reflects the interests of, and thus favours, the dominant/majority group. This is usually comprised of white, middle-to-upper-class males (Nieto 1992). The aims and content of education, therefore, are influenced by and reflect those interests. The assumption following this is that because not every learner belongs to that group, education based on or driven by those interests alienates or at the very least does not benefit those who do not belong to that group. Scholars, educationists and human rights groups have been trying to come up with alternatives to make education a meaningful experience for all learners.

Also, as the profile of learners in the schools changes, so too do the demands upon education professionals. Complicating the ability of the professional to adapt to the needs of this new student body is the fact that teachers and educational managers are predominantly from the older age group and were trained in traditional techniques that are not in line and, therefore, not effective with the students who often come from poor homes, not from the majority group, from the lower socio-economic class and with limited proficiency in the dominant language (Yates et al. 1998).

It is generally accepted that equal education is not determined by equal input but by equal output. Related to this premise is the notion that treating unequal people equally is as discriminatory and harmful as treating equal people unequally – hence education for diversity. Nieto (1992:26) observes that 'students are more different from one another when they leave school than when they enter, thus putting to rest the myth of schools as the "great equalizer"'.

Nieto (1992:xxiii) chooses the example of immigration as an alienating experience. She refers to the experiences of enslaved Africans, colonised American-Indians and Mexicans in the US. Here, 'immigration' may be used literally and figuratively. The principle or act of immigrating is central to the experience of other groups such as Africans, Coloureds and Indians of the formerly segregated South Africa, certain language groups, learners from poor communities and female learners as they move into the terrain of the majority where they become minorities. Even gypsies, nomads and other travellers, whose identifying feature is constant travelling and sometimes returning to same camping sites year after year, can be said to be an immigrating group (Holmes 1993).

The learners from minority cultures or populations feel alienated by the public schools. These schools are accused of promoting (intentionally or otherwise) one culture, implying its superiority over others. The 'immigrant' learners find

224

that the public school culture is different from theirs, and the school ignores or alienates them from their cultures. Even when integrated schools admit diverse learner populations in big numbers, the schools remain monocultural, monolingual and ethnocentric. As a result, other cultures and languages are either not acknowledged or suppressed. The minority learners experience 'othering' (Soudien 1997:18) or 'become invisible' (Vally & Dalamba 1999:22). Languages other than the dominant one are treated as problematic and seen as hindering the education process. Perspectives and contributions of other cultural groups are not taught. Prejudice and negative attitudes towards different communicative styles and socio-cultural expectations lead to stereotyping (Figueroa 1993). Diversity, at best, is viewed as interesting; at worst, as a deficit (Cushner et al. 1992).

Linked to alienation are experiences of racism and discrimination. Racism may be institutional or structural, cultural or individual:

- *Institutional racism* is manifested through laws, customs and practices resulting from and leading to racial inequalities.
- *Cultural racism* is based on a belief about the inferiority or non-existence of the culture of a group.
- *Individual racism* is personal and is based on a belief about the inferiority of certain groups in relation to others (Jones' categories cited in Nieto 1992:22).

In many instances, all three forms are present in each public school and learners of minority standing experience, individually, all three. Other factors leading to alienating experiences of schooling, and that may be linked to racism and discrimination are the perception of one's culture and language as inferior, and teachers' low expectations of (culturally) different learners (Nieto 1992:xxiii).

McNergney and Herbert (1995:254), applying Juvenal's framework (introduced about 2000 years ago), describe the different positions from which people view society and how these influence education. These are:

- 'viewing society from within versus viewing society from outside'

and

- 'viewing society from a position of advantage versus viewing society from behind barriers'.

These positions, therefore, greatly determine whether a learner will have positive or negative experiences at school, will naturally fit in or have difficulty fitting in, or forever remain 'on the outside looking in'.

For those in an advantageous position 'education can be a form of cultural capital' (McNergney & Herbert 1995:255). Learners from this group attend prestigious schools and, because of the added benefits that are part of the 'culture of power' (Delpit 1988), are assured admission to exclusive, prestigious colleges (McNergney & Herbert 1995). This greatly contrasts with what is experienced by those who view society behind barriers.

The barriers behind which some view society are barriers of poverty, caste, language, disability and a glass ceiling. Learners from the groups that view society from behind these barriers tend to attend poorer schools that are over-crowded, uninviting and lacking relevant and culturally appropriate instructional materials in under-funded school districts with diminished capacities to create educational opportunities (Nieto 1992).

Competence or limited competence in the dominant language is often the distinguishing characteristic between the norm and the 'other'. In countries like the US, Britain, Australia and some African countries where, for example, English is the dominant language in the education sphere, competence in the English language becomes the passport to opportunities. Language barriers have led to the identification of some learners as Limited English Proficient (LEP) students and the emergence of programmes such as English as a Foreign Language (EFL), English as a Second Language (ESL), bilingual education and multilingual education.

Ntshakala (1997:5), writing on the experiences of black learners in desegregated schools in South Africa, reported that the use of English in these schools as 'the language of instruction and socialisation ... becomes a problem for [these learners and] becomes a mechanism through which they are alienated'.

10.3.1 Assimilation and integration

Nieto (1992:38) takes the following view of assimilation: 'Because schools have traditionally perceived their role to be that of an assimilating agent, the isolation and rejection that come hand-in-hand with immigration and colonisation have simply been left at the schoolhouse door'.

Fyfe (1993:38) reports that the response to immigration in Britain, the rest of Europe, the US and Australia from 1950 onwards was to 'emphasise assimilation':

> Large groups of children with little or no English, from very contrasting social, economic and cultural backgrounds [were viewed] as 'problematic'. There was certainly a partial view of integration, in which the onus lay with the 'immigrants' to do the adjusting.

Foster (1988:144) cites the Australian *Report to the Minister of Immigration on the Migrant Education Programme for 1970-71* and draws attention to the language used in the Report:

> The ability of migrants to communicate is fundamental to their successful integration. Migrant education cannot be divorced from

migrant welfare. The development of the migrant education programme is evidence of the government's intention steadily to develop migrant education and welfare activities to secure for Australia the fullest economic and social advantage of migration.

The above rationale about the role of language influenced education policies all over the world (for example the US, Europe, Australia and Africa) in addressing learners who are different or deemed to be different from the 'norm'. These learners, characterised by coming from the 'outside' (country, language group, socio-economic class, mental and physical ability and/or ethnic group), and being in the minority (in numbers and status) in the school, had to be made to 'fit in'.

Foster (1988:144) explains that:

> by implication, the content of education was unquestioned. As long as the children learned the language of instruction, the knowledge transmitted in schools was assumed to be appropriate or relevant. The welfare role of education was quite explicitly assumed in [the Australian] government thinking at that time.

Christie (1990), reporting on her study on Roman Catholic schools as pioneers in admitting learners of colour in apartheid South Africa, also supports Foster by observing that since opening these schools to all learners had not been prompted by dissatisfaction with them, the teaching in the Catholic schools was never scrutinised. In a later South African study by the South African Human Rights Commission (SAHRC) (1999) on desegregated public schools, it is reported that pupils 'of the dominant racial grouping saw "minority group" pupils as the ones who needed to change and adapt to the school' (Vally & Dalamba 1999:24).

The aim of education, therefore, in the US and elsewhere, became 'integrating' the immigrant learners which, in this context, has the same meaning as 'assimilating'. In the US, the term 'melting pot' was coined. McNergney and Herbert (1995:253) explain the concept thus:

> Thoughts about culture in the US have been dominated by the metaphor of the melting pot. Immigrants, like ingredients, were to be added to the great cauldron (public education) and simmered over low-intensity educational fire until a perfectly blended soup was achieved in which characteristics of the individual ingredients disappeared.

In most cases of assimilation or the 'melting pot', the intentions were mainly good, even if sometimes misguided. Their proponents may have even been regarded as philanthropists. Most educators and policy-makers embarked on this with the intention of 'equalising' all learners by doing what they thought was best: 'I want the same thing for everyone else's children as I want for mine' (Delpit 1988:285).

According to Cushner et al. (1992:8):

> Both schools and the teachers who inhabit them are to a large extent 'culture-bound'. Indeed, one of the purposes of schooling has always been to transmit the dominant cultural beliefs, values and knowledge represented by these teachers to the next generation. In addition, it is a strong characteristic of most people – teachers included – to believe that their own cultural tradition represents the 'best' way.

Even where a different education system was established for 'immigrant' and other diverse learners, as in Migrant Education in Australia or Indian Education in the US and in Canada, the ultimate goal was that these learners would later join the mainstream. In other words, segregation was intended to aid their transition to mainstream by letting them work at their own pace without the pressure of competing with mainstream first-language learners.

The assimilationist approach to education was also influenced by a welfare maintenance mentality, in that these 'poor' learners had to be helped to catch up or reach the level of the 'normal' school population. David Wallace Adams (1988:2) describes this perspective in the case of Native Americans between 1880 and 1900 as viewing them as 'creatures of environmental and historical circumstance, fully capable of being transformed and assimilated once exposed to the "superior" influences of white society'.

It is important to note that assimilation or melting pot education has always had supporters from both the host, i.e. the dominant communities (the majority) and the immigrants (the minority). Rodriguez (1989:34), a Mexican-American and one of the supporters of assimilation, maintains that 'as America became an immigrant country, necessity gathered generations of ... immigrants. Assimilation was an honorable achievement, comparable ... with opening the plains, building bridges'. He also states that '[a]s education begins, diversity is the enemy of the classroom'.

For some parents of the diverse minority groups, it is felt that adopting the new culture is the only way for the children to succeed. Nieto (1992:xxv) feels that the children in the above instances are forced to choose between family and school and 'what inevitably becomes a choice between belonging and succeeding'.

Yates et al. (1998:25) concur with the above view and further state that students from minority groups 'understand that learning in school is equivalent to learning the dominant culture, and they believe they must give up their own culture in favour of the dominant culture to be successful in school'.

These writers also cite Ogbu (1990) who says that for students from minority groups to succeed academically in school they have to 'learn to think and act white'. Christie (1990:50) concurs and reports from her South African study that 'the assumption on the part of nearly one fifth of the black pupils [was] that it should be they who adjusted to the basically white schools' and 'for most open schools pupils' white norms and practices were the taken-for-granted basis for social interaction'.

The above situations are possible because even though the melting pot is supposed to mix different cultures and come up with a unique education with features from different cultures, the reality is that it is the minority cultures that disappear in the pot, with the flavour remaining that of the dominant culture. However, the proponents of the melting pot concept do not seem to have been concerned about the unmelted ingredient (the host culture) and the resulting unchanged flavour, probably explaining it as evidence of the strength of the dominant culture.

A reaction against the soup in the melting pot led to the idea of 'tossed salad' to replace the term 'melting pot'. That way all the ingredients remain intact and separate, with each contributing and maintaining its uniqueness to the whole unit (the salad). Alluding to this, Figueroa (1993:26) says that 'it is important not only to acknowledge the *existence* of cultural pluralism but to recognise it as being *valuable*'.

Efforts to devise curricula addressing the needs and abilities of immigrant diverse learners were criticised as being divisive and not in the interests of national unity. As late as 1991, for example, Kenneth Jackson, a member of the New York State Social Studies Review and Development Committee, disagreed with the Committee's findings which recommended overhauling the curriculum to address:

> the needs for multiple perspectives; for understanding indigenous social, political, economic and technological structures and the precolonial histories of indigenous peoples; for viewing effects as bidirectional instead of unidirectional (with the European participants as the actors). (McNergney & Herbert 1995:274)

Jackson argues that '[with]in any single country, one culture must be accepted as the standard' (McNergney & Herbert 1995:274). Rosenman (1989:41) offers a counter to Jackson's position and other opponents of education for diversity:

> While there is nothing wrong with a standard curriculum to promote unity, it is wrong to impose as correct a subjective curriculum teaching that the culture in power is better than any other. Even though that culture may make the rules of society and students may have to learn to play by those rules if they are to achieve success within the system, those majority values are not necessarily superior to other values that children bring to school.

Underlying education for diversity or multicultural education are the principles of democracy, equality, justice and freedom. By their nature, these principles are in conflict with assimilation, the melting pot and monoculture. These principles recognise the value in each culture and argue for space for each cultural group to practise its culture.

There is some slight variation in what people with disabilities are demanding, although the principles are the same as those above (democracy, equality, justice and freedom). The demand is for inclusive or inclusionary education in all schools, which is also integrated schooling, as opposed to separate, exclusive schools for learners with disabilities. This move, already in operation, has implications for regulation and allocation of funds, institutional (physical, curricular and staffing) restructuring and a new belief system.

As a response to inequality, discrimination, ethnocentrism and racism in education, as explained above, multicultural education and bilingual education emerged as outgrowths of the civil rights movement (Banks 1992 in McNergney & Herbert 1995; Nieto 1992; Squelch 1993). Multicultural education is based on the belief that the role played by one's culture in education is important. This belief is supported by governments, policy-makers, educators, learners and parents.

Multicultural education is informed by two contesting perspectives, namely 'liberalism' and 'radical structuralism' (Squelch 1993:36-37):

- The liberal view 'emphasise[s] aspects such as the development of self-concept, tolerance, and *"individual human rights"* and relates equal education opportunities to enable every individual to participate in education'.
- Radical structuralists, on the other hand, are against the liberal position because they believe the individualistic approach to be naïve. They are 'more deeply concerned about societal issues, particularly racism, injustices and stratification'.

An example of a liberalist approach to multicultural education is expressed by Figueroa (1993:26):

> Education is concerned with the development of [the] whole person as an individual *and* inseparably as an active *social being* in a specific cultural and socio-historical situation. Education is a process facilitating a growth of consciousness, a growth in critical awareness of self and of the other. It is concerned with initiation into value, symbolic, cognitive, communicative, affective, behavioural and social systems, faculties and skills. This includes the values, knowledge, skills, attitudes and behavioural patterns that a person needs to play an active and rewarding part in their society, and to interact constructively with others however different – to contribute to society's well-being and to making a living.

As an outgrowth of the civil rights movement, from the beginning multicultural education has had a radical structuralist function with the intention of changing society or the way society is configured. Through multicultural education learners would be educated for a democratic society, in contrast to education that reproduces, maintains or sustains inequalities. McNergney and Herbert (1995:272) describe education for diversity as education that is multicultural and social reconstructionist: 'This general approach to educate for diversity actively challenges social inequality and seeks to restructure educational institutions for the ultimate purpose of changing society'.

Both the liberalist and the radical structuralist approach are in line with the notion that education is never politically neutral. Neither mainstream education nor multicultural education is politically neutral. Multicultural education operates within a personal, historical, social and political context (Muffoletto 1995:30).

In summary, it emerges that the route to education for diversities has been through desegregated education, the melting pot, equal education for all, multicultural education, bilingual education and integrated education.

10.4 Some interventionist approaches to teaching diverse classroom populations in the 1990s

While most of what has been discussed in the above section, especially in section 10.3.1, can be considered approaches to teaching diversity there are direct interventionist approaches that need to be mentioned.

10.4.1 Forced bussing of learners

Forced bussing of learners from one section of town to another was one of the first steps to be taken, for example in the US, to facilitate desegregation. This is a radical approach that seeks to reconstruct society by giving learners from disadvantaged areas access to otherwise inaccessible schools which may be well-equipped and offer many educational opportunities. The practice of bussing is still happening in some societies, including the US, although there are indications of disillusion from the minority groups about its benefits.

The effectiveness of forced bussing as an interventionist strategy is also doubtful because this forced integration is for a very limited period (five to six hours a day, five days a week). The two groups (the bussed-in and the hosts) do not spend enough time together to integrate meaningfully. Forced bussing does not, in fact, reconstruct society, since school desegregation does not lead to residential desegregation (Contreras & Stephens 1997). The different ethnic minority groups continue to live in separate and unequal worlds compared to the majority. Thus, parents of the bussed-in learners remain geographically distant from the school and may not find it easy to interact with the school.

It is also reported that in the US, some white Americans, who are the majority group, expressed dissatisfaction with this ruling by removing their children from city schools targeted for bussing to suburban schools, and from public schools to private schools (McNergney & Herbert 1995). Of late, however, the group of white parents moving away from the city and city schools have been joined by other English-speaking parents, from other racial groups, who are not happy with the implications of large numbers of learners with limited English skills. These parents fear that with the extra time teachers have to spend with the learners with limited English proficiency, there will not be enough time to spend with English first language learners (Contreras & Stephens 1997). This fear is expressed by English first language speakers in South Africa too, with the latter also predicting an inevitable lowering of standards (Mda in print). Parents also remove their children from schools where there is forced integration to avoid racial and ethnic tensions and conflicts that are frequently experienced in such schools (Contreras & Stephens 1997).

10.4.2 Setting up separate schools

The problems experienced with forced bussing and forced integration have led to the setting up and maintenance of separate schools. Separate schools are likely to be private schools, suburban schools, or schools in exclusive residential areas. Some majority groups, as reported in section 10.4.1, do not want to lose what they already have by making adjustments for the new school populations. In Christie's South African study, an education official stated that they had 'no desire to destroy what [they] value and have taken years to build up' (1990:127). Also, the minority groups in the US would rather have equal funding for poor districts than forced integration in schools outside their areas. This is seen as a return to the practice of 'separate but equal'. In South Africa, after apartheid, there is a call for redress and equity for township and rural schools where racial integration is not likely.

In the early 1990s the first school exclusively for black males, in post Civil War America, was established in Baltimore, US. Other similar schools were established in Detroit, Milwaukee and Dade County (Florida), all areas with significantly large African-American populations (Greathouse & Sparling 1993:131). The African-American male-only schools or classrooms were established by African-American males in response to what is perceived as the plight of the African-American male in the US from birth to death. Statistical findings paint a grim picture of African-American males' demise resulting from high infant mortality rates, homicides, teen deaths, high dropout from school rates, unemployment and large numbers of them in jails. The males perceived to be mostly at risk are those from single female dominated, poverty-stricken homes and homes surrounded by violence (Greathouse & Sparling 1993:132). The social ills mentioned above are seen as structural and institutional racism against African-American males in the US. The idea of setting up single gender/race schools for the African-American males is to provide them with an environment where they can be affirmed, by positive African-American male teachers, who 'are better able to interpret young males' behavior and [who] can discipline them more effectively' (Greathouse & Sparling 1993:131).

In South Africa, schools are being established by conservative Afrikaners for exclusive use by Afrikaners. Unlike the African-American males in the US, Afrikaners constitute a powerful minority in South Africa, which feels that its culture, language and traditions are threatened by enforced integration. Since establishing these schools is within their constitutional right in South Africa, this is allowed, as long as they carry the costs for establishing and maintaining the schools (Constitution of the Republic of South Africa 1996). Using race as an admission criterion, however, is illegal and unconstitutional in South Africa, and so it would be impossible to establish schools like the US black male-only schools or classrooms in South Africa.

10.4.3 Affirmation

Related to separate schools is the use of affirmation of differences as an interventionist strategy. There is a growing interest in racial, ethnic, cultural and religious identity. The minority groups may, and do, assert their independence and difference. Thereby '[c]ultural and language differences become boundary-maintaining mechanisms between themselves and the dominant group' (Ogbu 1990:48).

In the US, the English spoken by African-Americans (a minority group) to whom English is a first language has frequently been studied and analysed. Since this variety of English was widely regarded as an aberration and a deficit, there have been programmes in the past to assist African-Americans to learn the acceptable dialect. Lately, however, there are moves among the African-Americans to have their variety of English which they call 'Ebonics' formally recognised as one of the American languages and therefore to be taught in American classrooms.

10.4.4 Increasing the heterogeneity of educational professionals

There is a concerted effort in some societies to recruit and retain educators from the minority groups. An important reason for this is to address the need for successful role models who belong to minority groups or who have disabilities because 'many racial and ethnic minority students and students with disabilities never see a teacher or an administrator who represents their culture or disability' (Yates et al. 998:33).

There is also a call to train and employ only multilingual and bilingual teachers for all diverse classrooms.

10.4.5 Multicultural education

Multicultural education has been discussed under section 10.3.1. However, since it is one of the major interventionist approaches to teaching diverse classroom populations, it is necessary to mention it again in this context.

Multicultural education is probably the most common form of education for diversity. There are, however, misconceptions about what it means. In South Africa, for example, some people refer to desegregated schools as multicultural schools, or as schools teaching multicultural education.

According to Squelch (1993:40-42) the goals of multicultural education are to:

- enhance equal educational opportunities
- develop the ability to identify with and relate to other groups
- reduce racial discrimination
- develop multicultural knowledge, attitudes and skills
- inculcate core values
- promote effective relationships between home and school.

Multicultural education may take the form of a programme within a school, an integrated approach for the whole school, or a separate, alternative school may be established to focus specifically on education for diverse populations.

Also according to Squelch (1993:42-46) the conditions for successful implementation of multicultural education include:

- early integration of learners
- design of appropriate, balanced and unbiased curricula
- use of a variety of instructional material that is both accurate and positively represents the different cultural groups
- use of diverse teaching methods
- multilingual teaching
- regular and varied forms of assessment
- healthy home-school relations.

Squelch (1993) proposes that the effectiveness of multicultural education in an education system or a school depends on:

- the area of emphasis or which goals are prioritised
- the level of integration of the programme within the whole school curriculum
- structural provisions for sustenance of the programme.

At California State University, Sacramento, which has a mixed student population, a separatist teacher education programme has been devised whereby student teachers from the minority groups are prepared separately from the student teachers from the majority group. This is done within the multicultural programme of the university.

Squelch (1993) also believes some criticisms of multicultural education to be that it:

- distracts learners from mastering basic academic skills
- emphasises racial and cultural differences which fosters negative attitudes and prejudices.

10.4.6 Bilingualism and multilingualism

The following models are identified by Skutnabb-Kangas and García (1995:226-227) as strong models in catering for multilingual classrooms:

- *The plural multilingual model.* This is typical of European schools. The languages of the different subsections are official and are regarded as majority languages. The students, who come from different national and linguistic backgrounds, are taught in the various languages with the intention of making them multilingual.

- *The immersion model.* This is designed for 'ethnolinguistic majority' learners. The learners are first taught through their second language and then through their first language. The goal is to make the learners bilingual and 'biliterate' so that they maintain their first language but also obtain access to the benefits provided by the other language. There is no intention to achieve equity.

- *The two-way dual-language model.* Both the majority and the minority students are taught in both languages, but the two languages are strictly separated. This model was developed in the US and uses mainly English and Spanish. The goals are pluralism, bilingualism, biliteracy and enrichment.

- *The maintenance model.* This is mainly for minority-group learners. Both the majority and the minority languages are used. The learners are first taught through their first language(s), while the majority language is taught as a subject. Ideally, the minority language remains the language of instruction throughout the learners' schooling. Often, however, the majority language also becomes a language of instruction, alternating with the minority one (Skutnabb-Kangas & García 1995).

10.5 Conclusion

The interventionist strategies discussed above, such as multilingualism, multicultural education, inclusion education (for learners and disabilities) and so on, all require commitment. They do not happen on their own. All the stakeholders – parents, learners, school administrators, communities and educators – need to be involved and committed. Skutnabb-Kangas and García (1995:234) emphasise the need for commitment and support for these programmes:

> A multilingual and pluralist school culture cannot exist in opposition to that of the societal context in which the school has life. ... in order for a school culture to have a long-lasting impact on a societal context by truly transforming citizens, it must be nurtured by societal aspirations.

While Skutnabb-Kangas and García are referring specifically to language, this is true for all the diverse needs. Often, the policies for equity and transformation are there, but the passion and aspirations of those who should be supporting and driving the initiatives are often lacking.

Teachers need to recognise the 'differences in learning styles and motivators', 'to find the learner's cultural and experiential wavelength' and 'to adopt practice accordingly' (Figueroa 1993:31). The point here is that although the learners of diverse backgrounds present learning styles and modes of behaviour that are unfamiliar and may even be unacceptable to educators, the educators still have to educate every learner in preparation for the interactions in which they will have to participate during their lives.

What needs to be emphasised is that programmes and approaches used in education for diversity should not just be politically correct, but, most importantly, must be educationally sound. The goal must always be to offer effective education to all learners.

These suggestions have implications for teacher education programmes. It is crucial for the curriculum in teacher education to prepare future teachers for an understanding of the social and political nature of curricula and schools, and to work towards improved tolerance and respect for all forms of diversity in society.

References

Adams, DW (1988) Fundamental considerations: the deep meaning of native American schooling, 1800-1900. *Harvard Educational Review*, Vol 58, No.1, February 1-27.

Banks, JA (1993) Education and cultural diversity in the United States. In A Fyfe and P Figueroa (eds) *Education for cultural diversity*. London: Routledge.

Capotorti, F (1991) *Study on the rights of persons belonging to ethnic, religious and linguistic minorities*. New York: United Nations Publications.

Christie, P (1990) *Open schools: Racially mixed Catholic schools in South Africa, 1976-1986*. Johannesburg: Ravan Press.

Cushner, K; McClelland, A and Safford, P (1992) *Human diversity in education: an integrative approach*. New York: McGraw-Hill.

Delpit, LD (1988) The silenced dialogue: power and pedagogy in educating other people's children. *Harvard Educational Review*, Vol. 58, No 3, August 280-298.

Figueroa, P (1993) Cultural diversity, social reality and education. In A Fyfe and P Figueroa (eds) *Education for cultural diversity*. London: Routledge.

Foster, LE (1988) *Diversity and multicultural education: a sociological perspective*. Sydney: Allen & Unwin.

Fyfe, A (1993) Multicultural or anti-racist education: the irrelevant debate. In A Fyfe and P Figueroa (eds) *Education for cultural diversity*. London: Routledge.

Grant, N (1988) The education of minority and peripheral cultures. *Comparative Education*, 24(2)155-1676.

Greathouse, B and Sparling, S (1993) African American male-only schools: is that the solution? *Journal of the Association for Childhood Education International*, 69(3):131-132.

Harber, C (1998) *Racism in two countries: racism and civic education for democracy in Britain and South Africa*. Paper delivered at the 10th World Congress of Comparative Education Societies (WCCES) at the University of Cape Town, Cape Town, 11-16 July.

Holmes, P (1993) Traveller education: structural response to cultural diversity. In A Fyfe and P Figueroa (eds) *Education for cultural diversity*. London: Routledge.

Kendall, F (1996) *Diversity in the classroom: new approaches to the education of young children*. New York: Teachers' College Press.

McNergney, RF and Herbert, JM (1995) *Foundations of education: the challenge of professional practice*. Boston: Allyn & Bacon.

Mda, TV (in press) *Integrated schooling in South Africa*. Cape Town: Juta.

Muffoletto, R (1995) Thinking about diversity: paradigms, meanings and representations. In RJ Martin (ed) *Practising what we teach: confronting diversity in teacher education*. Albany: State University of New York Press.

Nieto, S (1992) *Affirming diversity: the socio-political context of multicultural education*. New York: Longman Publishing Group.

Ntshakala, S (1997) Integrated schools must face issues. *The Teacher*. Johannesburg: Mail & Guardian Press.

Ogbu, JU (1990) Minority education in comparative perspective. *Journal of Negro Education*, Vol 59, No 1:45-57.

Rodriguez, R (1989) What is an American education? In JW Noll (ed) *Taking sides: clashing views on controversial educational issues*. Fifth edition. Guilford: The Dushkin Publishing Group Inc, 36-39.

Rosenman, AA (1989) The value of multicultural curricula. In JW Noll (ed) *Taking sides: clashing views on controversial educational issues*. Fifth edition. Guilford: The Dushkin Publishing Group Inc.

Soudien, C (1997) *'We know why we're here': the experience of African children in a Coloured school in Cape Town, South Africa*. Paper presented at the Annual Congress of the Southern African Comparative and History of Education Society. Livingstone, Zambia, 10-12 January.

Squelch, JM (1993) Education for equality: the challenge to multicultural education. In El Dekker and EM Lemmer (eds) *Critical issues in modern education*. Durban: Butterworths.

The Republic of South Africa Act 108 of 1996. *Government Gazette*, 378 (17678) 18 December. Cape Town: Government printers.

Vally, S and Dalamba, Y (1999) *Racism, 'racial integration' and desegregation in South African public secondary schools*. Report on a study by the South African Human Rights Commission (SAHRC). SAHRC: Pretoria, February.

Yates, JR; Ortiz, AA and Anderson, RJ (1998) Issues of race, ethnicity, disability, and culture. In RJ Anderson, CE Keller and JM Karp (eds) *Enhancing diversity: educators with disabilities*. Washington: Gallaudet University Press.

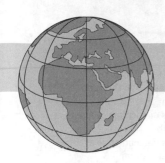

INDEX

243